From Arromanches to the Elbe

To those who served in 144th RAC/4th RTR 1944–5

From Arromanches to the Elbe

*Marcus Cunliffe and the
144th Regiment Royal Armoured Corps
1944–1945*

Charles More

FRONTLINE
BOOKS

FRONTLINE
BOOKS

From Arromanches to the Elbe

First published in Great Britain in 2019 by Frontline Books,
an imprint of Pen & Sword Books Ltd, Yorkshire — Philadelphia

Copyright © Charles More, 2019
ISBN: 978 152671 065 9

The right of Charles More to be identified as the author of this work has been asserted by him in accordance with the Copyright, Designs and Patents Act 1988. A CIP catalogue record for this book is available from the British Library All rights reserved.

No part of this book may be reproduced or transmitted in any form or by any means, electronic or mechanical including photocopying, recording or by any information storage and retrieval system, without permission from the Publisher in writing.

Typeset in Times New Roman and printed and bound by
TJ International Lrd, Padstow, Cornwall

Pen & Sword Books Ltd incorporates the imprints of
Pen & Sword Archaeology, Air World Books, Atlas, Aviation, Battleground, Discovery, Family History, History, Maritime, Military, Naval, Politics, Social History, Transport, True Crime, Claymore Press, Frontline Books, Praetorian Press, Seaforth Publishing and White Owl

For a complete list of Pen & Sword titles please contact:

PEN & SWORD BOOKS LTD
47 Church Street, Barnsley, South Yorkshire, S70 2AS, UK.
E-mail: enquiries@pen-and-sword.co.uk
Website: www.pen-and-sword.co.uk
Or
PEN AND SWORD BOOKS,
1950 Lawrence Road, Havertown, PA 19083, USA
E-mail: Uspen-and-sword@casematepublishers.com
Website: www.penandswordbooks.com

Contents

List of Illustrations vi
List of Maps vii
Acknowledgements viii

Chapter 1   Introduction 1

Chapter 2   Arromanches to Noyers 19

Chapter 3   Operation Totalize 42

Chapter 4   Advance to the Seine 63

Chapter 5   Holland and the Ardennes 81

Chapter 6   The Rhine to the Elbe..108

Chapter 7   The Experience of War..125

Chapter 8   Regimental Ins and Outs 149

Chapter 9   Conclusion 172

Abbreviations and Glossary..185
Notes 191
Sources and Bibliography 204
Index...210

List of Illustrations

1. Honeys and Shermans near Caen, July 1944
2. B Squadron tanks near Caen, July 1944
3. Outside Noyers: 'good tank going'
4. Preparations for Totalize, August 1944
5. Totalize: modern memorial at Cramesnil
6. 'Stonk Wood'
7. A knocked-out Tiger in Stonk Wood
8. Robert Thorne
9. Regimental officers
10. Alan Jolly
11. Marcus Cunliffe
12. The Calonne at La Vallette
13. The Aftwaterings Canal
14. The Ardennes: Hotton War Cemetery
15. The Ardennes: the road to Verdenne
16. Buffaloes near Marienbaum
17. The Rhine crossing: a message from Montgomery

Illustration Acknowledgements
Every effort has been made to trace, where possible, the copyright holders and obtain permission to reproduce the photographs that appear in this book. When this has not been possible, the author and publishers would be glad to hear from copyright holders so that due credit can be given in future printings.

1, 2, 4, 7, 17 – Regimental History
8, 9, 10, 11 – Private Collection
16 – Bovington Tank Museum
Other plates – copyright Suzanne Richards

List of Maps

2.1 The Battle of Noyers, 16–18 July 1944
3.1 Normandy, 25 July– 13 August 1944
3.2 Operation Totalize: The British Attack, 7–8 August 1944
4.1 Advance to the Seine
5.1 The Low Countries, autumn 1944
5.2 The Ardennes, January 1945
6.1 Rhine Crossing, 23–4 March 1945

Acknowledgements

A number of people have helped me during the course of writing this book and, as always, it is a pleasure to acknowledge this help.

For preliminary advice on the archival research, I would particularly like to mention Leah Richardson of the Special Collections Research Center, Gelman Library, The George Washington University. Shannon Bridget Murphy was of great assistance with Marcus Cunliffe's papers at the Gelman Library. Thanks also to Katie Thompson of Bovington Tank Museum Archives and to staff at The National Archives, Kew, and the Imperial War Museum.

Suzanne Richards took numerous excellent photographs; thanks also to Sam Richards for the loan of his camera. Martin Brown drew the maps, which he transformed from my very rough originals. And it was a pleasure to have the company of Suzanne and my wife Hilary in following the tank tracks of 144th RAC/4th RTR.

At Pen and Sword/Frontline Press, thanks to Martin Mace, Lisa Hoosan, Alison Flowers and Tara Moran for their work. Thanks also to Andy Cocks.

Chapter 1

Introduction

This book is about a British armoured regiment and its part in the Allied campaign to liberate Europe. It landed at Arromanches eight days after D-Day, fighting from then until the end of the war in Normandy, Holland, Belgium and Germany. It was one of many such regiments: a total of around forty served for all or part of the long campaign.[1] For 144th Royal Armoured Corps (or 4th Royal Tank Regiment as it became), the campaign ended at midnight on 8 May 1945. Most of its troops and vehicles were near Bremen, but one of its squadrons had been assisting an American division which crossed the Elbe near Hamburg. The Regiment ended the war strung out on the road which ran between the two north German cities. It had been in action for almost eleven months.

The Regiment was different from many because its campaign was remarkably well documented. The documents start with the regimental war diary, which all units kept, and which is in The National Archives in Kew. The 144th RAC's (the abbreviation will be used from now on) war diary is fuller than most, and is supplemented by a number of lengthy accounts of various operations which the Regiment undertook.[2] These accounts are sometimes personal, and sometimes extended versions of the third person descriptions in the narrative war diary.

They are complemented by *Blue Flash*, the history of the Regiment published in 1952 by Alan Jolly, its C/O throughout the campaign.[3] It is based in part on the war diary and its related documents, but also on other material and, of course, it includes Jolly's own commentary. Jolly was a formidable officer who went on to become a senior general.[*] Not surprisingly, the book is more informative than many regimental histories and is a valuable source in its own right. It is also written in a wryly

---

[*] Jolly ended his career as a full general and (1966–9) Quartermaster General to the Forces, in charge of Army supplies. He was knighted in 1968. (*The Times* obituary, 16 September 1977.)

humorous style, one that is familiar to those acquainted with British Army regimental magazines. It is at times very funny, and I have quoted from it freely, my excuse – apart from its humour – being that it is a rare book which few readers of this one are likely to have come across.

My interest in the Regiment was first aroused because my father-in-law, Captain Robert (Bob) Thorne, served in it. He was in command of A Echelon, which brought up supplies to the tank squadrons, and at the end of the war he received the MBE in recognition of his service during the campaign. In about 1990 I talked to him at length about his life, especially his army career, and recorded these conversations. These recordings, therefore, constitute another source.[4]

Bob had mentioned that a young officer in the Regiment went on to become a well-known historian. The young officer was Marcus Cunliffe. Cunliffe became a distinguished historian of the USA, and something from his obituary in *The Times* in 1991 lodged in my mind – that he had planned a novel based on his wartime experiences. However, for a number of years I pursued other interests. Then, a couple of years before writing this book, I put his name into Google and it threw up some fascinating information. As well as notes for the novel, his diaries and other material had been left to George Washington University. Subsequently I had some of these photographed (for practical reasons the notes for the novel were not included). This book has used the diaries he kept from August 1943 and went on keeping, with a gap in mid- to late 1944, until after the end of the war; they are supplemented by vignettes of particular scenes and personalities which had caught his attention and were written after the event. There is also an account by Cunliffe of Operation Totalize, a major operation in which the Regiment was involved, in The National Archives.[5]

My original idea for this book was to reproduce a variety of the sources available, with a linking commentary. There were two ideas behind this approach: to retell the story of the various major battles in which the Regiment was involved from the point of view of some of the participants; and to shed light on a variety of topics in which historians of the British Army are interested. Apart from that perennial focus of interest, leadership, the topics include tactics, equipment and morale. These aims still stand. But on looking through Cunliffe's diary, I realised that the book would not be quite the one originally envisaged, in which a variety of different individuals told the story. This is because Cunliffe himself supplied much of the material on which it is based. He wrote a large

INTRODUCTION

portion of the war diary, and the personal account of Operation Totalize. He was responsible for accounts of various battles in Normandy which were later used by Alan Jolly in *Blue Flash*.[6] And, of course, his diary and the material attached to it would form an important part of the source material. It was becoming clear that, although other participants such as my father-in-law would make a contribution, a fair proportion of the book would effectively be written by one man: Marcus Cunliffe. As he is such a major source, readers need to know more about him.

The Man
Cunliffe was born on 5 July 1922 and christened Marcus Falkner. The family lived near Manchester before moving to Newcastle in 1930. Cunliffe's father, Harold, was a man of enterprise: he changed careers from farming to running a profitable laundry business.[7] Odd hints in the diary suggest that father-son relations were not always harmonious, at least during the period in question. His mother, Kathleen, is not mentioned much.

Cunliffe attended the Royal Grammar School, Newcastle, where he was well taught, gaining a scholarship to read history at Oriel College, Oxford, in 1940. He spent five terms there before commencing officer training, and was commissioned into the Royal Tank Regiment in 1942. He joined 144th RAC in March 1943. His older brother Keith was already in it and they served together until the latter was wounded.[8]

Like the majority of junior officers in an armoured regiment, Cunliffe started as a troop commander.[9] As such he would have led a troop of three or four tanks within one of the Regiment's squadrons, the number varying according to the type of tank. At some stage in the spring or summer of 1943 he became Regimental Intelligence Officer, his position in August 1943 when the sections of the diary used in the book start.[10] Originally a second lieutenant, the lowest of the commissioned ranks, promotion to lieutenant was a matter of course. This was Cunliffe's rank by August 1943.

Cunliffe may have been chosen as Intelligence Officer because of his command of French combined with some knowledge of German, although this is speculation. On 17 September 1944 he switched jobs to lead the Reconnaissance Troop (Recce Troop), which comprised eleven smaller tanks. Again, although he remained a lieutenant, it was a relatively responsible role. Since Cunliffe did not keep his diary at that time, we

3

have no idea why the switch occurred. However, other tank officers' memoirs indicate similar changes of role.[11] Cunliffe had served for over a year as Intelligence Officer, and it was probably thought desirable to induct officers in different roles to maximise their flexibility. When in February 1945 the Regiment changed to operating Buffaloes (see below), the Recce Troop became redundant and Cunliffe reverted to being a troop commander in a squadron of Buffaloes. Cunliffe's position as Intelligence Officer and then commander of the Recce Troop meant that for a long period he was in the Headquarters Mess, with the C/O and a few other officers such as the Padre and the Medical Officer. Most other officers would be in Squadron Messes. This was, to Cunliffe, a mixed blessing. His reactions, to Alan Jolly in particular, are discussed in Chapter 8.

In August 1945 Cunliffe was attached to the military history team at the HQ of the British Army of the Rhine, where he worked on an account of 21 Army Group's campaign. The Group, led by Field Marshal Bernard Montgomery, commanded the two Commonwealth formations, British Second Army and First Canadian Army, in the campaign for the liberation of Europe. This led to Cunliffe's first book, with a co-author, Hugh Darby, *A Short Story of 21 Army Group*, published in 1949. He also, apparently, coined the titles for Montgomery's two early memoirs about the war: *From El Alamein to the Sangro* and *Normandy to the Baltic*.[12] It seemed only fitting to follow Cunliffe's lead in the title of this book.

Subsequently, having taken his degree at Oxford and after two years at Yale as a Commonwealth Fellow, he had a distinguished academic career. He was one of the pioneers of American Studies as an academic discipline in Britain, first at Manchester University where he became a professor, and then in 1965 at the young University of Sussex. From 1980 he was University Professor (a rare appointment) at George Washington University, in Washington DC. He died in 1990.

Cunliffe was primarily a historian, and among his extensive publications were several books on military history which will be mentioned later in this book. It is indicative of his wide range of interests, however, that his best known book is not strictly speaking historical at all: *The Literature of the United States*, first published in 1954 and subsequently going through a number of editions. It reveals an extensive knowledge of American authors, from the earliest period to the present day.[13]

Cunliffe had mainly studied British history at university – one doubts

INTRODUCTION

that there was much, if any, American history taught at Oxford in the 1940s – but according to his biographer, 'had been absorbed by American literature since his schooldays'.[14] Certainly his copious reading during his army career seems to have been mainly in literature rather than history. It is also clear from various entries in his diary that he had literary ambitions. There are references to possible topics for short stories, and one completed short story accompanies the diary.[15]

From comments in the diary, it is clear that Cunliffe's literary interests did not just encompass subject matter and plot but also technique. And it is also evident that, in terms of technique, the diary often serves as a surrogate for the fiction which, he felt, he had not time to write. Since his writings will be a significant part of the forthcoming book, this raises a question: is someone who was interested in the effect of writing on the reader as trustworthy as one who is only interested in recording the facts?

I think that, far from this making Cunliffe a less trustworthy observer, it makes him more so. The reasons are twofold. First, there is no reason to suppose that Cunliffe had any particular bias, beyond the obvious one that every individual has their own point of view. He was at times rather contemptuous of what he perceived as the average regular army officer's lack of interest in much outside their own narrow military world; but he does not set himself up in judgment on them as professionals, giving the impression that he thought the officers of 144th RAC, and particularly Alan Jolly, to be competent soldiers. Indeed he comments from time to time that it was he who was not a very good officer.[16] From a purely military point of view, he had no axes to grind, and we can be surer of that than we can for most observers because we have Cunliffe's own comments, made in the privacy of his diary, to inform us.

Second, Cunliffe's interest in technique, allied to a naturally attractive style, means that he was often a vivid describer of people, places and, in battle, actions. But his descriptions were effective as well as vivid. They were effective because Cunliffe observed more than most people, and expressed his observations in prose which is not only readable, but also precise. This entry in his diary of January 1945 relates to the tail end of the German Ardennes offensive – the 'Battle of the Bulge'. The British 53rd Division, to which 144th RAC was attached, had been counter-attacking the western end of the salient formed by the German advance. By the 9th, the date of the entry, the Germans were retreating. Cunliffe was making a journey, by jeep, over territory recently vacated by them.

This morning I went up through the single track in the woods, with the Colonel, who was looking for a brigadier. It is a poor, steep, inadequate track, never meant for a military [illegible]. It bears erratically upwards among thick firs, then appears quite suddenly at the end of the wood and meanders off across another little hill to the next valley. It was a dull cold morning; the woods were chilly and motionless – they exuded a steady cold, like an old meat-cellar deep underground. The snow was boringly ubiquitous. Up the track a long patient train of vehicles groaned and slithered, while a relieving infantry battalion moved up along the edge in single file. Once again my heart went out to them; the men so sturdy and matter-of-fact, trudging stubbornly onward to their next nightmare, their officers so energetic, so well-moustached, so full of livingness. A good many carriers had lost their tracks and were being edged aside by a bulldozer. Sappers were shovelling dirty brown earth across the whiteness, and flinging down freshly cut fir-branches in front of our wheels. The branches, crushed as soon as they were laid, gave out a bittersweet, aromatic smell – one of the odours of memory. The odour of Christmas trees, standing outside greengrocers' shops in the middle days of December. Cold, aromatic: a smell of the unusual, the expensive, the carefully-contrived.

Out of the wood, we were able to look across several miles of hilly, complicated ground, all under snow and much of it darkened by woods. It was very quiet, and very beautiful. The columns of infantry wound out from the trees, black against the snow, tiny and inexplicably purposeful. So was a tank, climbing a slope a mile in front of us. I remembered ants, toiling across the cracked parterre at home, in the blinding light of summer. What were they doing? Had they any consciousness of purpose? And what were any of us doing, among these bleak, lonely forests, these white uplands, remote from the crowded world, in a wild cul-de-sac of Europe?[17]

Cunliffe excelled at describing tableaux such as this. But his descriptions of action are also effective, and ring true. They do not seem exaggerated, and are full of detail. The diary suggests that he wrote preliminary accounts of notable events reasonably soon after they occurred, so the level of detail is not surprising.[18] Two excerpts from his personal account

INTRODUCTION

of Operation Totalize follow. The first part of Totalize, an operation in early August 1944, was an innovative night attack, launched at German positions to the south of Caen. The aim of this part of the operation was largely achieved, at a comparatively low cost in terms of casualties. Although the later parts were not so successful, the operation was a valuable step in precipitating the complete German collapse in Normandy which ended only two weeks later with the sealing of the Falaise pocket.

There is another personal account of Totalize which has become well known. It was written by Ken Tout, then a gunner in the 1st Northamptonshire Yeomanry, one of 144th RAC's sister regiments in 33rd Armoured Brigade. Tout's account, however, is an amalgam of his memories of a number of actions, in which Totalize serves as a representation of 48 hours of life in a tank. It also contains a lot of dialogue, which is no doubt typical but, given the forty years which had elapsed after the event, must be largely invented.[19] So Cunliffe's account is much closer to the event itself. Most of it is reproduced in Chapter 3. The two passages quoted here occur in the latter stages of 144th RAC's advance.

> A tank hit: one of the tanks a little way behind me was burning. I saw other tanks lumber away from it, in a hurry to get out of the glare, back into the sheltering obscurity. Wonder who it was. Who fired at it? You never know on these occasions. I remembered the training in England, where somebody waved a flag to represent an anti tank gun. When you saw it you rushed off into cover. You always saw it, and there was always cover on the training ground. How different this was. If you saw a gun, it was a safe bet that he'd seen you: and then it was just split-second luck which of you fired first. The odds were on the anti-tank gun.
>
> Soon afterwards, the infantry which 144th RAC had been escorting to their destination launched their attack. The defenders of the village which had been attacked were demoralised by the speed and suddenness of the Allied advance and soon gave up.
>
> The first infantry came back, with some prisoners. The prisoners were grey, haggard and docile. The Jocks [144th RAC was supporting 51st Highland Division] took their watches and then

told them to lie down on the ground. They obeyed gratefully. The attack had gone quite well; the village was captured; not many casualties; quite a lot of prisoners. One of the company commanders [of the infantry] had been killed though. An infantry officer told me about it: 'Poor old Bill – a Spandau was firing from the corner of the field, about a hundred yards from him, so he went after it – with a pistol'. The infantry was pleased; we were pleased; and although the day was sure to bring a counter-attack we did not worry too much about it in the first hour or so of daylight. By some marvel we had reached exactly the point to which it had been decided to bring the infantry. Out of all the chaos and anxiety of the night had come success, and the reassurance of sunlight.[20]

As with the passages above, I have used Cunliffe's diary mainly as a source of material on the Regiment and the war in general. There is a fair amount in the diary about his private life, for instance visits on leave to his family and to London, and after the war to Paris.[21] There was nothing very remarkable about these entries. He saw films and plays and met friends. He also had a girlfriend in London, and there seems to have been some sort of liaison in Paris, but he drew a gentlemanly veil over the details of these friendships. As the book is primarily about the military side of the Second World War, I have not included anything significant about Cunliffe's private life in it.

The Regiment
What about this regiment, 144th RAC, which fought in Operation Totalize and many other actions, and in which Cunliffe was a junior officer?

It had originated as a Holding Battalion of the East Lancashire Regiment, and was reinforced in the summer of 1940 by more East Lancashire men who had returned from France. One of them was Robert Thorne. Later in 1940 it became the 8th Battalion, East Lancashire Regiment, before being converted to armour in November 1941 – part of a drive to increase the proportion of armoured units in the British Army. It was then that it became 144th RAC, but the Regiment continued to have a high proportion of East Lancs men, and this Lancashire flavour is occasionally noted in Cunliffe's diary. The Regiment was originally equipped with Churchill tanks, then Shermans, switching back to Churchills before ending up with Shermans. Its role correspondingly alternated between 'tank' and 'armoured', the difference between these being explained shortly. Early in 1944 its long-standing C/O, Lieutenant Colonel S.T. (Jimmy) James, moved to another role and was replaced by Alan Jolly, who led it until nearly the end of the war.[22]

There was, therefore, a lengthy wait before the Regiment went into action. It seems, however, to have been well led during this period. Certainly Bob Thorne, who had been with the Regiment almost since its inception, thought highly of James. One can infer that it did not suffer from the staleness and inertia which might have resulted from such a long period of training. It is also worth mentioning that the Regiment had been warned for service in Sicily back in 1943. It had not gone, but had remained technically mobilised which meant that it was not raided for men and officers to strengthen other regiments going on active service. In the words of *Blue Flash*, this gave 'us a continuity and stability which had very beneficial effects on training and *esprit de corps*'.[23]

The Regiment's uncertainty about its exact role reflected a similar uncertainty in the higher ranks of the British Army, based on competing theories about the use of tanks. There had long been an enthusiasm among some senior officers for so-called 'infantry' tanks, whose chief role was to support infantry in their attacks. This meant that the tanks could be slow-moving, so there was more scope to equip them with heavy armour, improving their protection against anti-tank guns or hostile tanks. One result of this was the 'Churchill' infantry tank. This was quite a competent design, recovering from an initial reputation for unreliability.[24] However, infantry tanks were not much use in desert warfare and here the tank of choice had become the American designed Sherman. In British nomenclature this was a cruiser tank, intended for tank versus tank actions and the exploitation of breakthroughs.

When the Sherman first appeared in 1942 it was hailed with grateful thanks by Allied tank crews and commanders. It was reliable, in marked contrast to British tanks at that time, and effective against the German tanks of that date. This, together with its relative cheapness and its availability from the vast resources of American industry, led to the British as well as the Americans preferring it, although the British also continued to produce their own designs.[25]

By 1944 the Sherman's defects were becoming more obvious as it faced the newer German tanks now available. These were the Panther, fast and with a powerful gun, and the Tiger, heavily armed and armoured, although relatively slow and clumsy. The Sherman's armour protection was inadequate against their guns, as it was against the heavier anti-tank guns which the Germans now routinely deployed. This weakness was exacerbated by its tendency to burn violently when penetrated by an armour-piercing shell, leading to the darkly humorous nickname, 'Ronsons'. (Ronson was then the best known brand of cigarette lighter and, according to Bob Thorne, the firm had an advertising slogan – 'lights first time'. The Sherman's propensity to catch fire was sometimes put down to its being fuelled by petrol rather than diesel, but actually seems to have been due to inadequate protection for its ammunition bins.) The Sherman's 75mm gun itself lacked sufficient armour penetration capability to pose an equivalent threat to the larger German tanks.[26]

The problem with its armament stemmed, in part, from the tanks' initial employment in North Africa in 1942–3. Here the 75mm gun was effective because it was dual purpose, firing high explosive (HE) to deal with enemy infantry and artillery, and armour piercing shot whose penetrating power was adequate in combat with the German tanks of the period. By 1944, with the inception of the Panthers and Tigers, the latter was no longer the case, but it was too late to quickly change what was now a huge industry in its own right, namely the production of Shermans. The problem could be ameliorated, however, by equipping the tanks with the large and effective 17-pounder anti-tank gun. Shermans so equipped, of course, lost functionality in other ways, notably in their anti-artillery and anti-personnel role, and initially there were only limited numbers of such tanks. So the policy was to have one Sherman 17-pounder, called Fireflies, in each troop of four tanks. Later the proportion was increased.[27]

To the various British officers who were fixated with the concept of the infantry tank, the Sherman's weaknesses strengthened the argument for such tanks. There was no question about the type of tanks needed by armoured divisions whose role, it was envisaged, was primarily the exploitation of gaps in the enemy front. As this might involve rapid movement, it necessitated the use of Shermans or the British equivalent, Cromwells. The question was over tanks for the independent armoured/tank brigades whose primary role was to support the infantry. Eight of these started the campaign, and logically they would use Churchills. However, shortages meant that only three brigades could be so equipped for the Normandy campaign. To the War Office, this necessitated a distinction between tank brigades, equipped with

INTRODUCTION

Churchills, and armoured brigades, equipped with Shermans, each of which had to use rather different tactics.[28] Hence the alternating equipment of 144th RAC, which was part of 33rd Armoured (or, at times, Tank) Brigade. Presumably the War Office could not make up its mind about the type of brigade it wanted 33rd to be; or perhaps it was simply the shortage of Churchill tanks and the need for them elsewhere which dictated the Brigade's changes of role.

There were two problems with the War Office's distinction. One was practical – if the independent brigades' role was primarily to support the infantry, it would be difficult for the latter to adjust to the use of different tactics by their supporting armour depending on whether that was from an 'armoured' or a 'tank' brigade. The other problem was equally formidable – it was the fact that Bernard Montgomery, by late 1943 the commander of 21st Army Group, the headquarters of the invasion force, rejected the distinction between such brigades, arguing that they should be 'interchangeable and capable of supporting operations irrespective of their equipment'.[29]

On the whole, Montgomery got his way. However, John Buckley, a leading historian of armoured warfare, has also pointed out that, precisely because doctrine on the use of tanks in 21st Army Group was contested, it was therefore more flexible. Many commentators have criticised the British Army's lack of doctrine in the earlier years of the war, although as the tank argument shows the more accurate criticism might be of frequently changing doctrine. Buckley points out that doctrinal uncertainty might actually have been a good thing because it emboldened unit commanders to come up with their own solutions as appropriate to different fighting conditions. These varied in different parts of Normandy, and at different stages of the campaign. Timothy Harrison-Place, however, is more sceptical about the value of doctrinal uncertainty.[30]

All this is a background to the history of 144th RAC, but a necessary one. In theory, it was part of an 'armoured' brigade rather than a 'tank' brigade. In practice, it spent much of its time doing the same sort of infantry support work as tank regiments equipped with Churchills. However, at times it took on an exploitation role. One of the intentions of the book is to explore how 144th RAC itself perceived its role, how far it felt that its Shermans were adequate to its main infantry support job, and what sort of tactics it – and especially its commander Alan Jolly – favoured. This will shed light on whether doctrine was as mutable as

Buckley and Harrison-Place imply, and whether that was a good thing or not.

Although there seem to have been some differences between regiments, 144th RAC followed a fairly standard pattern for those equipped with Shermans. Regiments had three squadrons of tanks, designated A, B and C, each consisting of four troops with four tanks in each, one of which was a Sherman Firefly. There were also additional Shermans for squadron and regimental HQ personnel. The latter were part of 'Headquarters Squadron', under whose command there was also a reconnaissance troop of eleven smaller tanks. By 1944 these were American Stuarts; they had been used as cruiser tanks in the early days of 1941–2, and were fair-sized beasts. The British nicknamed them Honeys. Total regimental personnel numbered about 700.

Three regiments constituted a brigade. Non-British readers with some military knowledge will realise at this point that the usual idiosyncratic British military terminology is at risk of confusing them. In the UK, infantry regiments were embodiments of history and had some administrative functions. Each regiment would have a number of battalions – the number expanding in wartime – and battalions were the actual fighting units, three of which would be under the command of a brigade; in turn three brigades, with supporting arms, constituted a division. In the armoured branch, however, regiments were battalion sized units, which were also linked in brigades. (There were exceptions: if an armoured unit was part of the Royal Tank Regiment it was designated as a battalion; so when 144th RAC became 4th RTR in 1945, it ceased to be a regiment and became a battalion – but was otherwise exactly the same.)

Some armoured brigades were permanently part of armoured divisions, and in theory those of the independent brigades which were equipped with Shermans, such as 33rd Armoured, could fight with armoured divisions. In practice, however, the Brigade was usually allotted to an infantry division. It had spent a considerable time in England training with 49th Infantry Division and this was intended to be the division to which they would be regularly attached. In the event 144th RAC worked with them for precisely a week, and that was fortuitous, occurring when the Regiment was briefly assigned to the Division in late August, in the last stages of the Normandy campaign.[31]

In the early stages of the campaign 33rd Armoured Brigade was moved around but, during Totalize and for much of the time after it, the Brigade

INTRODUCTION

was attached to 51st Highland Division. In turn 144th RAC was attached to 153rd Infantry Brigade, one of the three in 51st Division. This systemic connection between infantry and armoured units was known as affiliation, and each of the Regiment's three squadrons were usually then allotted to one of the Brigade's three battalions.[32] As Jolly makes clear in *Blue Flash*, however, there were in his view limits to the extent to which tanks should be parcelled up and divided between infantry units.[33] Ideally, armoured regiment C/Os would take an overall view of the support they would allocate, although in practice, in the sort of dogged advance common in both Normandy and Holland, the allocation of a squadron to each battalion often made good sense.

This, however, is to anticipate. In early 1944, 144th RAC was still training in England. Most of their training so far had been for infantry tank work, since for most of the time after the conversion to armour they had been equipped with Churchills. Now, reequipped finally with Shermans, they spent some time training in an 'armoured' as opposed to 'tank' role, that is for mobile operations. Their specific brief was that 33rd Armoured Brigade 'might find itself replacing a brigade in an armoured division which had suffered heavy casualties'.[34]

By May, training was completed and the Regiment began moving south – it had been in East Anglia – to its 'Concentration Area' in Aldershot. It was part of the vast machinery of 'Overlord', the invasion of Normandy. Hundreds of units – infantry battalions, artillery and tank regiments, engineer companies, headquarters formations and all the vast logistical apparatus of a modern army – slowly moved towards the South Coast. At Aldershot there were numerous last-minute preparations. Telephones were attached outside tanks for communication with the infantry; this, one would have thought, might have been done earlier so that practice in their use could have been incorporated into training. Bins were fixed to the rear of the turrets in order to carry blankets, rations and bivouac tents. And, in the words of *Blue Flash*, 'there were those lengths of track to be welded to the outside of tanks to make the thin armour of the Shermans a little thicker'.[35] John Buckley suggests that this was unofficial although condoned by the authorities, but Jolly's phrasing seems to imply that it was official. Later analysis suggested that, unfortunately, it failed to improve the Shermans' resistance to German shells.[36]

By June the Regiment had finished its preparation and was waiting. It was in the middle of a rifle competition when, on the morning of 6 June, the news that the invasion had started was received. 'After lunch, the C.O. spoke to all officers in the billiards room of the officers' mess and later to all ranks in the riding school'. The Regiment finally left Aldershot on 9 June, arriving near Portsmouth, their embarkation port, around teatime. George Pearson, a driver with A Echelon, wrote: 'How well I remember those last few hours in England, how each village and town turned out to cheer us through and if we were lucky enough to stop we were simply showered with tea, cakes and cigarettes'.[37]

For four more days they waited, in what the war diary described as a 'period of tension and uncertainty'. A number of tanks were parked in Portsmouth streets, 'where the kindly inhabitants plied [the crews] with food and cups of tea, and even offered them beds'. Announcements about ship loading were made over a tannoy system: 'Several times an hour, day and night, one would hear it switched on – a tense pause while the operator blew into the microphone and then the announcement of the serial number of the craft to be embarked'.[38]

On 13 June the Regiment was finally called forward and loaded into Landing Craft Tanks (LCTs). Bob Thorne remembered sleeping 'very soundly in the captain's cabin' of one of the vessels in which they were embarked. The LCTs disgorged the Regiment at Arromanches on 14 June, by which time the famous Mulberry harbour, later known as Port Winston, was practically complete. The Regiment then moved to its own harbour, a 'huge field' according to Cunliffe, about 2 miles south of Bayeux. It was the first of many on the Continent.[39]

The Campaign
The military campaign in which 144th RAC played a part has had more written about it than most, and for obvious reasons. Together with the Russian campaign on the Eastern Front, it contributed to, and ended with, the liquidation of Hitler's Germany. Not surprisingly, initial accounts including Marcus Cunliffe's own *A Short Story of 21 Army Group* were mainly laudatory. Interestingly, however, an early personal account, Major Martin Lindsay's *So Few Got Through*, which told the story of the 1st Gordons, an infantry battalion which fought alongside 144th RAC for much of the campaign, stresses the savagery of the fighting, the heavy casualties, and the effectiveness of German resistance.[40]

Fairly soon, antidotes to the optimistic view started to appear. They

INTRODUCTION

were inspired by German commentators, many of whom were the self-same generals who had fought against the Allies in 1944 and 1945. Leaving aside a natural desire to portray themselves in the best light, the generals had another reason to elevate German fighting skills, while trying to fit this into a narrative in which Germany lost. The fighting skills, according to them, were a result of Germany's long military heritage, which, through training and the superiority of its military doctrine, had produced flexible and efficient armed forces. The defeat was the result of Hitler's interference in strategic and operational decisions; later in the war, the vast Allied superiority in resources also became a major factor.

This interpretation, which of course covered the whole war and not just the 1944–5 campaign in the West, implied that the generals were unsympathetic to Hitler and therefore conveniently distanced the *Wehrmacht* from the Nazi regime. Initially, the Western military commentators and historians who accepted it were unaware of the German army's complicity in the criminalisation of warfare on the Eastern Front by the execution of civilians, including many Jews, and other atrocities. Much of the evidence for these acts was hidden in Russian archives, unavailable until the 1990s. Not surprisingly, the generals' memoirs either did not mention the atrocities, or suggested their disapproval. It is only gradually that research has uncovered the extent to which generals implicitly or actively supported such acts, and units took part in them.[41] Nonetheless the German generals' emphasis on their military skills would have had no credibility as a smokescreen for their crimes had there not been something in their claims to superiority. In certain important military attributes, notably speed of decision-making and action, the Germans were superior to any Allied army throughout the war.

As the German generals offered their evidence, a shift occurred in many historians' approach to the Allied campaign of 1944–5. It particularly affected the early part in Normandy, when the Allies struggled for weeks to decisively break through the German defences. Much of the rest of the campaign until victory in May 1945 has attracted less interest, with the exceptions of the Arnhem operation, a notable Allied failure, and the Ardennes counter-attack which exposed Allied weaknesses before the Germans were finally thrown back. In other words, operations in which the Allies struggled have tended to attract more attention than those in which they succeeded easily.

FROM ARROMANCHES TO THE ELBE

This shift saw, instead of praise, criticism of Allied fighting skills. Historians drew attention to Allied weaknesses in morale, to Allied slowness in exploitation, to Allied failures in generalship.[42] This approach has its attractions, not least because some of its claims can be substantiated. It does, however, come up against the fact that the Allies won, and they did so comprehensively. By May 1945 the German war machine was shattered. And more recently, other historians have countered what they see as somewhat one-sided approbation of German military skills and censure of Allied ones, and developed a more rounded explanation of why the Allies gained military superiority. This takes into account their material superiority, but also pays due respect to their own military skills. It also puts into context the German generals' standard defence, which is that mistakes were due to Hitler.[43]

Although the focus here is on the Allied campaign in Western Europe from 1944–5, it will help to begin with the German attack which set off the greatest and most bloodthirsty military campaign of all time: Operation Barbarossa on 22 June 1941, the start of Germany's invasion of the Soviet Union. It is common to place 'turning points' in the war at some later date: perhaps Pearl Harbor on 7 December 1941, and the entry of the USA into the war; or the successful Russian resistance outside Moscow at the same time; or the Battle of El Alamein in October 1942 which marked the end of the German threat to the Middle East; or the Battle of Stalingrad, ending in February 1943. To some historians, however, the war's turning point – the point when Germany was doomed – was earlier than these. It was the moment when German forces crossed the Barbarossa start line.[44]

This judgment might be right or wrong, but there are cogent reasons for it. The German forces undertaking Barbarossa might have constituted the largest army ever assembled, but it was a giant with feet of clay. It was launched with limited artillery support, much of it horse-drawn; with limited numbers of high-quality tanks; and most notably with totally inadequate logistical preparation. The well-known shortages of winter clothing which condemned many German soldiers to frostbite or death in the winter of 1941–2 were only one part of this: transportation was lacking, petrol was short and food supplies were inadequate – the intention was to rob the conquered Russians of food, with the inevitable consequence of partisan warfare. Yet the attack was not launched by Hitler against the advice of his generals. On the contrary, many of them

INTRODUCTION

supported it and most thought that Germany would win, or at least crush the existing Russian forces.[45]

The casual and cavalier way in which the German army launched the biggest attack in history has lessons for an analysis of the 1944–5 campaign. Those historians who have lauded the Germans' fighting ability are in danger of missing a fairly major point. It is the winning of wars that counts; the winning of individual battles is only a means to that end. The winning of wars may be achieved by a few battlefield victories and by outmanoeuvring the enemy, as in 1940 when the Germans defeated France. But if these did not do the trick, as in Russia in 1941, then other factors came into play – the ones the Germans neglected in Barbarossa: depth of resources and logistical competence.

Historians who have espoused a more optimistic view of Allied capabilities see them as strong in precisely those areas in which the Germans were weak. They also, however, see the Allies as not just winning the war by the application of brute force, but rather as intelligently tailoring their fighting methods to take advantage of their own strengths and to minimise the effect of their weaknesses. The main points that are stressed by such historians are set out below.[46]

The Allies had by 1944 a huge superiority in aircraft and in logistical capability. They also had a large superiority in artillery and this was particularly true of the British and, by extension, the Canadians, who often fought with the British and used similar equipment. On the other hand, the Germans' larger tanks, the Tiger and the Panther, were better armed than most Shermans. The more heavily armed Sherman, the Firefly, was a partial countermeasure but the Allies knew that there would be problems. They also realised that their troops, many of them untested in battle, would need careful handling. The British were also well aware that their pool of manpower was running dry. With worldwide commitments, with a large air force and navy and a correspondingly large munitions industry, there were limits to the numbers who could be spared for the front-line infantry. Beyond a certain point losses could not be replaced. This necessitated a care with men's lives which might run counter to immediate operational requirements.

All these factors dictated a particular method of fighting, already honed in North Africa and Italy. The original British uncertainty over doctrine had been replaced by a fairly rigid formula. Large-scale artillery barrages and, sometimes, air bombardments would soften up the enemy before an advance. This advance might be led by tanks if the ground was right, but more often by infantry, if possible close behind a barrage and in conjunction with tanks. Command would be 'top-down' to ensure control over the advance. Allied, and especially British, command methods have often been subject to criticism by historians. These methods owed a lot to a deep-rooted tendency to control lower echelons rather than give them general objectives and let them get on with it – the preferred German method. Nevertheless there were also reasons for commanding in this way, notably the fact that, if troops were not as fully trained or battleworthy as was ideal, it might be wisest not to allow them too much initiative.

Tactics as outlined above were geared to the Allies' strengths. If something was yielded to the Germans in terms of speed and tactical astuteness, more was gained by playing to these strengths. Furthermore infantrymen's lives were conserved, although casualties were still heavy. But German casualties were heavier, because they consistently followed their well-established tactic of counter-attacking Allied advances. Here Allied artillery superiority was as or more important as when preparing for an attack, because once German troops were counter-attacking they were in the open and more vulnerable.

One important task of this book will be to assess the extent to which 144th RAC, and the battles in which it fought, accord with this analysis of Allied methods and their effectiveness. Was its training adequate to the specific tasks which it had? What light is cast on the performance of the infantry with which it fought? How far did Allied artillery play a part in its successes? How well did it cope with the superior firepower of some German tanks? Did the caution of many British senior commanders prevent possible gains or was it generally justified?

Chapter 2

Arromanches to Noyers

The First Month

When 144th RAC landed on 14 June, the Allies had already been in Normandy for eight days. They had achieved a great deal. The bridgehead stretched from 5–15 miles inland, and 50 miles of coast was in Allied hands. More importantly, the Germans had been unable to pose a serious threat after the first day. They had launched some major counter-attacks and sometimes regained ground, but the general direction of the Allies had been inland.

Nevertheless, there has been much subsequent criticism of Montgomery. In particular it has often been suggested that the events of those eight days did not fall out as he had planned. Typically, Monty himself claimed that they had done, writing, 'I never once had cause or reason to alter my plan'.[1] In fact, one of the basic principles of the plan, the early capture of Caen, had not taken place: the city was not fully under Allied control until late July. (Map 3.1) The plan had, however, called for only a slow advance from Caen after its capture, in a southerly and south-easterly direction. The main purpose of the Allied forces in this sector – primarily the British and Canadians – was to threaten German communications, thus provoking a strong reaction and absorbing the fighting capacity of the Panzer divisions. American forces to the west would therefore face less resistance and have a better chance of breaking out, as eventually happened. The Allies threatened German communications whichever side of Caen the British and Canadians were, so to that extent Montgomery's statement was justified. Even so, the initial failure to take the town probably prolonged the German capacity to resist.[2]

The need to threaten German communications, and thus provoke a German response, shaped the sort of fighting that the bulk of the British forces, including 144th RAC, were faced with during most of their time in Normandy. They and the Canadians mounted a series of attacks aimed at encircling Caen, occupying it and then threatening to break out to the south and east. These attacks were met by fierce resistance, both by entrenched German infantry protected by anti-tank guns, and by armour. This in turn meant that the initial battle experience of 144th RAC, in theory a dual purpose armoured regiment which could engage in more open armoured warfare as well as supporting infantry, was in the latter role. Subsequently, however, it took part in Operation Totalize, mentioned in the introduction, a night attack which gained several miles. Then, as the Germans retreated to the Seine, the Regiment's role became one of exploitation, although from time to time it had to revert to a slower moving type of fighting as it met resistance along river lines.

Soon after its arrival the Regiment was placed under the command of 7th Armoured Division, remaining with them until late June. At that point, therefore, the intention was to use it in a mobile role, rather than as infantry support. But in fact, it did not engage in any fighting for more than three weeks after landing. As Alan Jolly pointed out, this lack of action exemplified the strong situation the Allies were in. The 33rd Armoured Brigade was part of Montgomery's reserve, and would have been available had the Germans mounted a major counter-attack. Its mobility, therefore, was at that stage valuable for its defensive rather than offensive potential.[3]

On 8–9 July, having moved eastwards towards Caen, the Brigade took part in Operation Charnwood, the attack which would finally push into that city. The operation became notorious for the heavy bombing which preceded it which, while destroying much of Caen, did less damage to the German defenders.[4] Subsequently, further advances were held up by continued German resistance, in the southern suburbs and in the Colombelles factory district to the east.

The Regiment's part in this consisted only of a peripheral role in 59th Division's attack from the north. They reconnoitred towards Couvre-Chef, a northern suburb of Caen, found it empty and reported back. Nevertheless 59th Division was 'taking no chances' and Couvre-Chef was attacked behind a heavy barrage which, 'We watched with some derision'.[5] There is a hint here of the unnecessarily elaborate attacks and slow tempo of operations of which the British Army was often accused. The Regiment took a few prisoners and incurred no casualties, although subsequently it lost several wounded through mortaring. Nevertheless its experience, as yet, could hardly count as serious fighting. A few days later it moved westwards again. The British were to have yet another try at encircling Caen and evicting the remaining German defenders, and 144th RAC were to play an indirect part in this operation, named Operation Goodwood. (It continued a racecourse theme, since a previous attack in late June had been called Epsom.) Like several British operations in Normandy, Goodwood has a bad reputation among historians.

The strategic aim of the operation was straightforward. It was intended to finally clear Caen and to advance several miles beyond it, thus intensifying the threat to eastern Normandy. This area was the hinge of all German operations west of the Seine. It was the main route for their supplies and reinforcements. Furthermore, they still feared an Allied landing in the Pas de Calais, and saw eastern Normandy as a bulwark against an invading force there linking up with the existing invaders to the west of Caen. For both these reasons, they perceived eastern Normandy as vital. By increasing the threat to such a vital area, Goodwood would also distract German attention, and German forces, from the planned American breakout to the west. Named Cobra, this was to begin on 20 July (although bad weather, which would reduce the accuracy of the preliminary bombing, forced its postponement until 25 July). Goodwood, however, was a very difficult operation to mount because the British forces involved would have to form up in the limited space the Allies occupied east of the River Orne.

Goodwood has been criticised so heavily because the massed tank attack which was its main component suffered heavy losses and eventually came to a halt, in the face of strenuous German opposition, at the line of villages ringing Caen's southern edge. This was several miles short of its planned objectives. Even John Buckley, often a defender of British armoured forces' capabilities, is very critical. Nevertheless, a major part of the German defensive zone, which was up to 6 miles deep and backed by strong forces in reserve behind it, had been captured by the time the operation ended on 21 July. The initial phases of the main tank attack had broken through successfully, supported by Canadian and British infantry attacks on the west and east. The later stages of the main attack, however, had suffered heavily from unsuppressed German guns. In retrospect, the main criticism which can be directed at Goodwood was not so much its achievements, which were actually quite substantial, but the heavy cost in casualties, both human and tank.[6]

The 144th RAC was involved, not in the actual attack in the Caen area, but in one of the two subsidiary attacks which were designed to distract

German attention from the main operation. These took place along the front of the Odon salient, which had been created during Operation Epsom. (Map 3.1) The Regiment was, once more, to be working with 59th Division; for the purpose of the attack both had been transferred to XXX Corps.

Goodwood was to start on 18 July. The first of the subsidiary attacks, called Operation Greenline, was to start on the 15th; the second, Operation Pomegranate, in which 144th RAC took part, on the 16th. Neither attack is given much attention by the main histories of the campaign, but together they constituted a fairly substantial operation. After the war, when the British Army named its battles, they were united as the Second Battle of the Odon; Operation Epsom, in June, was the First. Greenline, which was mounted by XII Corps, stretched roughly from Maltot to Grainville-sur-Odon. Pomegranate, under the control of XXX Corps, extended the front westwards to Vendes.[7]

The Noyers Attack
The attack which 144th RAC assisted, and which was the most important element of Pomegranate, had as its objective the village of Noyers-Bocage. (Map 2.1) The name of the village is a clue to the problems of the attack. Much of the countryside in the vicinity is *bocage* country, characterised by sunken lanes, small fields and correspondingly numerous hedgerows on banks. This was easy country to defend against both tanks and infantry. Anti-tank guns, troops with hand-held *Panzerfaust* or *Panzerschreck* anti-tank weapons and even tanks themselves could hide behind hedgerows and in sunken lanes; similarly the infantry were confronted by hidden machine-guns and mortars. Allied tanks found it difficult to move cross-country even without opposition since the hedgerows and banks were themselves formidable obstacles. Churchill tanks, which had better climbing ability than Shermans, had the advantage here.*

---

* *Panzerfaust* and *Panzerschreck* were different types of hand-held anti-tank weapons, described in the glossary. Although the term *Panzerfaust* is often used in British writing on the campaign as a catch-all, the word used by 144th RAC was *Ofenrohr*, misspelt by them *Offenrohr*. It meant stovepipe, which was the nickname given to *Panzerschrecke* by German troops because of the cloud of black smoke emitted on firing. *Ofenrohr* will be used from now on for all such weapons as it seems appropriate to follow the Regiment's practice. *Panzerschrecke* were based on the American bazooka, and Robert Thorne referred to Germans wielding such hand-held anti-tank weapons as 'bazooka boys'.

Not all the country around Noyers was *bocage*. As a result the attack at Noyers afforded opportunities for different tactics to be employed at different times. The Regiment compiled a detailed report on it, so there is plenty of material for a case-study. While the battle itself was small-scale in relation to other battles in Normandy, examining it in detail yields valuable insights into British tactics in combined tank/infantry actions. There is not much in the literature about these actions unless undertaken by the armoured divisions; if there is, the focus is on the infantry. Yet independent tank or armoured brigades undertook many such actions over the course of the campaign.

In Chapter 1 it was pointed out that, according to both John Buckley and Timothy Harrison-Place, before the invasion there was considerable British uncertainty as to tank tactics in support of infantry. Nevertheless, both agree that certain features were stressed, although with different emphases at different periods. An ideal tank/infantry combination would consist of a troop of tanks leading, in order to suppress enemy positions. These would be followed by infantry who could clean these up further and take prisoners, and then by another tank troop, which would provide fire support for both the infantry and the leading tanks. According to Buckley, even in Tunisia with its open terrain this 'sandwich' method was sometimes found wanting, while in Normandy early disillusionment set in. Germans concealed in the *bocage* let the leading tanks pass then countered the infantry with machine guns; the tanks could then be dealt with, by concealed anti-tank guns or *Ofenrohre*. Buckley concludes that 'leading with tanks in the dense terrain of Normandy only worked when the enemy was weak or caught by surprise'. This is a little misleading because as will be seen – and as is apparent from observation when driving over the ground – terrain in Normandy is not always dense; there can be open stretches of country amidst the *bocage*. As a result, in certain circumstances it was possible to utilise the classic sandwich tactics with success. However, the circumstances were often not suitable and so we also see 144th RAC using other tactics to suit other circumstances. The Regiment's account of Noyers also contains evidence of Alan Jolly's strongly held views about the optimum size of units when supporting infantry, and material on other battle-related subjects such as command and control.[8]

During the battle the Regiment was in support of 177th Infantry Brigade, a unit of 59th (Staffordshire) Infantry Division. It was rare for a division to have a county name attached, as opposed to a regional name (e.g. Highland), and the name was a tribute to the wartime contribution of the north Midland county, although in fact several of the division's battalions were drawn from Lancashire, Warwickshire and, rather oddly, Norfolk. But 177th Brigade consisted entirely of battalions of the South Staffordshire Regiment.

The battle itself was scrappy, with intermittent bouts of heavy fighting. It will not be described in full, since its ultimate result was limited. Rather, certain stages will be analysed in depth. The terms 'Noyers' or 'the Noyers attack' will be used from now on as they were by the 144th RAC, even though the name has no official status. Indeed, as will be seen, Noyers itself was only briefly reached; but it was always the main objective.

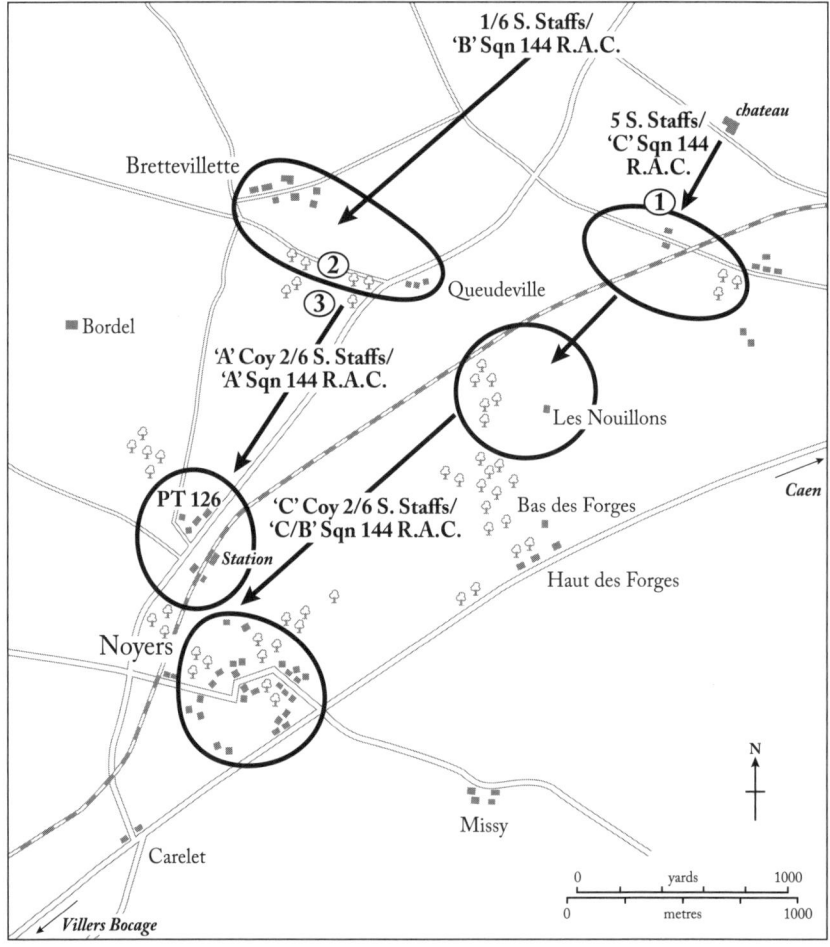

Map 2.1

ARROMANCHES TO NOYERS

With the attack due to start on 16 July, 144th's preparations began on the 13th with Jolly and the infantry brigadier making a joint reconnaissance and an outline plan. On the 14th plans were firmed up and squadron commanders liaised with the C/Os of the infantry battalions with whom they would be fighting. In the absence of any previous contact between 144th RAC and 177th Brigade, infantry platoon commanders and some NCOs and men came over on the 15th and 'examined the tanks and tank telephones and met troop and tank leaders'. As will be seen this induction was not sufficient. According to the account written by the Regiment after the battle, an innovation was the use of Flails, AVREs and Crocodiles under its command.* These fearsome machines are described in the Glossary. There was one troop each of the first two named, and two of Crocodiles. The preparations seem considerable for what was only one part of a diversionary attack, but the Germans had had over two weeks to dig in after Operation Epsom and, as would soon become evident, resistance was fierce. The German division involved was 277th ID, which had relieved 9th SS Panzer on 9 July. The German *regiment* on the front attacked was 989th GR. Later, however, elements of 9th Panzer were recalled.[9]

At 05.30 on 16 July the attack started. The first phase was on a two squadron/two battalion front and was intended to clear some hamlets prior to attacking Noyers itself. 'It was a hot summer day without a breath of wind and the early morning mist with the dust from the shelling made it extraordinarily difficult for tank commanders and drivers to see where they were going.'[10]

Both squadrons quickly lost a number of tanks on mines. The very large tank casualties reported for some large-scale British tank attacks, such as Goodwood, were inflated by casualties from mines. These very rarely resulted in the total loss of the tank, or in personnel casualties except among crews who were constrained to dismount and were then more vulnerable. It was the tracks or suspension units of the tanks which suffered, and these could normally be repaired. But the tank itself would be out of action, probably for several hours at least. So it was with 144th RAC at Noyers where, out of thirty tank casualties, twenty were caused by mines. The particularly galling thing about these was that the

---

* From now on quotes in this chapter will be from the Regimental account, unless otherwise identified.

majority were caused by British minefields. In spite of close co-operation with the infantry holding the sector, and promises to lift the mines, 'it appeared that they had no idea where each individual mine had been laid'. A further cause of chagrin was that the Regiment had been equipped with the mine-clearing Flails, but had been keeping them back for use on enemy minefields. If deployed in time on the British minefields they could have saved numerous tank casualties.[11]

On the right battalion front, where B Squadron was teamed with the 1/6th South Staffs, the initial advance on Brettevillette and Queudeville was in a loose sandwich formation. (The term 'sandwich' was not used in the Regimental account, but is a convenient shorthand for the method.) On reaching Brettevillette the tanks were to support from the left, as the hamlet itself was considered an unsuitable area for good tank support. The area is a tangle of little lanes, so this reluctance is not surprising. The implication is that, in the later stages of the attack, the tanks were to stand off the objective and 'shoot the infantry in'. Initially, however, although the infantry were described as following the tanks, 144th RAC's account also said that 'it was intended that leading tank troops should work closely with the leading infantry', implying that they were close together at this stage of the attack, rather than the tanks being some way in advance as in the classic sandwich method. Artillery support was by concentrations, probably because the *bocage* country meant that a steady advance behind a creeping barrage was deemed impossible.[12]

The right battalion had two axes of advance, each supported by two troops of tanks. On the left axis the infantry were soon pinned down by machine-gun fire and the leading tank troop lost two tanks on mines. Nevertheless, the remaining tanks 'were able to silence the machine guns temporarily, but the infantry did not appear to be able to take advantage of this to get forward'. There seems to be a hint here that lack of drive, rather than the temporarily suppressed enemy, was the reason for the infantry's stickiness. A third leading tank was then hit by an *Ofenrohr* and the fourth moved to rejoin the squadron. The other troop, No. 2, silenced some enemy positions in nearby houses but was itself steadily losing tanks on mines.[13]

When the troop was down to one tank, a Sherman Firefly, the rule book was thrown away. Sergeant Critchley, the tank's commander, advanced down a sunken lane (Map 2.1, location 2):

with both the tank Brownings firing and he himself leaning out of the turret firing his Sten gun and throwing hand grenades. Having run out of Browning and Sten ammunition, he borrowed a Bren gun from the infantry and continued firing with it from the turret of his tank.

He then reversed and advanced down the main road to the south, firing his 17 pounder into the enemy trying to reorganise in the woods . . . Although he had only A.P. [armour-piercing] shot from the 17 pounder this appeared to throw the enemy into confusion and the infantry were now able to advance and capture the position. [Map 2.1, location 3]

Clearly the speed of Critchley's action and his use of maximum firepower were decisive in confusing the enemy. This, of course, was the sort of thing at which the best German commanders excelled. It does not negate the worth of the careful advances, supported by artillery, which the British preferred. Such an advance had preceded Critchley's attack, had made considerable progress and may have disorganised the enemy. But clearly it had not suppressed them completely since the infantry commander, Major Barber, believed that his company would not have captured the objective but for Sergeant Critchley. It is only fair to note that Major Barber's company, whether or not it had been sticky beforehand, was capable of taking advantage of Critchley's courage and quick thinking. The latter was deservedly awarded a Military Medal.

Although his action was highly successful, it was, of course, also very risky. Another two troops of B Squadron were advancing, with more infantry, on the right hand axis. Lieutenant Borg, commanding No. 3 troop, attacked enemy positions in a similar manner, firing his Sten gun from the turret, and was killed.[14]

On this flank, the main tasks in the initial phase had now been accomplished. However, Lieutenant Potts, a troop commander whose tank had been hit by a mine, was not idle. He organised ground defences by dismounting his own tank's Browning and providing tank gunners to man a self-propelled anti-tank gun which had hit a mine. Finally, Potts organised other crew members to start lifting the minefield. British troops have sometimes been accused of relaxing after an advance, only to find themselves hit by German counter-attacks. Potts' initiative minimised the danger of such an attack succeeding.[15]

The infantry, having redeemed themselves by taking Brettevillette and Queudeville, and having agreed to the tanks being recalled, then requested their return to help clear up some alleged machine-gun positions. The 144th RAC's account was acerbic: 'No enemy were, in fact, found in this area, three more tanks were lost on mines, and another two hours were wasted'.[16] Jolly fought a constant battle of words, both here and in *Blue Flash*, against infantry demands for small groups of tanks to assist in local actions. He could have refused such requests, but presumably a desire to be helpful and perhaps the political calculation that backs had to be mutually scratched to encourage future infantry cooperation were factors in his decision-making. His objections to the practice were twofold: tanks were best used in larger groups; and such requests prevented tanks from returning in a timely manner to their temporary base in order to refuel, rearm and allow the crews vital rest.

Meanwhile, the left battalion front of the attack, comprising C Squadron in support of the 5th South Staffs, had been making for its initial objectives, orchards bordering the railway. (Map 2.1, location 1.) Marcus Cunliffe's brother, Keith, was a troop commander in this squadron. Again, numerous tanks were quickly lost to British mines, leaving only two on the right-hand axis of this attack. Here the value of having an entire squadron together was illustrated. The left-hand axis of attack found that its objective, an orchard south of the railway, was heavily defended, but on the right the objective was undefended. The squadron commander, Major Pickering, switched one troop from the left to reinforce his weakened right. They then circled to the north of the railway, crossed it west of the defended orchard and attacked the enemy successfully from that side.[17]

C Squadron and the infantry then continued to Les Nouillons. Here the now denuded squadron shot the infantry in to the hamlet itself and a wood nearby. This attack met with little opposition but there was more around a signal box and orchard to the north of the railway. As earlier, Pickering was able to concentrate his remaining tanks and engage the objective with HE. 'The outcome of this switch was immediately successful, and with the infantry and tanks working in the closest co-operation, the opposition was quickly quelled and a large number of prisoners taken.'[18]

Before the next phase of the operation, Jolly ordered Flails to clear an enemy minefield near Queudeville, and they soon exploded three mines.

The plan now called for 2/6 South Staffs, the third battalion in 177th Brigade, to 'pass through' and take over the infantry attack. Although the attack was less widely dispersed than in the first phases and would only involve one battalion, it involved two companies advancing, one on each side of the railway, and Jolly wanted to support each company with a squadron. Presumably this would give him and his squadron commanders flexibility and maximum firepower against strong enemy positions. After the heavy losses the two squadrons would be A Squadron, not hitherto involved, and a composite squadron consisting of the remnants of C Squadron, plus the surviving five tanks of B Squadron when they had been released from mopping up.[19]

By now it was late afternoon and the attack was launched at 17.30. On the right, A Squadron attacked in a classic sandwich formation. On this front, 'there was a thousand-yard stretch of good tank going' and as a result, 'A Squadron was able to put a training theory into practice, that even the thin-skinned Sherman tanks were comparatively safe if they followed closely behind the artillery barrage'.[20] In other words, there were two necessary ingredients for such an attack: 'no obstacles likely to hold up the tanks and cause them to "lose" the barrage'; and sufficient weight of artillery in the barrage itself. As a corollary, 'the leading tanks should keep close up to the line of the bursting shells, facing the far smaller risk of an unlucky hit from our own artillery rather than the certainty of casualties from German anti-tank guns'.[21] Infantry, according to Sydney Jary, could usually close up 50yd behind the barrage if fired by 25-pounders, as barrages usually were. Jary, as a Second World War platoon commander, had plenty of experience.[22] Tanks could presumably get even closer.

The Regimental account gives more detail. As in the morning attacks, A Squadron had two axes of advance, to the right and left of the road between Queudeville and the crossroads outside Noyers. Each axis had a troop forward and a troop back. According to the plan,

> Each forward troop was to push two tanks forward into the fringe of the barrage watched by the two remaining tanks. The barrage went forward at 100 yards in three minutes and the two rear tanks in each troop were to come up in the barrage with the two forward tanks just before the barrage lifted each time. The supporting troops [of tanks] were to support the forward tanks from a distance of

300 to 400 yards with a subsidiary task of assisting the infantry against any resistance not dealt with by the leading tanks. The infantry were to be further supported by the tanks putting down H.E. and Browning fire in all hedges and likely looking places of enemy resistance.[23]

The objectives of this attack to the right of the railway were Point 126, a group of houses about half a mile north of Noyers itself, and the railway station. (Map 2.1) On reaching them, the tanks would stand off and give covering fire into the buildings which the infantry would assault. The tanks would also watch the flanks of the attack. To assault the station the tanks needed to cross the railway and here air photographs were available.[24] This was a small example of the way in which the cornucopia of Allied resources, in this case reconnaissance aircraft, could be useful.

Plans were one thing, but the point about these was that they 'were carried out almost to the letter', with the tanks only needing to deviate slightly at one point because of a line of trees.

> Otherwise the troops [of tanks] moved exactly as planned. The infantry followed the leading tanks as close as the barrage permitted and were thus able to close with the enemy as he came out of his dugouts where he had taken refuge from the bombardment, thereby preventing the leading tanks from being fired on from the rear by undetected anti-tank guns. The enemy seemed dazed by the weight of the barrage and little resistance was encountered on the way to the objective. In the houses around Point 126 the enemy readily gave up when the infantry assaulted with the bayonet. It was not possible to carry out any exploitation as the infantry company was thin on the ground having started the attack considerably below strength.
>
> The right and left forward troops [of tanks] took up their positions as ordered on the objective and gave the assaulting infantry good fire support. About 70 to 80 prisoners were taken during the advance from the S. L. [Start Line] and in the buildings on the objective. Five 75 mm. Anti-Tank Guns were knocked out in front of the objective, the crews having no time to man them before the tanks and infantry were upon them. One Panther tank near the Railway Station was also knocked out by the left forward

troop, four of the crew, who were observed to bale out, being engaged with machine-gun fire.[25]

This was not, therefore, an attack which was predestined to succeed because it only faced thin defences. On the contrary, the defences were considerable; but British tactics, aided by plentiful equipment, were more than their match. Buckley's statement that the sandwich formation only worked in Normandy if the enemy was weak or caught by surprise therefore needs modification. With five anti-tank guns, the enemy was certainly not weak, and he could not have been caught by surprise since the British had been attacking since 05.30 that morning. Given a clear stretch of countryside and good artillery support, 144th RAC proved that the sandwich formation was alive and well.

The other attack was on the left of the railway, and was aimed at Noyers itself. It was less successful. Apart from the B Squadron tanks which, in Jolly's view, had been held back unnecessarily at Brettevillette, the C Squadron tanks had also been held by the infantry who had taken Les Nouillons. They were ordered to return to base for replenishment, so here Jolly seems to have overruled the infantry commander. Time had been lost, however, and when they returned once more to Les Nouillons to start the second phase, which like the attack on the right started at 17.30, the artillery barrage had begun and the infantry had started to go forward.

Given that this was an area of *bocage*, the use of a barrage rather than concentrations is puzzling. Any hope of the tanks catching up with it was gone when the two leading tanks moved forward to deal with machine-gun fire which was holding up the infantry. One tank ditched and the other was hit.* Major Pickering, the squadron commander, then made a reconnaissance on foot. Encouraged by A Squadron's successful hit on the Panther by the station, he believed that the opposition had been dealt with and decided to continue the advance. The infantry was slow to follow, however, and Pickering's tanks were in the lead when he was

---

* *Blue Flash* features a photograph of the first tank (facing p. 33) on its side, captioned 'Lieut. M. F. Cunliffe's tank'. It seems more likely that it was Keith Cunliffe's tank, since he was a troop commander in C Squadron. Marcus was at that time the Intelligence officer, whose role was at RHQ 'listening' to the battle (see Conclusion). The Regimental account described the commander simply as 'Lt. Cunliffe' ('Account', p. 11).

killed by a direct hit from an anti-tank gun, on the fringes of Noyers. His gunner immediately replied, knocking the gun out, and the infantry occupied some of the nearby buildings, supported by fire from the tanks. The advance on the village then stuck. The Regimental account continued: 'A stalemate situation now arose as the tanks could only shoot the infantry into the buildings and surrounding orchards, whilst the infantry on the other hand did not appear to be able to advance unless the tanks physically entered the buildings and orchards first.' But tanks would be unwilling to do either: in buildings and hedged-in orchards, with all their potential for ambush, they were extremely vulnerable to anti-tank guns and *Ofenrohre*. They could provide fire support, as they had done earlier at Les Nouillons and Point 126. Again, therefore, the account seems to imply that it was the infantry who were not doing their job.[26]

The battle petered out in the evening as the infantry, feeling that they could not hold some of the buildings near the station and on the fringes of Noyers which had been occupied earlier, withdrew to neighbouring orchards. There had, however, also been a successful attack on Haut des Forges, on the left flank, by the 6th North Staffordshires, who were temporarily under the command of 177th Brigade, and the 1st Northamptonshire Yeomanry who were a sister formation of 144th RAC in 33rd Armoured Brigade.

The Haut des Forges attack and A Squadron's successful attack on the 16th were the high points of the battle. The next day the attack on the right of the railway was resumed in the area south of Point 126 by the available tanks of all squadrons, which together equated to just one squadron. The houses here and elsewhere had been reoccupied by the Germans who were reinforced by the Reconnaissance Regiment of 9th SS Panzer, and they proved too difficult to dislodge.[27]

On the other flank, Jolly provided a scratch squadron of tanks which had been recovered and repaired to support the AVRES and Crocodiles. The attack only started in the late afternoon and followed the route Major Pickering had taken the day before. It met with some success, the AVRES blowing up some buildings and the Crocodiles then flaming them, 'which flushed a number of Germans'. However, it was dark by the time the outskirts of Noyers were reached due to the slow cross-country performance of the Crocodiles with their towed fuel tank. The attack was called off, but in the darkness the tanks could not find their way back and had to stay with the infantry. The next morning they had to return for replenishment and so were out of the battle.[28]

The 18th saw similarly ineffectual attacks in which several AVREs and Crocodiles were lost to an anti-tank gun. The steadily dwindling number of tanks and exhaustion on the part of the infantry may also have played a part in the failure of the attacks, as well as the impact of German reinforcements. With Goodwood well under way, the battle effectively stopped in mid-afternoon on that day. Before this happened, an unnecessary tragedy had occurred. Charles Veall, the Medical Officer, had felt frustrated at his lack of occupation in spite of the Regiment's steadily increasing casualty list. Armoured regiment MOs were liable to be in this position as wounded tank crews were frequently picked up by stretcher bearers from the infantry and taken to their Regimental Aid Post. Tank regiments had no stretcher-bearers and relied on an armoured half-track which could only be in one place at a time.

Chafing at his lack of activity, Veall had sought permission to pick up a wounded infantryman who had been reported by tanks as lying south of the railway. Jolly consented, with the caveats that Veall should go cautiously, should not go further than the railway embankment and must make contact with the tanks which had reported the casualty. Later, although his half-track had been flying a large Red Cross flag, Veall was found dead inside it with his driver, Trooper Collins, also dead nearby. Infantrymen in the vicinity reported that shots had been fired at the half-track as it passed them and Veall had been stopped and warned about the gun responsible. Nonetheless he had insisted on going forward. Jolly was obviously mortified at this, perhaps the more so as he had grudgingly given permission. Veall was a popular and efficient officer, but he had clearly exceeded his orders with disastrous results, and Jolly took the opportunity offered by the regimental account to read Veall's successor a lesson: half-track drivers and assistant medical personnel should bring in wounded men; Medical Officers' lives were too precious.[29]

Conclusion

Like Goodwood itself, Pomegranate and Greenline have not had a good press from historians, so far as they have been mentioned. Buckley cites an officer who referred to Greenline as a 'pointless muddle'. At first sight the Noyers attack, which was the single most important component of Pomegranate, also seems something of a failure. Casualties were heavy. In 144th RAC no less than five officers were killed and seven wounded, a heavy toll from an officer complement of about thirty-five. Added to these were the twenty other ranks killed and twenty-nine wounded, making total casualties of sixty-one. There was a net loss of seven tanks, allowing for those recovered and repaired. In addition four AVRES and Crocodiles were lost, all of which, having been hit and rendered immobile, were 'brewed up' by British tanks to prevent them falling into enemy hands. Over the four days from the 16th to the 19th, total British casualties in 59th Division were 1,250 killed, wounded and missing. Presumably, although it is not stated, this included 144th RAC which was attached to the Division for the attack.[30]

Nor do the operations on the Odon front, of which Noyers was one, seem to have had much success as diversions. If anything, they may have served as a warning to the Germans about the impending Goodwood operation. On the 17th, the HQ of Rommel, then commander of German forces in eastern Normandy and the Caen sector, reported that, 'The local attacks on July 15th between Maltot and Vendes [i.e. Pomegranate and Greenline] may be the prelude to the large-scale attack which is expected from the evening of the 17th for making a breakthrough across the Orne'.[31] Even more precisely, *Luftwaffe* HQ in the area predicted a major attack, 'decisive for the course of the war to take place south-eastwards from Caen about the night of 17th–18th'.[32]

To defend against the expected attack, Rommel already had four Panzer divisions ringed around Caen, and two infantry divisions.[33] The Panzer divisions were understrength but the Germans were well dug in. As a result, although substantial gains were made in Goodwood, it was effectively halted by the end of the second day. German reserves beyond those immediately available did not need to be deployed. So the fact that 9th SS Panzer was brought out of reserve to reinforce the Odon front had little, if any, effect on Goodwood.[34]

Whether they were a useful diversion or just a sideshow with no strategic value, Operations Pomegranate and Greenline together constituted a hard-fought battle, as the casualties testify. The Germans were well-established with considerable defences, but some of these had to be yielded. Their own losses were heavy. It is impossible to establish these precisely from the secondary sources available, but the 2,000 cited in the Wikipedia article on the Odon battle seems too low. For Pomegranate, the prisoner total can be reliably put at about 600, and for Greenline about 1,100. Given the weight of Allied bombardment and the number of German counter-attacks, which would have cost them heavily in casualties, it seems likely that the total of German killed and wounded would have been considerably more than 300.[35]

So the Odon battle as a whole had some positive result for the Allies in that it contributed to the overall reduction of German defensive strength. As a result of Pomegranate alone, 277th ID must have had its fighting value substantially reduced while 9th SS Panzer had to be brought out of reserve, diminishing its value for future operations. Collectively, Goodwood, Pomegranate and Greenline ensured that German attention remained focused on the Caen sector, and also wrote off a substantial proportion of the enemy's human and material resources. In so doing, they helped reduce the German capacity to withstand Operation Cobra, the American operation, which was the single most important attack in this period. Lieutenant General Hans Speidel, the Chief of Staff of Army Group B – the overarching German command in Normandy – thought that the British were planning a breakout, the Americans merely an extension of their front. As a result of his and others' miscalculations, on the eve of Cobra the British and Canadians, with 14 divisions, were pinning down 14 German divisions with 600 tanks, while the Americans with 19 divisions were opposed by the equivalent of 9 German, with 110 tanks.[36]

So Noyers played a part in the Allied campaign. It also – and this is of interest for us – serves as an exemplar of how an armoured regiment fought a battle in conjunction with infantry.

On a tactical level, the failure of the British to take Noyers itself, and their expulsion from the buildings surrounding it, probably owes something to a paucity of troops. Making the final two-pronged attack on 16 July with just one battalion, the 2/6th South Staffs, was ambitious, especially as it started the attack understrength due to heavy losses in Operation Charnwood.[37] By the 17th and 18th, when the Germans were reinforced, this dearth of troops was even more telling, while by now 144th RAC was running short of tanks. From the Regiment's account, however, the infantry at times may have been over-reluctant to make the final assaults on buildings and orchards.

This reluctance may also have had something to do with the lack of joint training between 59th Division and the Regiment. This was exacerbated by the failure of tank telephones, in spite of their prior introduction to the infantry. The telephones were apparently useful at first but then, due to lack of practice, the infantry 'failed to replace the handsets in the boxes provided' and as a result the telephones were dragged off by hedges. One squadron lost all theirs on the first day, conjuring up images of tanks careering through the Normandy countryside with telephone receivers trailing behind them.[38] Another illustration of the lack of familiarity between the various units was the infantry's persistent desire for tanks to remain with them for 'mopping up'. This habit did not disappear even when 144th RAC settled down with the 51st Highland Division, but it must have been easier by then for Jolly, working with familiar infantry units, to put his foot down and insist on tanks' return to base.

It is impossible to be sure who was to blame for the fiasco over the British minefields. The original British occupant of the area from which the attack was launched was 53rd Division. There was much mine-laying at the end of June during an enemy counter-attack, and that contributed to the imperfect records. Then 49th Division took over on 14 July, just before the attack, and held the position while 59th Division launched the attack. The lack of proper records and changes of unit obviously contributed to the muddle, but Jolly was adamant that 144th RAC had been told that the minefields were under control. It would clearly have been better if the lack of knowledge had been accepted, so that the Flails could have done their work.[39]

On the other hand, 144th RAC also paid testimony to effective cooperation with, and fighting by, 177th Infantry Brigade. This was particularly evident during the left-flank operation against Les Nouillons and the nearby signal-box on 16 July, and later on the same day the right-flank advance against Point 126 which achieved such success.

To the historian of a tank regiment, the most interesting thing about Noyers is the evidence in the Regimental account about the tactics employed during joint tank/infantry attacks. Timothy Harrison-Place has suggested that these were in an inchoate state on arrival in Normandy.[40] The evidence from the Noyers attack does not bear this out. First of all, the account was unambiguous about the merits of the classic sandwich formation if the conditions were suitable, as they were during A Squadron's attack on Point 126 and the railway station on 16th July: 'it is clear that the most successful part of the operation was that in which a standard "I" [Infantry] tank attack was staged'. The use of the word 'standard', and the earlier reference to a 'training theory' about the feasibility of this with Shermans, shows that the Regiment was well acquainted with the tactic. A point worth noting is that the 'sandwich' had very thin layers – in other words, tanks and infantry were close together. Earlier iterations of the theory had had the leading tanks much further ahead.[41]

Other tactics were also used. But contrary to Harrison-Place's claims, the account does not suggest that they were used because of uncertainty, or because 144th RAC was fumbling towards solutions for different tactical problems. The Regimental account, again, summarises the position. Tanks should lead an advance except where there were buildings or orchards, in which case they would stand off and give fire support to the infantry, or there were ditches or hedges to surmount, in which case the infantry would lead.[42] Roughly speaking, this corresponds with the Regiment's actions at various stages of the attack, as described earlier. Of course the Regiment had been in Normandy for a month and may have learned something from other formations which had already done some fighting. But there is no suggestion from the account that the various modes of infantry support, or mutual support between infantry and tanks, were unfamiliar. The inference must be that there was some acquaintanceship with them through training. John Buckley's conclusion, that tactics were flexible, seems the correct interpretation as to why different tactics were used at different times.[43] Of course 144th RAC and the other regiments in 33rd Armoured Brigade had benefitted from their additional training in 'infantry tank' tactics. It may be that other armoured, as opposed to tank, regiments had a steeper learning curve.

The Regimental account continued this analysis by adding a comment about different types of tank, and the passage sheds light on contemporary understanding of Allied tanks' strengths and weaknesses. According to the account, the success of the attack on Point 126,

> seems to show that there is nothing incompatible in Shermans carrying out the normal well-tried 'I' tank technique when co-operating with infantry. The argument that Shermans must 'sit back' because of their 'thin skin' is open to question, as no allied tank nowadays can rely solely on its armour to provide protection. Even Churchills will be penetrated without difficulty at the short range common in most parts of Normandy if they are not properly supported by artillery, as was shown by the fate of the Crocodiles [Crocodiles were modified Churchills] on 18th July.[44]

The writer – either Jolly himself or someone setting forward his views – went on:

> The idea should be discarded that tanks can gain any serious degree of immunity from anti tank guns by reason of thickness of armour (existing types only being considered) or by their own fire and movement (although this is an important adjunct). Tanks must be closely supported by artillery so as to keep the enemy anti tank gunners below ground until the armour can close with them and destroy them. Unlike infantry, tanks can advance close to the barrage and are therefore on top of the enemy before he can man his weapons.

He then mentioned the artillery's role in tank-on-tank action. 'Against tanks, the same degree of protection cannot be expected but artillery fire should serve to keep enemy tank commander's hatches closed and upset the gunner's aim, thus giving the Sherman a chance of closing the range and fighting on more equal terms.'[45]

Jolly was mainly focused on the appropriate tactics against anti-tank guns, but the final part of the passage refers to tank-on-tank action. Numerous historians have written about the 'problem' of pitting Shermans against Panthers and Tigers. As Stephen Hart has pointed out, however, the problem has frequently been misspecified. No Allied tanks, including Churchills, were proof against Panthers and Tigers. On the other hand, Panthers and even Tigers were vulnerable against Sherman Fireflys (and against the British 17-pounder anti-tank gun, which was the gun mounted in the Firefly). In other words, the problem was not so much Allied tanks' vulnerability, although Shermans' propensity to catch fire was an issue, as the lack of lethality of the Allies' standard tank armament, the 75mm gun. But so long as there were a reasonable number of Fireflys available, the 'problem' of unequal lethality was not that serious. To put it another way, there was not nearly as much of a mismatch between Allied and German tanks as some have suggested. At Noyers a Panther was knocked out by the Regiment. As will be seen, in Totalize a number of Tigers were destroyed – and by Allied tanks, not anti-tank guns. The Regimental account shows that Jolly grasped the fundamentals of this more balanced analysis of the Sherman's capabilities and limitations.[46]

Jolly then included further advice about tank positioning. Tanks should lead an advance except, as discussed above, where there were buildings or orchards, in which case they would stand off and give fire support to the infantry, or ditches or hedges to surmount in which case the infantry would lead. But he also added an important further prohibition to this – tanks should <u>not</u> lead unless there were two troops available, the second to watch the front troop and the infantry. The rear troop could then be stationary, tank gunnery being far more accurate from a stationary position. The 'two troops' rule was 'an order in 144 RAC'.[47] In practice, both at Noyers and in later actions, the rule was at times broken for various reasons; but, where possible, it remained one of Jolly's basic precepts. It helps to explain why Jolly was so insistent that tanks were used in squadrons. Since two troops constituted a half squadron, any advance on two axes was automatically going to need a full squadron. Even where only one axis was required, the full squadron gave flexibility. This was evident at Noyers during C Squadron's initial advance towards Les Nouillons on 16 July. This was actually on two axes, but on two occasions Major Pickering, realising that there was little or no resistance on one of them, was able to switch the majority of the tanks on that axis to the other. This was especially valuable when, as was likely to occur, casualties reduced the number of tanks available.

    Keeping squadrons together also aided command and control of the entire regiment. During periods of action, Jolly would exercise control as far forward as possible. There was a Main Regimental Headquarters, staffed by the Adjutant and Intelligence Officer, whose prime task was to 'listen' to the battle and pass on situation reports at frequent intervals. Jolly himself had a separate Command Post, usually consisting of two scout cars, one for him and one for a liaison officer, and two tanks, one of which was a control tank with the necessary radio links. During Noyers, the Command Post was initially with the C/O of 177th Infantry Brigade, then moved between the HQs of the two battalions taking part in the first phase of the attack, then stayed with the HQ of the only battalion, 2/6th South Staffs, involved in the second phase. Battalion-level decisions could therefore be taken immediately.[48] To expedite decisions down the line squadron commanders had a radio set tuned to the infantry battalion frequency, although with Jolly actually at the infantry battalion HQ himself this was used only infrequently. More important was a Reconnaissance Officer at infantry company HQ, with a scout car and '19' radio set – the standard tank set which provided for contact with individual tanks and with HQ. This, in Jolly's view, was the 'only really satisfactory method of communication', apart from personal contact. Presumably this was because the officer could relay messages direct from the infantry company commander, either to Jolly or to the local squadron commander. However, only a limited number of such officers could have been deployed at any one time. The standard infantry '38' sets in troop leaders' tanks which were netted to forward infantry platoons were not used because, 'Troop leaders have too much else to think about'.[49]

Troop leaders had a great deal to think about, since they were at the sharp end: leading their own troop, receiving instructions from the squadron commander, commanding their own tank and finally liaising with the infantry on the spot. It is not surprising, therefore, that they seem to have operated with the turret hatch open, giving them a wider conspectus of the battle. The number, and manner, of troop commander casualties strongly suggests that this was their usual modus operandi.

The death of Lieutenant Borg while firing his Sten gun has already been mentioned. Major Pickering – a squadron commander, of course – was in his tank when killed, while the rest of his crew were uninjured. This suggests that he was exposed above the turret line. The same happened to Lieutenant Hotson who was killed on 17 July. On the 18th, Captain Simmons was wounded in the head and subsequently died. Lieutenant Thomas had also been wounded in the head on the 16th, although he survived.[50] The evidence is less clear as to whether all tank, as opposed to troop, commanders were similarly exposed on a regular basis, although Sergeant Critchley must have had had his turret hatch open when he demoralised the enemy at Queudeville. Other tankmen's memoirs suggest that open hatches were the norm, at least for troop commanders.[51]

After the war, Jolly recorded some of his impressions of the Noyers attack: 'my main impression of the early stages is of how extraordinarily difficult it was to obtain information about what was happening'. Staying at 177th Brigade HQ was not much use and so he spent most of his time between the two battalion HQs. The lack of visibility due to mist and to the dust raised by shelling was a further problem.[52] Nonetheless, it is a tribute to the original plan that, in spite of lack of information and the initial lack of visibility, so much on the first day was successful. As noted earlier when 144th RAC had watched an elaborate attack on a village outside Caen which they knew to be empty 'with some derision', the

British had a reputation, at least among some German commanders, for slowness of movement and over-elaboration. Yet these had advantages. While the infantry provision in the Noyers attack may have been deficient, there was no shortage of tanks. So in spite of the heavy losses on minefields, the infantry always had substantial tank support. In addition, the British had their usual massive artillery support. As a result, for instance during the successful attack on Point 126 on 16 July, the Germans 'seemed dazed by the weight of the barrage'. If the attack petered out in subsequent days due to the Germans bringing in reinforcements while the British did not, this was a testimony to Pomegranate having some success as a diversion.

Chapter 3

Operation Totalize

The succession of operations in the Caen sector had fixed German eyes there. On 25 July the Canadians launched another, Operation Spring, in the salient which Goodwood had created to the immediate south of Caen. It made only marginal gains but continued to distract the enemy, whose forces remained concentrated in the east, facing the British and Canadians.[1] Against the Americans, conversely, their line was stretched taut. So when at the same time as Spring the Americans launched Operation Cobra, the Germans finally broke. By the end of July American units had reached Avranches at the base of the Cotentin peninsula. German units along much of the American front crumbled. With nothing behind them, there was now practically no effective enemy resistance in the whole of north-western France, to the west and south of Mortain. In the first week of August American tanks, racing along French roads in an advance reminiscent of the Germans in 1940, had almost reached Le Mans in the east and Brest in Brittany's far west. German forces held out there, and in a few other fortified enclaves on the coast. (Map 3.1)

Meanwhile the British and Canadians continued the sort of slogging fighting against entrenched defences which had characterised their campaign so far, and of which Noyers was a typical example. As before, the strategic aim was to threaten enemy positions, and supply routes, to the south and east of Caen. The Germans were forced to devote resources to their defence and had that much less chance of hindering the American advance. Operation Spring was followed on 30 July by the British Operation Bluecoat, further east where their sector adjoined the Americans. This led to advances of up to 10 miles and disrupted German attempts to reinforce their left flank against the American onslaught. There was to be no breakout for the British forces, however. After its initial success the attack met skilful German defence and stopped. With a continued necessity to distract and tie up German units, Allied attention switched again to the Caen sector.

OPERATION TOTALIZE

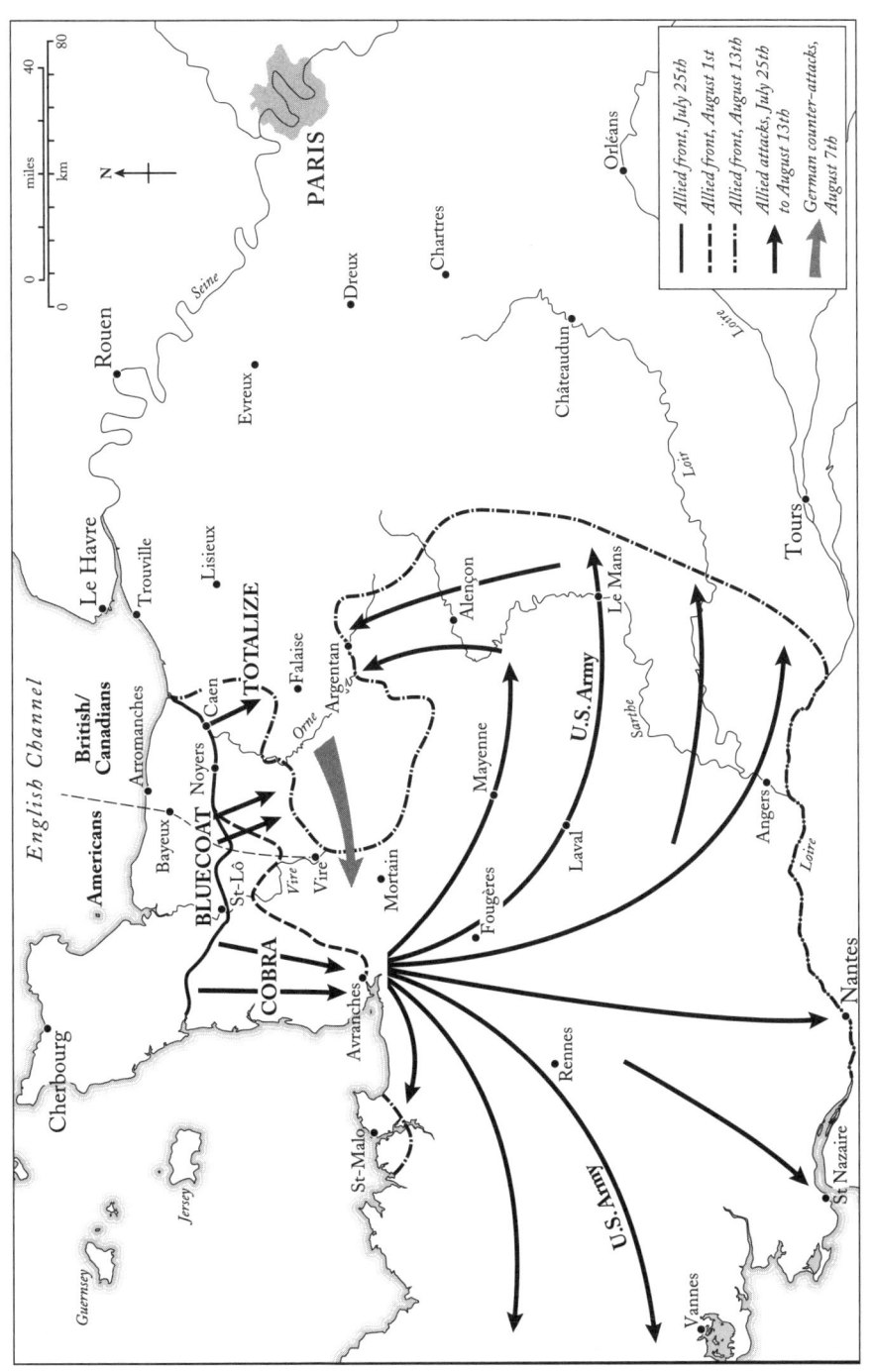

Map 3.1

The tempo of action for 144th RAC also stepped up, after a week's rest following Noyers. They moved north-west, round the northern edge of Caen and past the 6th Airborne Division's landing zone where they had seized the bridges across the Orne river and canal on D-Day. Still to be seen, in late July, was 'the fantastic sight . . . of hundreds of their gliders parked where they had landed, practically nose to tail'.[2]

The Regiment ended up in a defensive position just to the south-east of Caen, and only a mile or so from the enemy. As Allan Jolly described it, 'here was open, rolling country, not unlike Salisbury Plain'. It was dotted with villages and hamlets which the Germans had made into strongpoints. The Regiment's crews lived in dug-outs beneath the tanks. The Germans in the vicinity had plenty of fight and reasonable quantities of ammunition, resulting in daily shelling which caused a number of casualties. After a week of this, on 3 August, 144th RAC moved north of Caen to prepare for Operation Totalize.[3]

Operation Totalize

Totalize was essentially an operation in the mould of previous ones around Caen.* Its prime purpose, by breaking through the crust of defences the German had constructed, was to intensify the threat to eastern Normandy and thus, as before, limit the German capacity to mobilise forces against the American advance.

The same problem with which the Goodwood planners had wrestled assailed those preparing Totalize. The mixed Canadian, British and Polish force which constituted Totalize would have to advance across open countryside, in which the Germans occupied well-entrenched fortified villages with good fields of fire. The operation was put in the hands of Lieutenant General Guy Simonds, commander of II Canadian Corps. He had to square the circle and break through the German defences, while avoiding the heavy tank losses of Goodwood.

Simonds is usually regarded as one of the most innovative and successful Canadian commanders, and he came up with an original plan for the operation. Totalize would be a night attack, thus neutralising the German artillery and anti-tank guns as they would be blind. Night would, however, also pose considerable problems for the attackers. Night tank

---

* As the operation was Canadian-led, its name used the North American spelling with a 'z', although British sources sometimes use the British spelling.

attacks were not entirely new – one had been successful in the Battle of Tebaga Gap, in North Africa, in March 1943 – but were certainly unusual; furthermore the Tebaga Gap attack had been premised on moonlight, whereas no such assumption could be made about northern France.[4]

The Canadian attack was to incorporate another novelty: some of the infantry were to be carried with the tanks in armoured personnel carriers (APCs). This seems to have been their first, or almost their first, use. Those in 1944 were makeshift. They were constructed from American self-propelled guns, nicknamed Priests, which had been lent to the Canadians and were about to be returned as they were being replaced by British-model artillery. The Americans agreed to a temporary dismounting of the gun and the use of the resulting hull as an APC (though the term itself was not yet used). They were, inevitably, renamed 'defrocked Priests'. Later they and their successor models were called Kangaroos. Simonds laid claim to the idea of using Priests in their new form.[5] Although the use of Kangaroos was an innovation, most troops in the operation were actually carried by more orthodox vehicles, such as Bren-gun carriers which were unarmoured, but tracked, or Canadian armoured trucks.[6]

Subsequent to the night attack, which constituted Phase 1, Totalize called for two armoured divisions to pass through and exploit towards Falaise. This chapter will focus on the night attack, in which 144th RAC took part.

The front of the German fortified area centred on the little village of Tilly-la-Campagne. Tilly had already been the site of fierce fighting during Operation Spring, and the Germans had twice won it back with counter-attacks. The first phase of Totalize aimed to not only seize Tilly, but ten other fortified localities. The seven forward ones ran from May-sur-Orne in the west, via Tilly, to La Hogue in the east. Behind that was a reserve line of four, from Caillouet to St Aignan-de-Cramesnil. (Map 3.2) Not only were the villages fortified, but German artillery in the low hills behind and to the east of the defenders could bombard advancing columns while their tanks remained hidden from Allied artillery and aircraft in nearby woods and copses.[7]

The Allies benefitted, however, from recent changes in German dispositions. A few days earlier, when the American reached Avranches, Hitler had conceived his attack on the American salient, which at that time stretched down the west coast of the Cotentin peninsula. This was the so-called Mortain counter-attack, as it was to be launched from the

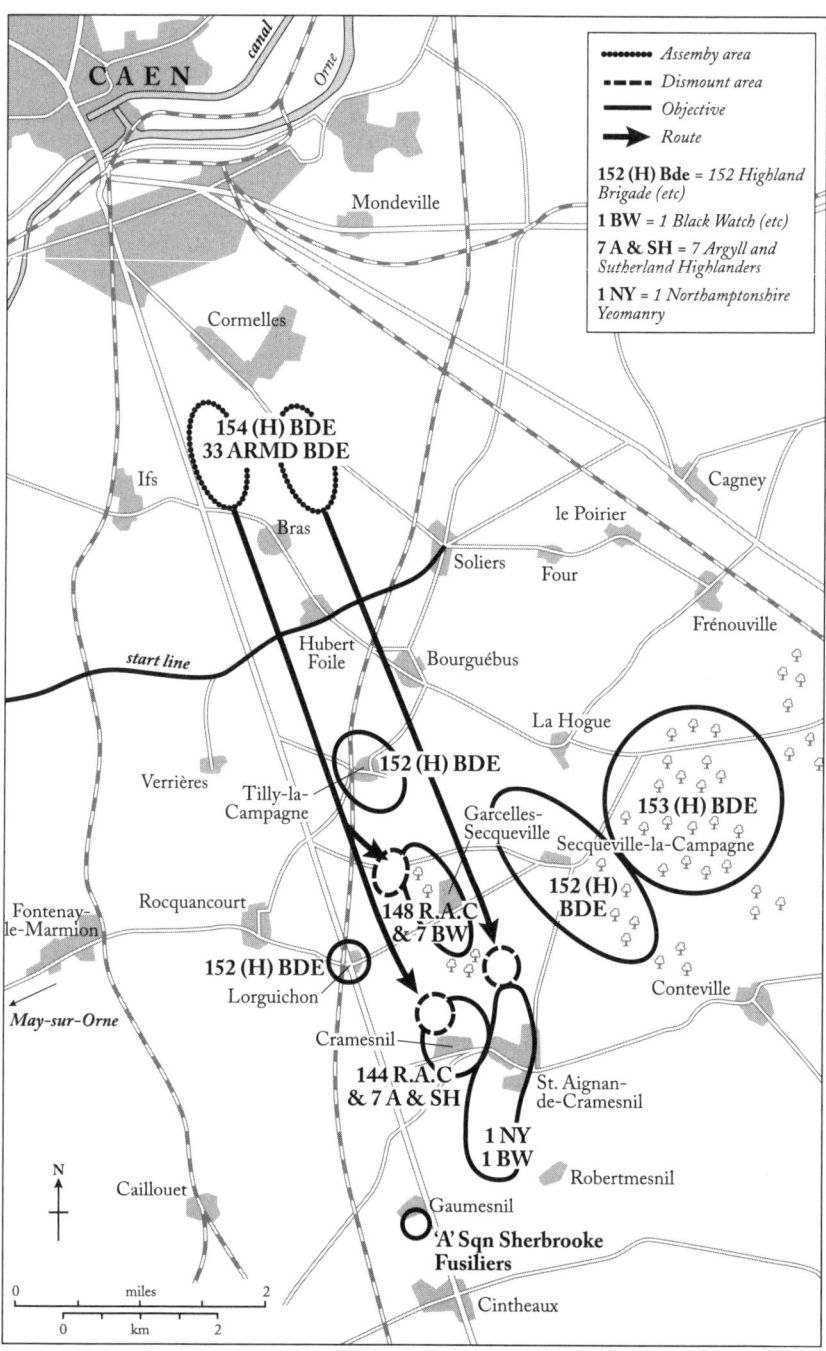

Map 3.2

OPERATION TOTALIZE

Mortain area – although the Americans had captured the town itself on 2 August. The attack was far-fetched when conceived, and even more so when it was launched. Constant Allied interdiction from the air meant that attempts to assemble an adequate striking force were doomed to failure. And by moving his armoured units west, Hitler made their ultimate escape more difficult – or in many cases, impossible.

To carry out Hitler's plan and simultaneously oppose Bluecoat, Gunther von Kluge, the new German commander in the West, had pulled the 1st and 9th SS Panzer divisions from their positions south of Caen.[*] They were replaced by the 89th and 271st Infantry Divisions respectively.[8] It was 89th ID that would man the defence line which was directly threatened by Totalize. On the right of the German line 12th SS Panzer, the infamous *Hitlerjugend* division which was responsible for numerous atrocities, was also replaced by an infantry division and moved back into reserve behind 89th ID Their tanks were supplemented by the 25 Tigers of the SS 101st Heavy Tank battalion, famous for its tank ace Michael Wittman. So the Germans continued to have some armour available for counter-attack, but less than when Totalize was being planned.

The 89th ID was by no means the weakest of German formations, although it had much less combat capability than a Panzer division. It had an experienced commander in Lieutenant General Konrad-Oskar Heinrichs; its troops were mostly fairly young and had had reasonable opportunities for training in Norway before it moved to France; it only had a modest number of anti-tank guns of its own, but a detachment of the formidable 88mm guns was also available; like most German formations, it had plenty of machine guns and mortars. It was not mobile, relying largely on horses for transport, but that hardly mattered for a defensive battle. However, like increasing numbers of German divisions it only had two *regiments*, rather than the three which had once been the norm. Consequently its own reserves were limited; for large-scale counter-attacks it would have to rely on 12th SS Panzer and the Tigers of 101st Battalion.[9]

---

[*] Von Kluge had taken over from von Rundstedt, the C-in-C West, whom Hitler had sacked (for neither the first nor last time) in early July. Then Rommel, who commanded Army Group B which controlled the armies in northern and north-western France, was seriously injured after an Allied air attack on 17 July and von Kluge stood in for him as well.

In the night attack, the Allies would have at least twice the German front-line strength: 2nd Canadian Division would be supported by 2nd Canadian Armoured Brigade, and 51st Highland Division by 33rd Armoured Brigade. For the purposes of the operation, both were attached to the First Canadian Army. (For political reasons, Canadian leadership of one army was thought desirable. But with limited numbers of Canadian troops, British units had to serve in the Army in order to bring it to a reasonable size.) The second phase of the attack would be carried out by 4th Canadian Armoured and 4th Polish Armoured Divisions, the latter also attached to the Canadians. In spite of the resources of the Allies, the strength of the German positions and the lack of any cover for an attack made Totalize a formidable proposition.

Simonds' main worry was direction-finding. In a later lecture on the attack he said:

> the features on the ground did offer some assistance: there was the main Falaise road, the railway which would provide a guiding line on the 2nd Cdn Div front in the later stages of the advance and the Lorguichon works; in addition, the villages stood out clearly in the open country. But against this it was mid-summer and there was the problem of the dust from the bombing and artillery bombardment; in fact, there was no certainty that any of these landmarks would be seen for more than few yards at night. So we devised every possible means to assist the columns to keep direction, including Bofors firing over the columns and an improvised direction-finding apparatus . . .[10]

Jolly in *Blue Flash* enlarged on the direction-finding apparatus, by which the regimental navigator heard a series of dots on the wireless if he was too much to the right, and a series of dashes if too much to the left. 'To use the method at all successfully required a great deal of practice and concentration. One was the enemy of the other, as the more the navigators practised the more tired they became, and the less they were able to concentrate.' Bob Thorne remembered meeting Bobby Osbourn, the lead navigator, after the battle. Osbourn's tank had fallen into a bomb crater soon after the attack commenced, so he missed much of the battle, but even so he was 'so weary' that he kept falling asleep. In addition to these aids there was 'movement light' provided by a group of searchlights pointing towards the clouds in the direction required, and compasses – the latter seem the obvious answer but 'the inaccuracies of tank compasses were well known'.[11]

The night attack was to consist of two divisional fronts: the British troops to the left of the Caen–Falaise road, and the Canadians to its right. The objectives of 51st Highland Division are shown in more detail on Map 3.2. The 144th RAC, supporting 7th Argyll and Sutherland Highlanders of 154th Brigade, was to take the lead. Its target was Cramesnil, which was one of two villages, the other being St Aignan, furthest from the start of the attack. The 148th RAC and 7th Black Watch would be in line behind them; they would peel off and attack Garcelles Sequeville. Another column would take a course more to the left, or east, and attack St Aignan. The 152nd and 153rd Brigades would follow on and consolidate. The Polish and Canadian armoured divisions were to pass through the ground won and continue the attack. (Map 3.2)

Each column consisted of a 'solid phalanx' of tanks, four abreast with a mere 6ft between each tank. Near the front were flail tanks, equipped with a huge rotating drum and chains for mine clearance, bulldozers and other Royal Engineer tanks; after the first squadron came the Regimental Headquarters Squadron to which Marcus Cunliffe was attached. Then another squadron of tanks, the APCs carrying the infantry and then the final squadron of tanks. The whole column was some 350yd long.[12]

Jolly described the scene just after 9 in the evening of 7 August when the columns formed up:

> The tightly packed column of over 150 vehicles was drawn up . . . looking more as though the occasion was a review than a battle. 148 RAC and 7 Black Watch followed behind us and formed up on our left as there was no room for them between the tail of our column and the built-up area behind . . . the route [to the Start Line] was marked by a double line of green and amber directional lights.
>
> It was a perfect, still summer's evening, and everyone was very quiet while we waited until it was time to move off. At ten minutes to eleven, as the light was just beginning to fail, the silence was broken by the engines starting up and we began to move slowly up to the Start Line.

Reaching the Start Line, the tanks accelerated to 5mph in order to keep close to the artillery barrage which opened up shortly afterwards. The air bombardment had already started.[13]

Meanwhile Lieutenant General Harry Crerar, the commander of First Canadian Army, was briefing war correspondents on the operation. He reminded them that it was to be fought on 8 August, twenty-six years to the day after the start of the Battle of Amiens. This was a First World War Allied attack involving Canadian, Australian and British units which resulted in a shattering defeat for the Germans and marked the beginning of their long retreat which ended on 11 November 1918. Ludendorff, the German chief of staff, had called 8 August 1918 'the black day of the German Army'.[14]

As the column of tanks neared Tilly, which it was to bypass, the barrage started and 'the column was immediately enveloped in a dense cloud of dust which reduced visibility literally to a few yards'. The lead and reserve navigators could not pick up the wireless direction-finding and, anyway, the leader's tank soon fell into a bomb crater while the other two collided. The arduous practice they had put in was wasted. It was difficult, Jolly wrote, 'to imagine the complete and utter disintegration of the column which occurred in the thousand yards [after the opening of the barrage]'.[15]

Marcus Cunliffe's account of the battle gives one tank commander's experience of how this disintegration could take place.[16]

> I listened anxiously for word from Bob Osbourn as to his progress. He had reported passing the start line, and since then had made two or three comments on progress. The last had said that visibility was getting very bad. In a moment I found out what he meant. The column ran into a haze of dust so thick that I could hardly see the tail lights of the tank in front of me, even though we were almost bumping into him. The shells had raised the dust, and the tanks were churning it up. The air reeked of cordite; my mouth felt as parched as if I had drunk nothing for three days. This was madness, I thought; suicide. We could see nothing and should just keep trundling on until we ran into serious trouble. We did keep trundling on. Someone bumped us from behind. Nothing fired on us. The haze seemed to grow worse. I had not the least idea which way we were going, until the red Bofors tracer came over, gliding

across the sky like a miraculous portent. We were still O.K. for direction.

From now on the description of the operation comes from Cunliffe's account; a few details differ from the account in *Blue Flash*, but nothing seriously.

At that stage the navigators ran into trouble. The tank in front of Cunliffe halted briefly before setting off again.

> We followed as closely as we could for a hundred yards. Another flight of Bofors trace to reassure us. The tank in front halted again, then slewed off to the right (all this hazy in the extreme; I only knew it had turned right because its lights disappeared and we almost ran into its side) to follow the others. I thought this must be wrong, but reassured myself that it was being done to avoid the craters and that we should soon be back on course again.

After a short time, however: 'All other tanks disappeared, so that you were quite certain that you were alone, and badly off course. A nice feeling, in the midst of enemy territory: and a nice start to our famous adventure! I cursed the bright boy who had thought of the barrage and neglected to consider the dust that it would raise.'

Cunliffe worked out that if he went too far to the right he would strike the Caen–Falaise road, likely to be covered by anti-tank guns. The railway was to his left and the column had to cross it, so his 'best bet was to bear left until I hit the railway, trust to luck that I hadn't gone too far, and hope to pick up my whereabouts by discovering the crossing place'. At that point he saw another British tank and stopped. The tank was from A Squadron, the leading squadron, and was commanded by Corporal Browne.

> We were both pleased to see one another, and even more pleased to realise the haze was clearing a little. While we discussed the situation, another tank soldier came walking across to us. It was a Canadian, seeking his own regiment. 'What outfit are you from?' he asked. I told him we were the column on the left of his: he had wandered a long way off his course and had better stick with us, unless he was specially eager to rediscover his own unit. 'Hell no'

he said. 'I've got a 17 pdr Sherman: it might come in handy. I'll stick with you guys.' [Cunliffe told the Canadian and Browne to follow him and set off again, making a hard left turn.]

The fog was lifting. I saw red tracer sail over. When you're not on course, it's very difficult to tell the exact line of the tracer, but it seemed to me to be over on our left.

He noted that this tallied with the fact that the Canadian had crossed the Caen–Falaise road; Cunliffe and Corporal Browne may have almost reached the road, to the right of their intended line, before making their left turn. He saw the railway embankment in front of him and met other tanks who were rendezvousing in its vicinity. Then they reached their designated crossing point, recognisable because of a railway hut.

I jumped down to the ground to have a word with anyone else who was about. It was quite peaceful: no one was firing at us and we were not firing at anybody either. Not quite what I had expected – although I hadn't any idea what to expect. I met Steve, a B Squadron officer, very excited and very belligerent, brandishing a Sten gun and telling everyone he had shot up some Jerries round the building. I didn't believe him, because it seemed much too peaceful, and because one part of my mind refuses to take war seriously, even in grim moments.

A grim moment soon came. Robert Reid's [commander of A Squadron] tank crossed the railway, closely followed by two others. All the other tanks revved up in preparation to getting into line again. Then – a bang, a shower of sparks and a cloud of smoke from Robert Reid's tank. It stopped and I saw little black figures leap out from it, and begin running back towards us. The second and third tanks were also hit, and the third began to 'brew up' in the usual horrible way, the glare of the flares illuming the whole scene. It was a nightmare after Breughel or Hieronymus Bosch: fire, death, darkness, retribution. No sign of an enemy soldier: that would have been something concrete and reassuring: just the thuds as the three tanks were hit, out of the darkness. Just the little railway building, the burning tank, the other tank-shapes backing apprehensively into the shadows, (I reversed also: a hundred yards was too small a distance between me and Robert Reid's tank). Then the Shermans began firing, blindly, at the enemy they could not see. They smashed the little building with HE [high explosive] shells; they poured torrents of machine gun fire into the hedges in which the Germans were probably lurking.

The deputy C/O, Tom Lovibond, found another crossing and led the way across it. 'He was followed rather slowly by the rest: that crackling, exploding tank had made everyone wary, perhaps too wary. He turned through a hedge, got on course again, and began to advance across a vast open field firing his machine gun at a wood about a thousand yards ahead.' Lovibond stopped again to complain that no one was following him: 'He and the C.O. lashed the regiment verbally . . .'. Lovibond's tank was then hit, but not seriously and he continued with the others following him.

Now we were on the move again, bowling rapidly over the level open ground, I could see Tom's tank just in front of mine, and two or three others on either side. The others appeared to be bunched up a little way in the rear. The night was so cleared up that I could see a good many stars, while the Bofors tracer was coming over to reassure us. We were going the right way, even if it wasn't exactly certain where we were, landscape looks so anonymous at night; it did not seem possible that the black bar of trees ahead could have any name, or be recognisable in daylight. It seemed to have a night time existence of its own.

   Our tracer whacked among the trees as we drew nearer to them. All the other tanks were shooting also at the wood, which was our only 'target' and loomed so dark and menacing that I hoped the Panzer Division whose wood the R.A.F. had bombed had not been hiding in this one all along.

   A hundred yards from the skirt of the wood. Tracer from behind whined past us; much to our rage, we were being fired <u>at</u> by some of the rear tanks, so much so that I had to duck inside the turret several times. (Next day we found that some of their bullets had riddled the bin on the back of the turret). We came up on the air to complain about being dosed with bullets, but the other tanks continued to sweep the whole neighbourhood, stabbing the black night with these lethal strings of red tracer.

Up against the wood, we found a thin skirt of trees at its left-hand end. It was a combined Hedge-cum-ditch, over which we lurched painfully. The nose of the tank rose ponderously, then dipped again abruptly into the ditch, rose and fell again with a jar. I hung on to the rim of the turret, breathing a sigh of relief when we were safely over. No-one likes to get his tank stuck at such a moment.

We found ourselves in an open field, dotted with small mounds, with another belt of trees along its left hand boundary. Where were the enemy? Among the trees? Dug in, somewhere in the field? No-one was firing at us, thank Heaven. As we ran on I suddenly realised how happy I was. In the dust haze, despair had put a weight down in the pit of my stomach: I had seen our whole enterprise doomed to disastrous failure. Then, at the railway crossing, despair had given way to personal alarm. I had seen then that we could reassemble the column and keep direction, but that we were going to lose some tanks, one of which might well be my own. But now, after a clear run of twenty minutes without any kind of trouble, I was filled with contentment. I saw everything more clearly than ever before, felt the beauty of the night as keenly as a poet, and was sure that my brain had become so clear that I could understand anything in the whole world. This exaltation often comes in action, when the edge of living is made razor-sharp by fear and by excitement. I found myself talking gay nonsense to my crew over the intercomn., till they must have thought I had gone bomb happy. Our two Brownings [machine guns] were rattling from time to time, as the front one shot up the next hedgerow and the turret one was traversed to fire at the wood on our left. We ran among the mounds – they proved to be hayricks – with a wary eye for slit trenches. At last I saw some, took a Sten gun that was slung on the top of the turret, and tried to let off a magazine into the trenches. Nothing happened. I banged and tapped and swore but still nothing happened. I gave it to the gunner, who played with the gun, then said 'nothing the matter with it, sir' and handed it up to me.

At the next hedgerow I saw more trenches and again tried to fire the Sten down into them; again without success. It was only when we got clear through the hedge that I remembered the two grenades that I was carrying in my bosom. I must use them when the next opportunity arose.

We kept on going. Direction I maintained by looking back at the Pole star, which shone modestly through the glittering Plough and Cassiopeia. The Bofors tracer helped, but was so high up that you couldn't be sure of its exact line. To the left, among the trees, a house. Or rather a ruin, a farm without a roof. A few rounds of Browning. The gunner said 'shall we give it H.E. sir?' H.E.? oh, yes, good idea. The driver heard the conversation and halted. The gunner fired, the shell exploded in the ruin, the gun clanged, the spent case fell out against my leg, the loader slipped another into the breech. We gave the farmhouse two or three more, then moved on. Tom Lovibond was now a little to my left, while two or three other Shermans were to my right and just in rear. Looking behind I saw the remainder coming on across the plain, illuminated by burning hayricks. An impressive enough sight.

My front machine gun got a stoppage. Separated case. The front gunner had to take it out of its mounting and play around with the gun, while we jolted along across the field. Then my turret gun jammed. The same trouble. I swore under my breath. The gunner got it across his knee with a screwdriver. We had to switch on the light in the turret for him to work by, and I wondered how much the light showed up my head to a hostile world. What luck to have them both stuck. What if we met some Germans?

Fortunately we didn't. The guns were repaired and soon firing again. Next worry – how far had we gone? I had not the wildest idea. Then how should we know when to stop? If we continued until we ran into the village – the infantry's objective – we should probably all be shot up. I hoped that somebody would have a better notion of where we were than I had. It had seemed so easy, on the air photos, to pin point oneself. Yet now, there were trees and hedges everywhere, black, ragged, shapeless clumps of them, that didn't fit in to the neat picture of the route that I had formed. Another hedgerow – a bad one, with a nasty little ditch. Tom got through it on my left. I emerged into a small paddock whose far side was barred by a formidable wall of hedge. Half right was another building of some sort. We fired hastily at it, Browning and then H.E. It looked nasty. In fact, I didn't like this paddock at all. It seemed a sort of cul de sac, just the place where enemy tanks might have harbour. I halted and thought about life for a moment, wondering whether we could be at the outskirts of the village. Everything was so damn dark . . . the black shadow along the hedge . . . the silent wall of hedge all round me . . . Bob Secretan's voice in my earphones, loud and a little excited – 'Twenty one has just been blown to bits' – Twenty-one? That was the number of Tom Lovibond's tank. He couldn't have been more than two hundred yards to my left . . . The Colonel told us not to go any further for the moment, so I decided to reverse out of my little paddock before someone took a bang at me. We began to crawl backwards. Just as we reached the hedge through which I'd come, and were poised on the earth bank in the middle of the hedge, someone began to drop heavy shells on us. Ours or German? The question seemed irrelevant; all I knew was that they were heavy calibre and far too close.

I halted the tank and ducked down, while these monsters crashed around us. Uncertainty again: I didn't feel so happy now. Whoosh – bang. Whoosh – bang. I closed the lid of my tank. Utterly helpless feeling, stranded in a stonk on the top of a bank. Bob Secretan's voice again: 'I can see twenty- two. He's stopped and looks as though he's been hit. There's a hell of a stonk coming down.' Twenty-two? With a shock I realised that I was twenty-two. I wondered whether my brother had heard the message, so came up on the air to say that I was alright.

As soon as the shelling ceased, I opened the lid and reversed back into the open field, where a number of tanks were gathered. Some of them were driving to and fro in apparently aimless circles, so as not to present too easy a target. Good idea: I told my driver to do the same.

The C.O.'s tank was somewhere very near to me: his voice sounded very loud on the air. He sounded calm and confident, although this must be an agonising experience for him. It's difficult enough to command an attack in daytime, when you can see something.

He called up Mac, our L.O. [Liaison Officer] who was with the infantry somewhere behind: 'Are friends ready to come up and do their stuff?' Mac's voice, Scottish, cheerful: 'Yes, friends are ready.

OPERATION TOTALIZE

Will come up now'. Were we at our correct debussing place? I couldn't believe that we were. Perhaps the C.O. knew. Even if he were uncertain he was quite right to call up the infantry. There was just the faintest tint of dawn in the sky and it might be tough for both ourselves and the infantry if they didn't get moving in the few remaining minutes of darkness. Moving where to? I felt utterly bewildered by all these hedges.

It was at this point that another tank was hit and caught fire, as described by Cunliffe in the passage quoted in the Introduction. But this was soon followed by the successful infantry attack on Cramesnil, the aftermath of which was also detailed in the Introduction. The other villages en route were also subdued successfully, although Tilly, attacked by an infantry battalion, proved difficult to take at night and had to be finished off the next morning. The Canadians on the right had even more difficulty in keeping direction, some of their forward tanks driving straight through Rocquancourt, then still held by the enemy, when they were meant to bypass it. Others, like the Canadian who joined 144th RAC, strayed to the east of the Caen–Falaise road. Nonetheless by morning most of them had reached their objectives.[17]

Nine men from 144th RAC were killed, including three in the tank which Cunliffe had witnessed brewing up after the railway crossing and four more in the tank hit near Cramesnil. Trooper Sydney (Sid) Moore was the only crew member to escape from this. Exhausted, he had been sitting in the tank leaning forward, and thought that he would have been killed if he had been sitting upright. As it was, he managed to pull himself out, in spite of leg injuries and severe burns to his hands.[18] Tom Lovibond, a popular officer, had also been killed when his tank was hit. In spite of these losses, the overall casualties suffered by the Regiment, in comparison with the gains made in the attack, were very low. Other units, too, had suffered relatively lightly given the strength of the German defences. Total tank losses were less than 20 from the 300 attacking; this compares, for instance, with the 9 144th RAC lost in the Noyers operation, a far smaller affair albeit lasting over 3 days.[19]

While casualties during the advance were relatively light, the 'complete and utter disintegration' of the column which Jolly referred to in the post-war Battlefield Tour, and which Cunliffe's adventures seem to confirm, appears one of the most striking features of the Allied advance.

Jolly wrote about it in similar fashion in *Blue Flash*, and one or the other of his accounts have been the source for much post-war writing on the Totalize advance. But taken at face value Jolly's accounts are misleading, because they imply that Totalize only succeeded because of luck: because somehow, in spite of the chaos, a miracle occurred and everyone got to their destination.

In reality, the 'chaos' of the early stage of the attack was succeeded by relative order. More important than the disordered start was the fact that, quite quickly, the column regrouped successfully and landed the infantry virtually unharmed at the correct place. In 144th RAC's case this was Cramesnil where forty Germans were captured, the infantry suffering just three dead.[20] And as noted, the other attacks by both the 51st Highland Division and by the Canadians were similarly successful. The infantry were transported safely, and relatively swiftly, in part by the use of APCs.

As Brian Reid, who has produced the most comprehensive history of Totalize, wrote:

> The fact was that, for every horror story of vehicles colliding or falling into bomb craters or going astray and joining other columns or being brewed up, the vast majority arrived at their objective areas after having driven through the prepared main defensive zone of an enemy infantry division. Although there were serious incidents, for many drivers and their passengers in the columns it was a case of following the tracks and lights and keeping alert, until somebody in authority at the end of the movement told them where to go and what to do.[21]

Cunliffe's account gives some clues as to what went right about the planning for Totalize, as well as what went wrong. Clearly the biggest problems were caused by the dust and the craters resulting from the barrage. Once the tanks had 'lost' the barrage – in other words it had advanced more quickly than they had and left them behind – the dust subsided and visibility returned. Jolly cast some doubts on the necessity for a barrage in his discussion during the Battlefield Tour, while accepting that one might sometimes be required, and the historian can only come to the same ambivalent verdict.[22] The barrage must have helped to demoralise the Germans and it no doubt killed and wounded a few, although the purpose of artillery barrages was more to keep heads down and shake the enemy's morale than to cause material damage, especially as 89th ID was thoroughly dug in. However a night advance by such a concentrated force, without a barrage, might well have caused the same degree of temporary demoralisation and confusion without loss of visibility.

In spite of the dust, however, the belt and braces approach of Totalize to navigation meant that there were still enough directional cues. In Cunliffe's case, these were the overhead tracer and the narrow gap between the main road and the railway, which meant that the distance he went off course was bounded. Later he navigated partly by the stars, although it seems unlikely that every tank commander could do this. Cunliffe found features on the ground hard to recognise, but Jolly's account in *Blue Flash* suggests that once visibility returned, he was able to use the map to recognise where they were. Cunliffe's account also suggests that he successfully fulfilled one of the roles of an officer – taking responsibility – when he ordered Corporal Browne and the Canadian tank commander to follow him before taking what turned out to be the correct course back to the railway. However small a part he played in the overall affair, it depended on personnel at all levels doing their job effectively.

Anthony Beevor has described Totalize as a failure, but this is inaccurate. The night attack was a striking success which ripped apart the first and most formidable German defensive zone between Caen and Falaise. The zone would no doubt have fallen eventually to a more orthodox attack but it would have incurred far more Allied casualties and probably have taken longer, giving the Germans more time to escape eastwards via Falaise.[23]

What was a failure was Totalize's second phase. The 144th RAC's only part in this, along with other British units, was a successful defensive action which will be described shortly. The offensive part of the second phase was meant to be a continuation of the attack towards Falaise by the 4th Polish Armoured and 4th Canadian Armoured divisions. For a variety of reasons this went wrong. A faulty plan was one, inexperience by the armoured units concerned another, the veering off course by American planes which delivered a heavy bombing attack on Canadian rear areas a third, and tenacious German defence a fourth.[24]

The failure to reach Falaise, or at least the heights to the north commanding the town, has been excoriated by various historians because it allowed large numbers of Germans to escape eastwards who would not have otherwise done so. But this criticism takes for granted the success of the night attack: without it there would have been no possibility of the Allies getting to Falaise quickly. Beevor also points out that the failure, or partial failure, can be interpreted in another way. On 8 August Kluge had been terrified by the implications of the night attack but cheered up on the 9th after the failure of the second stage. It gave him, he thought, another opportunity to realise Hitler's plan to attack westwards towards Avranches, the first attempt having been repulsed. Kluge still had no faith in the plan, but thought he ought to try it. He therefore temporised for a few more days, thus ensuring that more German troops and equipment could be caught in the pocket.[25] The ultimate verdict must be that a complete success for Totalize would have been better even if it speeded the German retreat, since it would have sealed the pocket sooner. Nonetheless, the Totalize night attack was, on its own, a considerable success, even if the operation as a whole did not justify Crerar's hopes for it as another Battle of Amiens.

From 144th RAC's point of view, the defensive action on 8 August, the day after the night attack, virtually completed its part in the battle. By mid-morning the Regiment was ensconced in defensive positions around Cramesnil. Some Canadian troops were on its right, holding Point 122 just to the east of the Caen–Falaise road. The 1st Northamptonshire Yeomanry, one of its sister battalions in 33rd Armoured Brigade, was positioned to its left in St Aignan, with some of their tanks forward in an orchard, south-west of the village. Also forward, just to the west of the road in Gausmesnil, was a Canadian tank unit, A Squadron of the Sherbrooke Fusiliers. The Allied forces formed the rim of a loose pocket and, perhaps by accident rather than design, had laid a well-concealed trap for any German counter-attack (Map 3.1).[26]

The first significant counter-attack emerged from the woods south of the Allied positions, at around 12.30. The forward troop of Northamptonshires could see three Tigers in line ahead on the Caen–Falaise road, moving north. The Tigers were focused on the Canadians, with their guns pointing west. The Sherman Firefly of the forward troop, under the command of Sergeant Gordon and then, after he was injured, Lieutenant James, claimed successful hits on three Tigers in succession. Credit for some superb gunnery, at a range of about 800yd, goes to Trooper Joe Ekins, the Firefly's gunner. Almost simultaneously the

OPERATION TOTALIZE

Sherbrooke Fusiliers' A Squadron saw a group of Tigers, plus self-propelled (SP) guns and half-tracks carrying infantry. They engaged them and claimed two Tigers and other tanks and SP guns. It seems likely that these were in the same group as those engaged by the Northamptonshires. The 144th RAC also engaged German tanks, claiming one Tiger and one Mark IV.[27]

The 1st Northamptonshires went on to see further action since a separate, large-scale, German attack by elements of 12th SS Panzer developed to the left and centre of St Aignan. After heavy tank losses on both sides, the Germans, in desperation, mounted an infantry attack which got nowhere and also suffered heavy losses. While 144th RAC lost 2 Shermans and suffered 5 dead and 9 wounded in the defensive fighting on 8 August, the Northamptonshires lost 20 tanks, 12 killed and 51 wounded. In return they claimed fifteen tanks, including more Tigers, and five self-propelled guns, and inflicted numerous casualties on the Germans. The tank claims were probably rather too high, as most such claims were. For instance, the Germans lost a total of five Tigers that day, while the combined Allied claims imply eight. Nonetheless the day's honours belong to the Northamptonshires, with support from 144th RAC and the Sherbrooke Fusiliers. Far more important than the loss of Allied tanks was the failure of the German counter-attacks, while the Germans could spare their tank and SP gun losses less than could the Allies.[28]

This defensive action has become famous for one thing: its association with the German tank ace, Michael Wittman, the temporary commander of the SS 101st Heavy Tank Battalion on 8 August. To the British, Wittman became well known because of his exploits at Villers-Bocage in the early stages of the campaign, when he had destroyed a number of Allied tanks and other vehicles. Wittman's role in this was probably exaggerated, but he was undoubtedly skilful and had an excellent gunner. German propaganda, looking for heroes, puffed up his achievements further.[29] Wittman's skill could not prevent him being one of the German victims on 8 August: he and his crew were all killed when their Tiger exploded. Wittman's fate has usually been attributed to Trooper Ekins. Brian Reid, however, makes a good case that it was A Squadron of the Sherbrooke Fusiliers which destroyed Wittman's Tiger.[30] The fate of Wittman and who was responsible for it are details. What is more to the point is that historians have frequently assumed that it was only the Allies who exhibited a lack of understanding of tank tactics, or that the Germans' speed of action made them superior soldiers. Wittman's fate and the fate of the other German counter-attacks on the 8th shows that the careful preparation by different Allied units of their defensive positions trumped the speed of the German reaction – or in other words, that speed was not the only attribute needed. Tactically, Wittman seems to have exhibited a carelessness about his flanks which suggests that his previous successes may have been down to luck as well as judgment.

Chapter 4

Advance to the Seine

After the defensive action following Totalize, the Regiment continued to advance in concert with the Canadians on their right until 15 August, when they crossed the River Laison near Ernes and turned east. (Map 4.1) The 144th RAC and the rest of 33rd Armoured Brigade were now semi-permanently attached to 51st Highland Division. This, in turn, was part of First British Corps, which was itself still under First Canadian Army.

First Corps was responsible for the advance to the Seine over the whole of an area which extended northwards, from the approximate line St Pierre-sur-Dives–Rouen to the Channel coast. The pursuit of the enemy in this part of Normandy is barely mentioned in most books. Even the Official War Histories of Britain and Canada have very little about it. Lacking the drama of the American advance and the fighting in the Falaise Pocket, it seems to have fallen into a historiographical vacuum. Yet it was important for two reasons. Early on, it extended the northern boundary of the Pocket and therefore prevented the Germans trapped in it from escaping northwards. Once the Pocket was eliminated, the speed of the Allied advance dictated how many men and how much material the Germans could move across the lower Seine.[1]

The troops concerned would not have been aware that they were subsequently to be neglected by history. To them, the advance contained plenty of drama as well as more light-hearted moments. It also gave rise to some episodes, involving both civilians and the enemy, which were vividly described by Marcus Cunliffe.

For the first few days, the Germans were still trying to hold on to the remains of their defensive positions south of Caen and resistance was considerable. By 18 August, however, Walter Model, the new German C in C who replaced the sacked von Kluge, had concluded that counter-attacking or even holding where they were was impossible, and that there should be a general withdrawal to beyond the Seine.[2] Having just been installed, Model had more clout than Kluge and Hitler had to agree to his

FROM ARROMANCHES TO THE ELBE

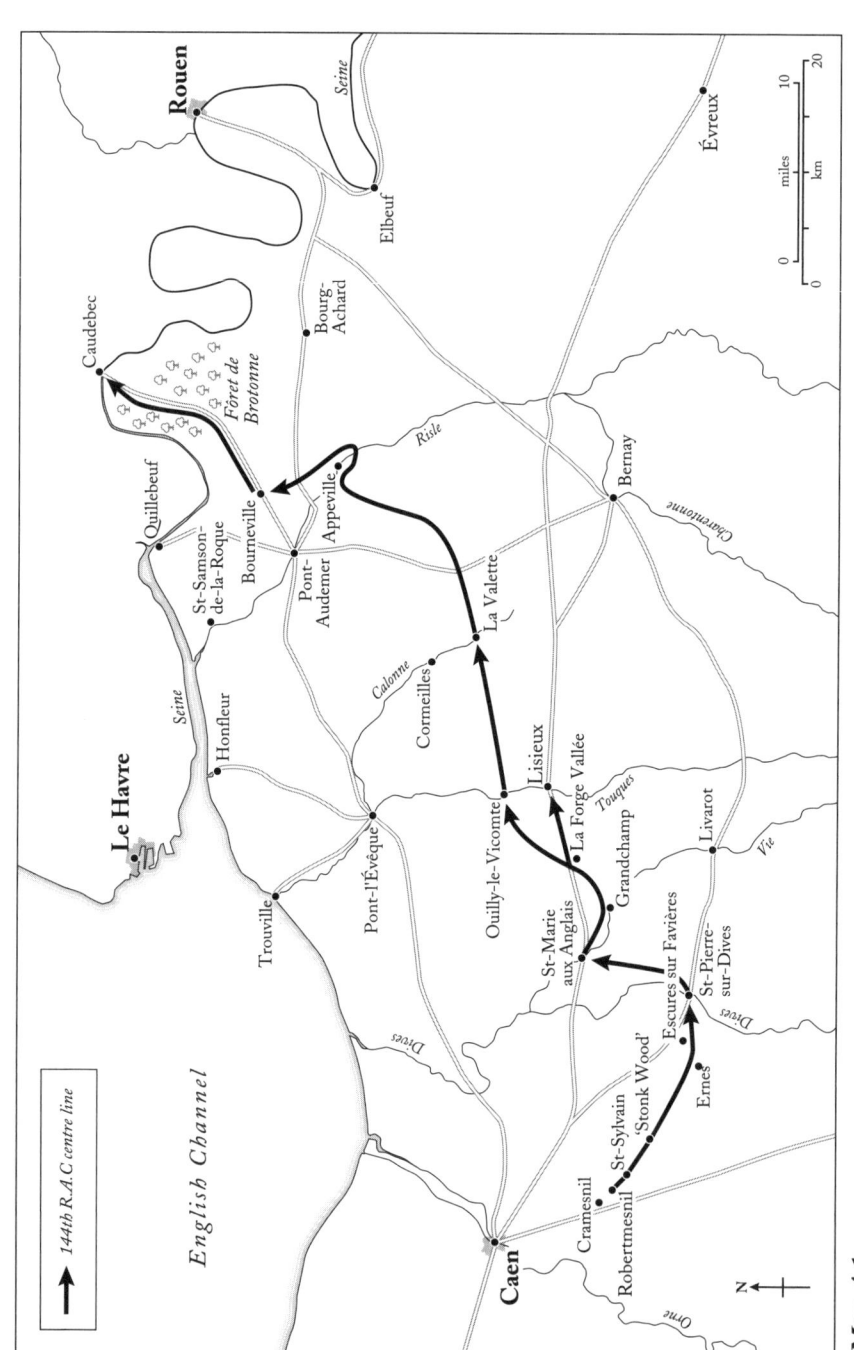

Map 4.1

ADVANCE TO THE SEINE

plan. Even so, it was too late to save much of the German Army, caught in the maelstrom of the Falaise Pocket. So while the Canadians had the satisfaction of reaping the harvest of Falaise, and the Americans that of advancing rapidly, 144th RAC and other British units were engaged in I Corps' unglamorous little campaign. The Corps was pushing at a door which periodically swung back as the Germans retreated, then stuck as they held at a river line. The resistance, however, was not of the same nature as it had been during Totalize. Then the Germans had layers of well-prepared defences; now their defences were improvised as they retired. Nevertheless, they had considerable forces between Caen and the Seine, and could put up a fight when they wanted to. To 144th RAC and its associated infantry, the experience was of an advance which was relatively rapid compared with the slogging of Noyers, but was punctuated by the need to overcome German points of resistance.

The drama of Totalize over, the Regiment spent 9 August resting. The next day they moved to Robertmesnil in a defensive role and while doing so came across evidence of the failed German infantry attack on the Northamptonshire Yeomanry and their associated infantry battalion: 'quite a dozen dead Germans in every sort of ungainly posture'. Jolly noted that seeing such an 'obvious dividend' from Allied artillery fire was unusual, because the Germans were usually well sheltered in trenches and dugouts.[3]

A few local advances had been made while the Regiment was resting, including the capture of St Sylvain by the Polish Armoured Division. St Sylvain was in a hollow and of no tactical significance; the country beyond it was more important. The 51st Highland Division's task was to attack a wood beyond the village, from which the enemy had good observation over much of the ground just occupied. At the same time, the Canadians were to seize Quesnay Wood, on the direct road to Falaise. The attack on Quesnay Wood was a failure, and marked the end of Totalize.[4] The British attack, however, was a success and laid the ground for further advances. As so often the case with Allied successes, this operation is virtually unknown. The 144th RAC supported 154th Infantry Brigade who carried out the attack on the night of 10/11 August. The Regiment was not involved in the attack itself – tanks would rarely participate in a small-scale night infantry operation such as this one. Its task was to navigate the streets of St Sylvain, starting at 04.30, arriving at the wood at first light in order to consolidate the infantry position. As anyone who has tried will know, it is remarkably difficult to find the correct road in St Sylvain, even in the twenty-first century and in daylight.* Half the Regiment missed the turn, but fortunately the mistake was quickly discovered and the tanks turned round, even though several heavy stonks came down and, in *Blue Flash*'s words,' traffic control did not seem a very healthy occupation'. Meanwhile, the infantry had successfully attacked the wood, although its further reaches remained in German occupation.[5]

The wood, originally nameless to the Regiment, quickly gained a name: Stonk Wood. The Quesnay Wood attack having failed, 154th Brigade had made the main lodgement in the remains of the German defensive screen around Falaise and retaliation was to be expected: '"Stonk" after "stonk" came down with great weight and accuracy. . . . one of the infantry battalion commanders, who had been through the North African and Italian campaigns said, after the war, that it was the heaviest shelling he had experienced at any time, either before or after'. Meanwhile, the troop commanded by Sergeant Critchley, who had helped the early stages of the Noyers attack to succeed, knocked out a self-propelled gun and a half-track. Critchley was wounded in the shoulder but nonetheless returned with five prisoners. Then the Germans mounted two local counter-attacks, which were successfully beaten off. The second was supported by a Tiger which had been lurking in the woods and had put several 144th RAC tanks out of action, one with all the crew killed. The Tiger was finally knocked out by a Firefly.[6]

The infantry were by now very thin on the ground after the casualties of the last few days, and for once Jolly accepted uncomplainingly that the tanks should stay forward during the night: 'The sight of the tanks withdrawing would certainly have had a disastrous effect on infantry morale'. The next morning appeared peaceful, but the peace was deceptive. A violent stonk arrived and crews took shelter beneath their tanks. When the bombardment finished, Marcus Cunliffe and his crew, bar one, crawled out. The exception was Corporal Callwood, who had been killed by a piece of shrapnel passing between the bogies. Later that morning Keith Cunliffe was severely wounded, losing an arm as a result.[7]

What transpired on 12 August must have been the nearest that Marcus Cunliffe came to death, with the shelling he experienced during Totalize

---

* It is the Conde-sur-Ifs road, D183.

a close second. But I have not come across any subsequent reference in his diary (which he did not keep at that time) of that morning in Stonk Wood, and it is not the subject of any of the vignettes of episodes in the Normandy campaign which he wrote later. Perhaps it was simply too personal. In one day, apart from his own close call with death, his brother was wounded. And at the end of the war Cunliffe listed in his diary those he had liked who had been killed: Callwood was one of them.[8] In his role as Intelligence Officer, Cunliffe wrote the war diary: this has the briefest mention of the events.

While the tanks were stuck in their forward position, supply was a particular problem. A Echelon, under Bob Thorne's command, receives the occasional favourable mention in *Blue Flash*. Here it is praised for forming dumps in a hollow just behind the wood to which tanks could fall back to refill with ammunition and water. Food was not a significant problem as each tank carried tinned rations for three days. The Bedford 3-ton lorries of A Echelon would drive from 'railhead' – which in Normandy would probably not be an actual railhead but simply a main dump. The run up from the railhead, often made at night, was known in the Regiment as the 'night train'. A sub-unit of A Echelon, A1 Echelon, took the supplies on the last stretch, which allowed most of the transport to sit back away from the immediate threat of shelling. Bob Thorne remembered A1 Echelon as being largely crewed by troops from the A-A platoon, who were not needed in their original role.[9]

The Regiment pulled back from Stonk Wood on 13 August and spent the day reorganising. The wood continued to attract German attention, however. The 148th RAC had replaced 144th and their CO, Lieutenant Colonel R.C. Cracroft, was killed there later in the day. By a sad coincidence, 148th RAC was broken up immediately after this. British casualties in the campaign had been so heavy that a number of formations were disbanded at this time to bring others up to strength. The 59th Division, who supplied the battalions partnering 144th RAC at Noyers, was one such. The Regiment received 142 reinforcements from 148th RAC, making up losses from the previous days of heavy fighting. From the Regiment's point of view the reorganisation was positive. The men it received were trained and experienced; crews were kept together as much as possible so they could seamlessly fit in.[10]

The next day the Regiment moved forward again to the vicinity of Stonk Wood, now some way behind the front. After a brief period of confusion early on 15 August, in which it was discovered that the next objective had already been taken, the Regiment was breakfasting when: 'our brigadier arrived in his tank full of breakfast and the cavalry spirit and asked why the hell we weren't getting on'.[11] The Regiment pushed on several miles through Ernes to Escures-sur-Favières, a spread-out series of hamlets. It was, if only briefly, operating as an armoured unit tasked with exploitation, with limited infantry support. Accompanied by only a few dismounted troops from the 2nd Derbyshire Yeomanry, 51st Highland Division's reconnaissance regiment, 144th RAC started to clear up the area which was defended in some strength. A number of prisoners were taken and it was almost certainly at this point that a tragic incident occurred which was described later by Cunliffe; his account is reproduced in Chapter 7, 'Prisoners'.[12]

As there were still Germans in and around Escures, one squadron was left to assist in winkling them out; in fact the Germans pulled out that night with little more resistance. Meanwhile, the rest of the Regiment pushed on towards St Pierre-sur-Dives, a fair-sized town and communications centre a few miles ahead. During the day it had advanced about 7 miles as the crow flies, but considerably more by the roundabout route which had been taken, and had fought a minor battle at Escures into the bargain. Cunliffe, writing the war diary, rarely permitted himself to stray beyond a factual narrative, but the speed of the advance loosened his pen. He wrote: 'the remainder of the regiment bypassed the woods and plunged on astride the main road to St. Pierre-sur-Dives, in a twilight falling rapidly to darkness'. In a tactical aside, *Blue Flas*h noted that, as they proceeded along the main road, they came under artillery and mortar fire from the direction of Percy-en-Auge, a village to the left. One squadron fired smoke to screen the left flank, which successfully halted the fire. Apart from Totalize, it was one of the few occasions when the Regiment bypassed existing German positions in order to reach a more distant objective.[13]

The Regiment's gallop towards St Pierre continued. They had been told to halt for the night but, Jolly relates, he had been 'stung by a previous remark that the Regiment had been "slow all day"', and decided to press on. The remark presumably came from 33rd Armoured's brigadier, H.B. Scott, and the passage is a little dig back at him, as was Jolly's earlier comment about Scott arriving 'full of breakfast and the cavalry spirit'.[14] Jolly's sallies were restrained examples of the settling of accounts between units, or between subordinates and commanders – or vice versa – which is remarkably common in post-war memoirs, regimental histories and the like. A striking, and potentially much more offensive, example will be discussed shortly.

Reaching a farmhouse, and with memories of the hut at the railway crossing during Totalize which concealed Germans, C Squadron, in the lead, fired at it: 'as the buildings began to burn, men could be seen against the flames running in all directions to escape the hail of machine-gun fire directed at them from the tanks'. The next day abandoned guns, half-tracks and horse drawn transport were found at the farm. The Regiment finally halted on the outskirts of St Pierre, resuming operations at 05.30 on 16 August. The bridges over the Dives had been blown but the tanks were able to ford the stream, to find the town virtually deserted. By 08.30 it had been captured, with the assistance of the Derbyshire Yeomanry carrier platoon. A few prisoners included a paymaster – 'unfortunately without any pay' – who motorcycled into the town, unaware that it was in British hands. In the main square, 'a number of enthusiastic inhabitants fortified our intelligence officer [Cunliffe] with calvados and regaled him with stories of the enemy's departure'. Apparently a badly shaken German had arrived in the middle of the night with stories of '150 tanks' waiting to attack the town. In reality there were about twenty-five. The attack on the farmhouse had paid dividends.[15]

Unfortunately, the 'holiday atmosphere' in the main square was halted at about 10.00 by a heavy stonk. It may have been this which badly damaged the eleventh-century market hall, later rebuilt. I can well remember sitting outside a cafe with Bob Thorne in 1989, looking at the hall. He recollected that when he was there forty-five years earlier the roof was off and the tiles lay in heaps on the ground.[16]

As the Regiment arrived in St Pierre, the bulk of the German Army was fighting for its existence in the Falaise Pocket. (Map 2.1) Falaise itself was entered by the Canadians on the same day, 16 August, narrowing the pocket still further. Within it were an estimated 100,000 German troops, 'the remnants of fourteen divisions with stragglers from a dozen more'.[17] By now the Americans had advanced far to the east, and were fighting the enemy in Chartres. Their front formed the southern boundary of the pocket. To the north, I Corps, with 51st Highland Division as the southernmost component, was pulling the mouth of the pocket further east while the Germans retreated in the same direction. As the German units moved, dodging the Allied bombers and rocket-firing Typhoons, the distance they had to travel to escape the constriction of the ever narrowing pocket remained the same.

To Alan Jolly, satisfying although the capture of St Pierre was, it was something of a missed opportunity because of the lack of organic infantry or artillery units such as would have been available to an armoured regiment within an armoured division. Had these been available to 144th RAC, Jolly suggested that it could have pushed eastwards from St Pierre immediately and caught the Germans before they could prepare their next defensive position; he pointed out that it was not until 10.00 that their artillery was ready. St Pierre's market hall might have been spared and the Germans kept on the run.[18]

As it was, the Regiment pulled back from St Pierre while the infantry consolidated. This did not require much effort, as the Germans had departed. In the meantime B Squadron, left behind in Escures-sur-Favières, spent 16 August helping an infantry battalion, the 1st Gordons, secure another crossing place on the Dives to the north of St Pierre. It transpired that the bridges had been blown and, in boggy ground, a number of tanks got stuck. The details are unimportant but what make this little manoeuvre interesting is the extraordinary attack launched, after the war, on one of the Regiment's officers by the acting CO of the Gordons, Major Martin Lindsay.*

As was noted earlier, accusations against other units were freely bandied about in post-war publications. The author came across an egregious instance when writing the history of the Battle of the Ypres–Comines Canal, one of the battles fought during the retreat to Dunkirk. In this case the 1st Battalion Oxfordshire and Buckinghamshire Regiment (Ox and Bucks) accused the 8th Battalion Royal Warwickshire Regiment (Warwicks) of retiring early. It is clear when all the accounts were collated

---

* Lindsay, originally a Regular Army officer, was a well-known Arctic explorer, returning to the army during the war. He was a Conservative MP before the war, and again afterwards. Recently a critical memo he wrote after the Norwegian campaign of 1940 has been discovered. Politically well-connected and independent-minded, Lindsay showed the memo to Clement Attlee, the Labour leader; it was apparently influential in leading Attlee to oppose Chamberlain in the famous debate of 8 May 1940 which led to Churchill becoming Prime Minister. (*The Times*, obituary, 7 May 1981; *The Times*, 5 October 2017, p. 17, referring to Nicholas Shakespeare, *Six Minutes in May* (London, Harvill Secker, 2017).)

that the Ox and Bucks' belief that the Warwicks had retired was mistaken. The belief was no doubt genuinely held, but it also acted as an excuse which helped to explain their own retirement. They ended the day further back than the Warwicks whose line, given their heavy losses, remained commendably far forward. In other words, the Warwicks fought a more effective battle than the Ox and Bucks, which did not stop the latter making accusations which seem almost libellous.[19]

The book in which Lindsay made his accusation, *So Few Got Through*, was published just after the war in the form of a personal diary.[20] The blurb suggests, however, that it was constructed as such for publication, rather than being entirely written at the time. ('The author . . . tells his epic story in diary form'.) Certainly much of it reads as if it was written at leisure as a book, rather than nightly in a billet in unsatisfactory light after a day in action. Equally, the detail in it suggests that it was based on contemporaneous notes, and to that extent it should be reasonably accurate in representing Lindsay's perception of events at the time.

His accusation was more limited than the one made by the Ox and Bucks, which damned an entire battalion, but because of this also more personal. According to Lindsay, one of B Squadron's troops sent out to reconnoitre the bridges on the Dives had 'got nowhere' after an hour; 'the squadron commander admitted to me that the troop-leader was windy and useless'. Jolly, who defended the Regiment against another of Lindsay's accusations later in the campaign, made no mention of this one in *Blue Flash* but merely pointed out that the going was bad and tanks were getting ditched for no purpose. And of course, since the bridges were blown, the troop leader's inaction was understandable.[21]

What is remarkable about Lindsay's attack, apart from his reporting a presumably private comment made to him by Major Bob Secretan, the squadron commander, was that many of those who had served in 144th RAC could have identified the troop leader concerned. One would have thought that common decency would have led to some toning down of the criticism in print, especially as the dereliction of duty, if there was any at all, seemed insignificant.

The Regiment had fought with the 51st Highland Division from Totalize onwards, but this was the point where it began a semi-continuous link-up, known as affiliation, with that division's 153rd Brigade. Apart from Lindsay's 1st Gordons, usually linked with B Squadron, the Brigade consisted of the 5th Black Watch (A Squadron) and the 5/7 Gordons

(C Squadron). Of the other two regiments in 33 Armoured Brigade, the 1st Northamptonshire Yeomanry was usually affiliated with 152nd Brigade, and the disbanded 148th RAC's replacement, the 1st East Riding Yeomanry, with 154th Brigade. The Division awarded the regiments collectively their flash – the interlinked initials 'HD', in red on a blue background, worn on the shoulder. This was, as Jolly said, 'quite illegal' as 33rd Armoured Brigade was still technically an independent formation. The gesture was intended, and seemed to have worked, as a morale booster, and was presumably initiated by Major General Thomas Rennie, the new commander of the division who had been appointed because of the division's perceived inadequacies early in the campaign.[22]

Affiliation to infantry units was commonplace among the artillery, dating back to the First World War, and it is puzzling that it took so long for this to occur with tanks. Buckley suggests that lack of a settled relationship between infantry units and tanks remained a problem throughout the campaign. It would be interesting to know whether this judgment is correct and 33rd Armoured Brigade exceptional in becoming affiliated, or whether affiliation became more common at this stage.[23]

Affiliation had clear advantages – familiarity with the different practices which every unit evolved, irrespective of what 'doctrine' might call for, and also familiarity between officers and men in the units involved. Of course this could cut both ways, as Lindsay's criticism of the B Squadron troop commander shows. Although he was soon to aim another barb at 144th RAC, elsewhere Lindsay praises the Regiment. He mentions one occasion when he took Alan Jolly's advice on an attack plan. Much later, after fighting in Holland and the Ardennes and when 144th RAC was to be converted to an amphibious 'Buffalo' regiment, there was a farewell party between 1st Gordons and B Squadron. Lindsay concluded that: 'We have had the squadron supporting us on most of our operations since Normandy, and could not wish for a better'.[24]

After the Dives, the next line of resistance was the River Vie at Grandchamps-le-Chateau. Crossing this and occupying the high ground beyond involved a complicated little action on the night of 19/20 August in which all three battalions of 153rd Brigade were involved, supported by the Regiment. It is described at some length by Lindsay. It is indicative of the effectiveness of the German defence that the 1st Gordons alone suffered nearly fifty casualties, many of them from shelling and mortaring. The Regiment suffered just three, all wounded. It was a stark example of the way tank crews were insulated from the effect of shell, mortar and machine-gun fire. On the other hand, neither this nor the other river crossings to come saw the fierce and continued counter-attacks which marked, for instance, Noyers and Totalize. The German resistance was aimed simply at slowing the Allied advance; there were not enough resources to halt it.[25]

For the next few miles, the enemy fell back fairly rapidly. On the way, 1st Gordons and a troop of A Squadron approached the tiny hamlet of La Forge Vallée, no more than a few scattered dwellings. Its chief claim to fame was as the home of a large stud farm managed by an Englishman called Sam Ambler. Lindsay relates that on the afternoon of 21 August he received a message from Ambler, who was 'expecting me to visit him'. Ambler was then sheltering from the expected battle – which did not materialise, as the Germans had withdrawn – in a cave, and Lindsay was 'so intrigued by this impertinent cave-dweller' that he visited Ambler, who was 'sitting like an Eastern potentate on a divan (of horse rugs)'. Ambler produced a bottle of champagne which had apparently been given to him by a German officer to share with the first Englishman he met – an oddly chivalrous gesture. Lindsay reported that the stud was owned by an American named Strasburger. The horses were 'hidden away on small, obscure farmsteads'. The stud farm is still there, looking extremely smart. It must be the one then owned by Ralph B. Strassburger, an American businessman and racehorse owner and breeder, and described in his Wikipedia entry as at Lisieux. Lisieux was in fact only a few miles away, and it was the next destination of 153rd Brigade and the Regiment.[26]

The approach to Lisieux marked the first time recorded in *Blue Flash* that 144th RAC carried troops on its tanks. Tanks were not going to advance much faster than infantry on foot in the painstaking attacks mounted in the *bocage* country, for instance at Noyers, so there was no particular need for additional transport for the latter. Totalize, as has been seen, saw the first use of APCs, and these were to become increasingly important. But for the time being there was a shortage of obvious means for carrying troops cross-country, or along roads if lorries were not available. There were the ubiquitous Bren carriers, but they might be needed for other purposes and had limited space. The alternative was for troops to ride on the tanks themselves. Although this was common on the Eastern Front, there were British concerns about tank riding before the invasion: it was considered very dangerous. A proposal to carry King's

Shropshire Light Infantry men as tank riders in the planned dash to Caen on D-Day was regarded as highly unusual. The speeding up of British and Canadian progress in the later stages of the campaign meant that, in the absence of APCs, the earlier qualms were ignored and tank units started to carry riders. In the advance to Lisieux, two troops of C Squadron lifted a company of the 5/7th Gordons with them. Later there were other instances.[27]

The initial stages of the advance on 22 August were promising. To Jolly, there was a feeling of unreality: 'Was this really war, or were we on manoeuvres, and the battles of the last two months just a dream? The countryside was untouched and the wooded hills had given place to orchards and well-kept farms'. The air of unreality was enhanced as the acting infantry brigadier, Henry Hovell-Thurlow-Cumming-Bruce, was 'nonchantly leading the advance into Lisieux, followed at a respectful distance by his nervous tank and artillery C.O.'s'.[28] Cumming-Bruce, officially CO of the 1st Gordons but temporarily commanding 153rd Brigade (which was why Lindsay was temporarily in command of the Gordons), was 'a slightly unorthodox military figure with his rather old-fashioned curly moustache, white framed horn-rimmed spectacles, and slight stoop'. He seems, however, to have been an effective enough officer, since he was promoted to command 44th Infantry Brigade at the end of 1944, when still only 34.[29]

Lisieux was to see another confused action. On arrival C Squadron found an intact railway bridge over the River Touques, The town had been heavily bombed and rubble blocked the streets, so a tank acted as a battering ram to make a hole through one of the remaining houses in order to reach the bridge. Once over, the tanks met heavy mortar and small arms fire but, as on the approach to St Pierre, successfully screened themselves with smoke. In a lighter interlude, 'we met our first member of the Resistance, a Frenchman of great enthusiasm and courage who wanted to take command of the operation, including our tanks'. There followed uncertainty as to whether 7th Armoured Division would take over clearing the town. According to Jolly, the armoured division 'claimed it was <u>their</u> battle', but after a brief abortive attack 'they disappeared as mysteriously as they came'. Jolly saw this as a missed opportunity. If an attack supported by artillery had been put in during the evening, he thought that it might have succeeded. As it was, there had to be a costly clearance operation the next day when the Germans had regrouped.[30]

ADVANCE TO THE SEINE

There is a suggestion here that I Corps, who were presumably responsible for the uncertainty over who was to mount the attack, considered the combination of infantry division and armoured brigade as inferior to a specialised armoured division. In fact, the infantry having been lifted on tanks, the 51st Highland Division and 33rd Armoured Brigade together were acting like an armoured division: tanks, infantry and artillery were on the spot and available for the attack if it had been mounted.

The action the next day was the occasion of another of Lindsay's over-the-top broadsides. His 1st Gordons, who were helping to clear Lisieux, had a foothold on a hill on the far side of town, supported by one tank. Artillery support had been refused, initially because of the danger of hitting the 7th Armoured Division who were still in the vicinity and then because the 1st Gordons were too close to the Germans, so the barrage might hit the former rather than the latter. The exasperation Lindsay expressed in his diary seemed to be because he had promised his companies, exposed on the hill, that they would have further tank support, but it was difficult for the tanks to get up the hill. 'I got so angry that I jumped into the co-driver's seat in the tank belonging to the second-in-command, who was in charge in the absence of his squadron-commander . . . and ordered him to proceed'. The tank then broke down, which was hardly the fault of 144th RAC. According to Lindsay, 7th Armoured Division, who finally appeared in force, found no difficulty in getting up the hill.[31]

Jolly's view was rather different. His rejoinder to Lindsay was mild, although it contained a sting: 'There were times when we made mistakes, as did our friends in the 51st Highland Division, but this was not one of them'. He pointed out that tanks had severe disadvantages in street fighting due to their vulnerability to ambush, although they could support infantry by covering them from corner to corner, firing into upper windows. In this case, C Squadron had managed to get two tanks up the – very steep – hill, one of which had been hit and three of its crew killed. The remaining tank, 'perched like a fly on the wall', was giving the infantry fire support. In Jolly's view, the tanks should 'never have been given' the job of getting onto the hill. Neither account makes it clear who ordered the first two tanks up, but perhaps Jolly was referring to the later unsuccessful attempts, which were clearly ordered by Lindsay himself. In the absence of the C Squadron commander, Lindsay overrode the second-in-command, who was presumably trying to keep to Jolly's precept that tanks should not attack in penny packets but in troops, enabling them to give each other mutual support.[32]

As before, some of Lindsay's and Jolly's disagreement reflects the different perceptions of each party. But one suspects that Jolly knew rather more what his tanks were capable of than Lindsay. The latter made a rash promise to his men, could not fulfil it in spite of ordering the tanks to do something against their better judgment and then vented his frustration on 144th RAC.

For a time the Regiment was to leave the Highland Division, who had a few days' rest. It was well earned. Infantry casualties during the campaign had been appalling. 1st Gordons, for example, lost 133 killed or died from wounds up to 3 September, over 15 per cent of their original strength. By comparison 58 of 144th RAC's men were killed, about 8 per cent of the original strength.[33]

Instead of 51st Division, 144th RAC was teamed with 49th Infantry Division and, for that purpose, was temporarily under the command of 31st Tank Brigade.* Lisieux now taken, I Corps was operating in full pursuit mode. Once more, the tanks carried riders, this time from the 7th Duke of Wellington's Regiment, of 147 Brigade. On 24 August they had the thrill of advancing for 10 miles or so through a just liberated countryside, and the ecstatic reaction of the inhabitants is described in Chapter 7, 'The Costs of War'. The war then intervened, and a crossing of the River Calonne, against light opposition, was made at the tiny hamlet of La Vallette. The crossing involved the tragic part-demolition of a farmhouse; the description by Cunliffe is reproduced in the same chapter. On 25 and 26 August the Regiment advanced another 14 miles, from the Calonne to the River Risle at Appeville. The limited opposition melted away before there was any serious fighting, and casualties between the 24 and 29 of August were minimal. The Risle was crossed on 27 August and the Regiment, with the battalions of 147th Brigade, fanned out north-westwards and northwards, advancing to Pont-Audemer and towards the Seine itself. Jolly and Cunliffe, probing ahead in a scout car,

---

* 31st Tank Brigade was in the process of conversion to a specialist role operating 'Crocodiles', and two of its three regiments had already been detached for that purpose. (Wikipedia, accessed 16.10.2017.)

ADVANCE TO THE SEINE

reached the river at Quilleboeuf to find a mass of enemy equipment. Cunliffe's description is also in Chapter 7, 'The Spoils of War'.

Rapid as 144th RAC's advance was in the final few days, it was slow compared with that of forces further to the south. By 20 August the Falaise pocket had been closed and British and Canadian forces hurried towards Rouen. American forces had covered much greater distances – usually against no or very little opposition – and by the 26 August, with the French 2nd Armoured Division, had taken Paris. Two days later, when 144th RAC closed up to the lower Seine, the river up to and beyond Paris was almost entirely in Allied hands.

The one significant exception was the Forêt de Brotonne, lying to the south of a large bend in the river west of Rouen. *Blue Flash* describes an advance made with considerable trepidation by a column of the Regiment's tanks, lifting infantry of 49th Division, down the main road. With the possibility of ambush by *Ofenrohre* or anti-tank guns constantly in mind, extensive 'prophylactic' machine-gun fire was used to brass-up the surrounding undergrowth. In the event there was little opposition, in spite of the enemy possessing a number of 88mm guns which were subsequently captured. The Germans were completely demoralised and surrendered easily; 2,000 prisoners were taken in the area.[34]

There was one last act for the Regiment in Normandy, although the campaign is usually taken to have ended when the Allies reached the Seine. That was the capture of Le Havre, on the north bank where the river meets the sea. France's second largest port in peacetime, its capture was important because of its potential value for supply. Like the earlier advance through northern Calvados, however, the capture gets relatively little attention from most historians.

The neglect is understandable since the Allies had more exciting things happening elsewhere. By early September Le Havre's German garrison was isolated, because the Allied advance had swept onwards. On 4 September American forces reached the Meuse. In an even more dramatic dash, British XXX Corps drove forward over the Somme and through the Pas de Calais to reach Brussels and Antwerp by the same date. At last the British, after their months of attritional warfare, were able to emulate the American breakout which had started at the beginning of August. The story is almost a romance: the capture of Heinrich Eberbach, commander of German Seventh Army and the most senior German general taken in the campaign so far, in his pyjamas at Amiens; the four-day, 330-mile drive of the Guards Armoured Division to reach Brussels on 3 September; the capture of Antwerp and its docks on the 4 September. Unfortunately, German control of the north bank of the Scheldt estuary prevented the use of the port for several months.[35]

The failure to establish full control of the Scheldt made the possession of other ports, such as Le Havre, even more vital. The Regiment's part in its capture will not be described in detail as there was not all that much action. It will be more interesting to look at the evolving pattern of inter-arms cooperation, which had come a considerable way since Noyers.

The Le Havre assault, against defenders who were well dug-in with outer and inner defence layers, took some time to prepare and the infantry and tank assault only started on 10 September. As so often with Allied attacks on urban areas, there was a heavy preliminary bombing attack with, consequently, a large civilian death toll. The bombing was as much to weaken German morale as to cause physical damage to the defences. The Allies believed, rightly as it turned out, that enemy morale was already low. It was not helped, one imagines, by the usual Hitlerian orders to fight to the last man. There was also extensive Allied leafleting aimed at the Germans, and in that and other ways the assault was more sophisticated than earlier ones. By now the Allies had more specialist supporting tanks. The initial assault, by 152nd Brigade of 51st Highland Division, was accompanied by Crabs (mine-clearing tanks with flails) and AVREs, including ones which carried fascines – huge bundles of wood – which could bridge anti-tank ditches. In the follow-up assault 144th RAC's B squadron, supporting the 1st Gordons of 153rd Brigade, included two troops of Crocodiles and further Crabs and AVREs. By now the Regiment had reverted to working with 51st Division, although the attack also included 49th Division, supported by 34th Armoured Brigade. The Regiment also supplied squadrons to support other battalions of 153rd Brigade which would exploit after the breakthrough.[36]

Although 153rd Brigade's advance suffered the usual traffic jams and mishaps, the minefields were gapped successfully and, once through them, there was relatively little opposition. Both *Blue Flash* and Martin Lindsay record prisoners surrendering in batches. Lindsay wrote: 'it was most encouraging to see that they were being led by their officers. They lined up in front of me. "There you are," I said to the men who were near me, "the Master Race. Help yourselves." They soon had a fine collection of watches, fountain pens, pocket knives, and not a few French francs.'

ADVANCE TO THE SEINE

A little later he records the acquisition of further spoils of war. 'All the Jocks are smoking cigars and B Company has found a very nice little car.' However, he himself was unlucky: 'I still haven't any German field-glasses, which is my principal war aim.'[37]

The fighting was mostly over after the initial advance. In the account of operations he wrote for Jolly in the autumn of 1944, Cunliffe recorded the aftermath.

> A dense, cheering mob of Frenchmen gathered round the tanks, comforting proof that no enemy remained. An 'O' Group . . . was held in a small restaurant. It was a noisy hilarious scene, farce threatened to overcome the more serious problems of war. The Maquis [Resistance], together with odd civilians, were all eager to give information and suggest plans of campaign, all determined to get a word in first and therefore all speaking at once. One woman provided a torch, an invaluable street map, and some very excellent cognac.

Jolly also wrote amusingly about this incident in *Blue Flash*, his account obviously based on Cunliffe's; it gave him an opportunity to indulge one of his favourite pastimes, joking at the expense of the French Resistance.[38]

In spite of the farce, the capture of Le Havre was a triumph, apart from the heavy civilian casualties. There were 11,300 prisoners and British casualties were minimal. The 1st Gordons, for instance, had just three killed and fourteen wounded – tiny by comparison with infantry casualties in most battles. The 144th RAC suffered no casualties at all. Damage to the port was heavy but not irreparable, and within a month it was operating effectively.[39]

Jolly had some reflections on the success of the assault. Low German morale, weakened further by bombing and artillery fire, was a factor, and he pointed to others. The Allied plan was sound, because the attack was both concentrated and came from an unexpected direction. The availability of specialist tanks was particularly important. The Germans had covered the minefields with machine guns, with the anti-tank guns in defilade to engage tanks which got through the mines. But since the Crabs were impervious to machine-gun fire, and indeed could engage the enemy as well as clear mines (not usually at the same time, so some tanks would fire while others flailed), the minefields could be gapped without much difficulty. Then infantry and tanks would pass through the minefields, surmount anti-tank ditches with the help of the specialised AVRES and turn up where the Germans did not expect them. Fortified by the Crocodiles, which terrified the enemy even when they were in concrete emplacements, these tactics precipitated rapid surrenders. Finally, the Germans lacked any mobile armoured reserve with which they could have countered incursions.[40]

Although I Corps' campaign ended with a triumph, the advance beforehand could be criticised as too slow. There were reasons for this beyond the control of the Corps. John Buckley has pointed out that Montgomery saw this advance as subsidiary, as most of the German forces were escaping further south, and consequently there was less pressure from above. The retreating Germans were not as demoralised as those to the south who were fleeing from the Falaise Pocket. Finally, the enemy facing I Corps were able to use the rivers intersecting the terrain to good defensive effect. The relative slowness of the advance may not have mattered much, anyway. The Germans' heavy equipment losses before the river crossing were almost as great as in the Pocket, and they escaped with only a tiny fraction of their guns and tanks. A fair number of men crossed the Seine but, given the speed of the Allied advance from the end of August, it seems likely that many of those who escaped were captured soon afterwards before they made it back to Holland or Germany.[41]

Chapter 5

Holland and the Ardennes

After Le Havre, the 144th RAC was fortunate enough to have five weeks without action, time in which it could reorganise and train. Along with numerous other formations, it had been 'grounded' and its transport used to supply the troops who had advanced into Belgium and then Holland and then fought the ultimately unsuccessful battle for Arnhem – Operation Market Garden. Thirty of the Regiment's 3-tonner lorries were on supply duty between mid-September and early October, covering 2,000 miles and carrying a total of 1,500 tons. It was just about 100 miles a day on average for the time they were away, no mean achievement given that this had to encompass loading and unloading and the vagaries of French roads overcrowded with other military transport.[1]

This is not the place to discuss Market Garden, or the merits of the idea which lay behind it – Montgomery's attempt to accelerate the Allied advance towards Germany by attacking on a narrow front, rather than focusing on the opening up of Antwerp's docks by clearing the banks of the Scheldt.[2] Our concern is with the results: although the Allied airborne troops failed to hold on at Arnhem itself, the entire operation drove a huge wedge-shaped salient some 50 miles deep into the German front. (Map 5.1) In the course of doing this, the Allies successfully crossed several major rivers, notably the Maas (Meuse) and Waal, even if they did not hold the 'Bridge Too Far' over the Rhine at Arnhem. As a result, they could now exploit eastwards, up to the Rhine, and westwards without having to make further major river crossings. There were, however, still German forces south and west of the Maas which had to be cleared, and the low-lying nature of the countryside meant that numerous smaller waterways had to be crossed when any significant advance was made.

While 144th RAC was grounded, training continued, notably three days' shooting practice. Jolly noted that the standard of shooting had deteriorated. In the small-scale battles since Totalize most firing had consisted of 'brassing-up' nearby hedges and woodland, as in the Forêt de

Brotonne, and speed of reaction rather than accuracy was the prime requirement. The Regiment was also involved when Germans were alleged by the Resistance (renamed the Forces Francaises de l'Interieur, or FFI) to be hiding in dug-outs near Fécamp and Bruneval, towns along the coast from Le Havre and near the Regiment's quarters. Two squadrons carried out a sweep, both unsuccessfully, leading the FFI to suggest that the Regiment should search the sewers of Fécamp. Jolly countered with the suggestion that the Resistance should post sentries at the exits from the sewers. Judging by this and other references, Jolly had little time for the FFI, viewing them as, at best, an amusing irrelevance. The FFI declining his suggestion, he deployed one of his sardonic put-downs. They 'seemed to think that anything to do with fighting Germans was our business and not theirs'. Soon afterwards, the Regiment was called forward to Holland, and the Germans, if they existed, were left in the sewers.[3]

Holland

On 11 October 144th RAC started a move of 300 miles which took it to St Oedenrode, in the middle of the Allied salient. (Map 5.1) There it rejoined 51st Highland Division; once more, it would be supporting 153rd Brigade.[4] After the failure to hold the bridge at Arnhem it had been accepted – if reluctantly by Montgomery – that the Allies faced a further winter of slogging through prepared enemy defences. To combat these without excessive losses the Allies needed to use their huge advantage in resources. This was impossible with the existing transport system. Le Havre was now open and, in the south of France, Marseilles could be used after the American landing in August. But these ports were now hundreds of miles from the front line. Furthermore, the railway network of the Pas de Calais had been bombed heavily as part of the build-up to D-Day, so transport across the region still had to rely on the roads. It was essential to clear the banks of the Scheldt and open up Antwerp.

While it was the Canadians who bore the main brunt of this operation, British forces were involved in the attacks which supported it. Twelfth Corps, to which 51st Highland Division and 33rd Armoured Brigade were now attached, and other corps attacked the western edge of the salient so that German troops in south-west Holland were kept fully engaged. The Brigade participated in Operation Colin, which aimed to capture Tilburg and 's-Hertogenbosch and advance the salient to the lower reaches of the River Maas.[5]

HOLLAND AND THE ARDENNES

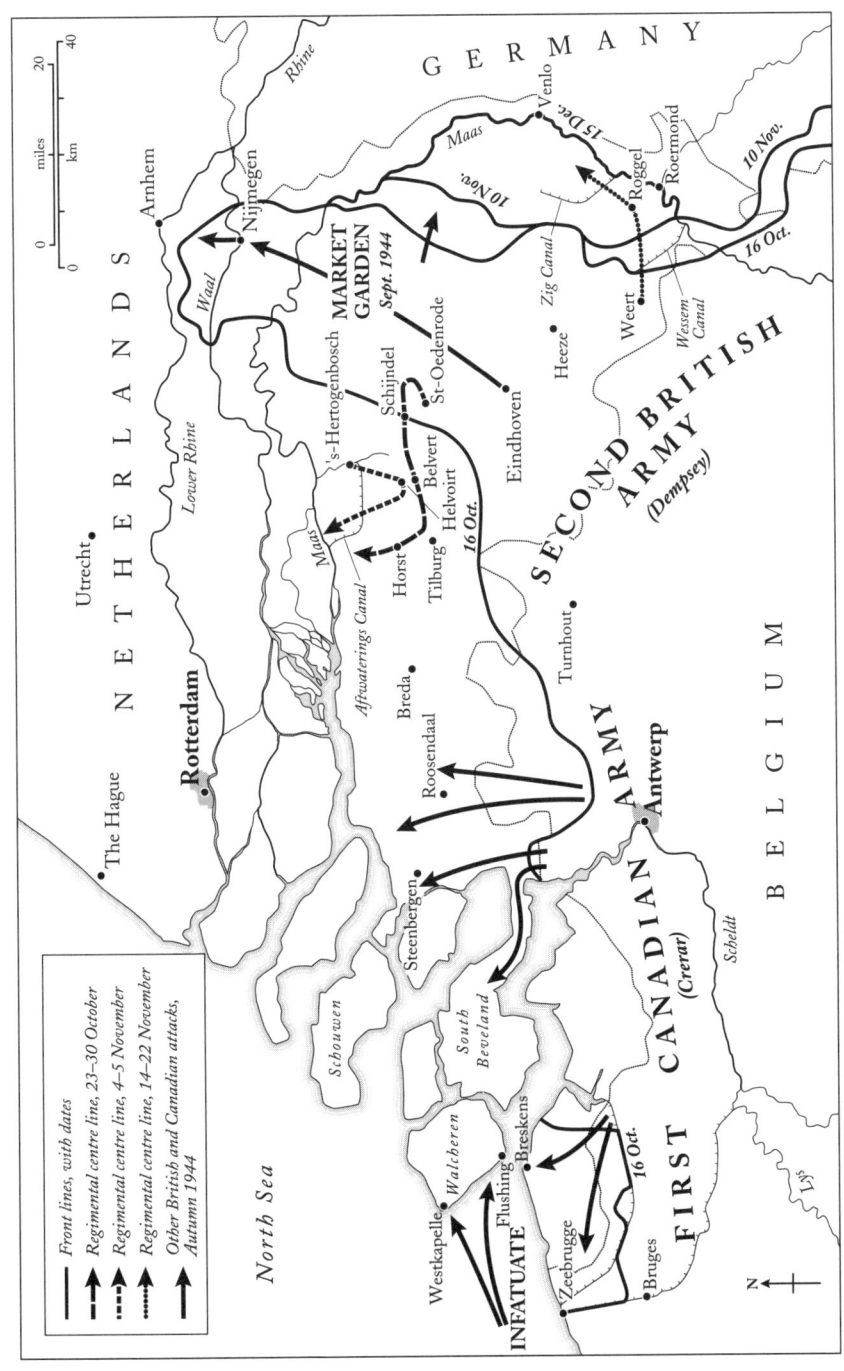

Map 5.1

FROM ARROMANCHES TO THE ELBE

The operation started on 23 October and was completed by 5 November. The 51st Division was flanked by 53rd Division to the north and 15th Division to the south, with 7th Armoured also participating. The Regiment's centre line lay just south of 's-Hertogenbosch and took it to Sprang, to the east of the city. In a second stage, it moved to the outskirts of 's-Hertogenbosch, crossed the Aftwaterings Canal and cleared up to the Maas at Herpt. (Map 5.1) Rather than pursue every turn it made through the watery Dutch countryside, some significant features will be discussed.

By now the Allies were lavishly equipped with special purpose armoured vehicles of all kinds. Their value was illustrated in the crossing of the Aftwaterings Canal. The enemy held most of the north bank and on 4 November armoured bulldozers built up ramps along the southern bank, shielded from the enemy by the bank itself and by smoke. A and C, Squadrons, reinforced by Crocodiles, mounted the bank at 16.30 and 'poured a hail of lead and drenching flame on to the far side'. Under its cover 1st Gordons successfully crossed in assault boats.[6]

During the preparations for this B Squadron had detoured to 's-Hertogenbosch, parked in the suburbs and 'drank coffee with the inhabitants'. They then crossed the canal and drove along the north bank towards the British crossing point. There was a potential obstacle in the form of a subsidiary dyke, which was presumably why this was not chosen as the main attack route. The Squadron was accompanied by two AVREs, one carrying an 'enormous fascine' and another a 30ft box-girder bridge. These successfully bridged the dyke, allowing the tanks to cross it and continue along the canal to join the Gordons. Later the other squadrons moved to 's-Hertogenbosch and took the same route to rejoin the infantry, rather than wait for a larger bridge to be completed across the canal by the Royal Engineers. Jolly described it as a 'very neat little operation made possible by the use of the assault bridge'.[7]

An action during the first stage of Colin, involving A Squadron, also drew Jolly's approbation. No AVRES or other special purpose tanks were involved in this. The 5th Black Watch were attacking Horst, and were supported by the squadron which directed an artillery concentration on two anti-tank guns while moving two troops of tanks in a flanking operation. Jolly saw this a classic example of the use of an entire squadron to outmanoeuvre the enemy and carry the advance forward, with no loss to the Regiment. The Black Watch wrote that the squadron, 'gallantly cleared the situation' with its two troops which 'brassed up the wood and area, from which the enemy was firing, with good results'.[8]

Jolly felt, however, that Operation Colin was less successful than it should have been. The initial attack on Schijndel had been preceded by a considerable amount of artillery support, but the town was largely unoccupied. Mounting a prepared attack here was, to Jolly, a waste since it was obvious that the first defensive line would be on the River Dommel, 3 miles further on. On 25 October opposition at Belvert on yet another waterway led to a hiatus as 7th Armoured Division – 144th RAC's bête noire at Lisieux – was again scheduled to pass through and carry on the attack. They materialised and went away again, and no attack was made that day. Instead the Regiment successfully supported 153rd Brigade in an early morning river crossing on the 26th. However, the operations after the productive river crossing became bogged down for lack of full-scale artillery support, with several of the Regiment's tanks lost.[9]

When they were told to pull off the road for 7th Armoured, Jolly reflected that this occurrence had become rather a joke: 'All that resulted was a thorough traffic jam with their tanks and ours double-banked down the road'. Cunliffe, by now commanding the Reconnaissance Troop, recorded his perceptions of the events in his diary; parts of his description are reproduced in the section entitled 'Waiting' in Chapter 7. As the above account suggests, much of war was waiting and Jolly's criticism was, in part, because he thought that with a better plan some of it would have been unnecessary. 'It was no good piling up more tanks. What was needed was a proper plan for the concentrated use of the tank, artillery and infantry resources already available, of which there were ample.' And again, to Jolly it seemed that informed scrutiny of the map would have shown that opposition would come when they advanced after the crossing on the 26th.[10]

Of course, Jolly was writing after the event and things may have been less obvious at the time. But it remains true that, although Operation Colin successfully cleared a large area and took about 3,500 prisoners, numerous Germans escaped northwards from the Tilburg area and crossed the River Maas before the Allies sealed it off.[11] Leaving out the attack on Tilburg itself, the operation occupied two infantry divisions with their supporting tanks and, of course, 7th Armoured Division. The advances on each day were limited to a few miles, against a retreating enemy. It is difficult not to agree with the implication of Jolly's comment about 'ample' resources – that 7th Armoured Division was redundant and that attempts to use it which were then aborted may have slowed things down rather than speeding them up. If the final part of the operation had been quicker, more Germans would have been trapped.

Operation Colin had been finished for only a few days before the Germans were finally evicted from the banks of the Scheldt. Once the estuary had been swept of mines, the docks at Antwerp could be used and British attention could turn again to their ultimate target, Germany. The eastern flank of the salient created by Market Garden ran parallel to an earlier stage of the River Maas, where it ran northwards out of Belgium before its turn west to the sea. After some initial Allied advances in the area, attention had turned to the Scheldt and south-western Holland. Then in late October the Germans put in a significant counter-attack on the eastern flank. It was stopped but the Allies were left some way short of the Maas. German forces to the west of the river continued to pose a threat and the next step was to clear them.[12] Twelfth Corps, including 51st Division and 33rd Armoured Brigade, moved eastwards to take up positions for an attack towards Venlo, where the German counter-attack had driven a salient into the Allied front. They were about to embark on Operation Mallard.[13] (Map 5.1) There was, in fact, little enemy opposition as the Germans evaded a battle here and fell back in front of the Allied advance. The latter was notable only because of the ever-greater use of specialised armoured vehicles. The main impediments, apart from the ubiquitous waterways, were mines, and the Flails were particularly useful here. There was not much call for orthodox tank action, and instead the Regiment found itself mainly providing fire support.

This was well illustrated in the first action, the crossing of the Wessem Canal near Weert on 14 November. On a two-battalion front, each battalion was supported by the fire of a squadron of tanks plus six Crocodiles. Furthermore, the spare squadron, as well as the tanks of RHQ and of a Flail squadron, were used to supplement the artillery by predicted fire at a crossroads 3 miles away. Using tanks as quasi-artillery was not their prime purpose, and illustrates the lavishness of the Allies' material resources by this stage of the war.[14]

Cunliffe wrote an account of the day in his diary.

> I joined in the RHQ shoot, having nothing better to do. Shortly before H Hour we were lined up, a thousand yards from the canal,

HOLLAND AND THE ARDENNES

looking out on a sallow, dismal landscape in which nothing moved. There was nothing to be seen except farms and fields, stretching away in an indistinct vista. The canal could not be made out. No sound except a truck on the move.

Punctually at four the silence was shattered, first by the odd gun firing just behind us, then by troop after troop, battery after battery. [This was artillery fire, not fire from the tanks]. Looking over my shoulder I saw the flames of the guns stabbing out everywhere. A moment later the prodigious bang of the charge reached me, and the shells whined viciously overhead. Then, later, the long rumble of the explosion, all along the canal. I saw fountains of greyblack earth go up. The air trembled with airbursts, which then announced themselves as tiny black smokeclouds, lingering along the canal like so many blobs, forlorn and ugly as trees seen in silhouette through a mist.

Smokeshells descended on the far side of the canal. Soon it was veiled, and the shells screamed into the opaque wall that marked the objectives. On the right, tanks led forward in single file, moving purposefully into the fog. Besides them the leading infantry, also in single file, marched towards the obstacle. They looked very tiny, insignificant in all the fiendish din, and very brave. In a few minutes the clockhands of their fate would have moved round. They would be pushing out their flimsy assault craft, scrambling up the sodden bank, over the top to ——— what? Some murderous Spandau perhaps, or the sharp menace of mortar-fire. Work for bayonets, moments of terror, death for a friend. . . .

Mortars, machine-guns, Bofors guns, all joined in the barrage. And then, like a final huge crash of drums in a symphony, the tanks. Arthur Hall raised a red-white-blue flag, gazed around to check that all had seen it.[*] It streamed in the wind, bravely. An Errol Flynn gesture; and I think Arthur, competent yet conceited, was aware of it. Impressively he cut away his hand. The immediate air above our ears cracked and rocked, turned sour with cordite. Somebody was firing too high; he shot away the telegraph wires in front with his first round. A dog, scampering delicately down the muddy road, fled in abject terror. My tank reeled back; empty

---

* Major Arthur Hall, C/O of A Squadron which took part in the shoot.

rounds clanged to the floor; cordite fumes curled in the turret, acidly unpleasant, catching at the eyes.

We fired in batches of five rounds. Then comparative silence; the Errol Flynn performance began again, and another thunderclap. The tanks and infantry had disappeared into the grey wall; the only hint of their existence came through my earphones, in the jargon that was grown so familiar –

'Hullo, How 4, are your supporting your friends?'

'How 4 – yes – it's damned hard to see anything in this smoke but they're getting across nicely. I can see them on the other side. No opposition that I can see: Over.'

'How 4 – Roger – keep it up – Out.'[15]

There was limited opposition on the other side which was cleared up the next day. On 16 November the advance continued several miles, via Roggel towards the Zig Canal. With the enemy disappearing, the Reconnaissance Troop under Cunliffe had, in Jolly's words, the 'exhilarating, if somewhat alarming, experience of being the spearhead on the 153 Brigade front'. Cunliffe's description of this is reproduced below. The patrol was reinforced by a troop of Shermans and infantry in Kangaroos, an example of how these once-scarce vehicles were now becoming common.[16]

The final advance to the Zig Canal (now called the Uitwaterings Canal) the next day was marked by the use of tanks, as well as Flails, for mine-clearing. The mines in question were the anti-personnel *schu* mines which the Germans were now sowing lavishly. Flails took the lead to detonate the larger mines, but it was thought that flailing would not set off the smaller *schu* mines so Shermans followed the Flails. Presumably their and the Flails' weight would explode the mines which were too small to damage the tanks' tracks.* The Canal itself, a rather insignificant affair by Dutch standards, was crossed easily with the tanks' role, again, being to provide fire support. This was the Regiment's last significant part in Operation Mallard, since the salient had now been driven in and the Allies had closed up to the Maas on the eastern, as well as the northern, flank.[17]

---

* One method which was tried to counter *schu* mines was to push a garden roller with an exceptionally long handle over them!

A 'Honey' tank of the Reconnaissance Troop and some 'B' Squadron tanks near Caen, 8 July 1944. (Regimental History)

Tanks and crews of 'B' Squadron waiting to go into action near Caen, 8 July 1944. (Regimental History)

Outside Noyers – 'A' Squadron's advance on the afternoon of 16 July was directly towards the camera. On their left was the railway, now a dual carriageway road. Their centre line, a secondary road to Cheux, is just off-camera to the left of the photograph. This was not *bocage*: instead there was 'a thousand-yard stretch of good tank going', still evident today (Chapter 2).

Operation Totalize; Tanks of A Squadron moving to the Forming-up Place south of Caen, 7 August 1944. (Regimental History)

Just outside Cramesnil, 144th RAC's destination in Operation Totalize, the local communes have erected this silhouette of a Sherman to commemorate the battle.

'Stonk Wood' from the St Sylvain road (D183). The wood's commanding position on a hill made it a target for German retaliation when it was captured. The author is on the left.

'Stonk Wood'; the Tiger knocked out by Corporal L. Eckersley's tank, 11 August 1944. (Regimental History)

A portrait of Robert Thorne, probably taken in 1940, when he was a newly promoted captain.

A group photograph of officers of the 144th. Alan Jolly sits in the centre, front (first) row. Marcus Cunliffe is standing, third row, sixth from left of the photograph; Robert Thorne is standing, second row, third from right. Of the forty-three officers in the photograph, nine were to be killed: Major Tom Lovibond (on Jolly's right); Major Pickering (front row, third from right); Captain Guillemette (second row, second from right); Captain Simmons (second row, fifth from left); Captain Charles Veall, the Medical Officer (front row, end right); Lieutenant Barnes (third row, third from right); Lieutenant Borg (back row, fourth from left); Lieutenant Jones (back row, fourth from right); 2nd Lieutenant Hotson (back row, end left). Two other officers who joined later were also killed. Among those wounded was Keith Cunliffe, Marcus' brother (back row, end right).

Alan Jolly – a close-up from the officers' group photograph.

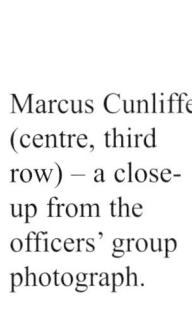

Marcus Cunliffe (centre, third row) – a close-up from the officers' group photograph.

The crossing of the Calonne at La Vallette. On 24 August Marcus Cunliffe and Alan Jolly descended into the valley; the bridge was blown and there were mines on the road and the verge. 'On the far bank the valley side rose up like a green wall. It towered above the stream, so that standing down in the valley-bottom you felt tiny and helpless, at the mercy of whatever lay hidden above you in the thick tree-growth' (Chapter 7). The mines are gone and the bridge has been rebuilt, but Cunliffe's description of the valley still holds today.

The north bank of the Aftwaterings Canal, looking east towards s'Hertogenbosch. On 4 November, A and C Squadrons, reinforced by Crocodile flame-throwing tanks, poured shells and liquid fire over the canal from the south bank. Simultaneously B Squadron motored along the towpath on the north bank, having crossed at s'Hertogenbosch.

Hotton War Cemetery in the Ardennes, where there are the graves of ten soldiers from 144th RAC, together with British infantrymen killed in the fighting, and airmen whose aeroplanes came down in the area.

Above Hotton War Cemetery on an appropriately wintry day: the road to Verdenne. To the left, beyond the wooded hill, is the Waharda Ridge which was the ultimate goal of 144th RAC and the accompanying infantry. Jolly wrote that the forest 'looked thoroughly unsuitable for tanks [and] … we therefore felt certain that we would have to attack it before long'.

A group of 4th RTR's Buffaloes in the Assembly Area for the Rhine crossing: woods near Marienbaum. (Courtesy of The Tank Museum)

The Rhine crossing. A personal message from Field Marshal Montgomery to 21st Army Group being read to the battalion before the operation by the Commanding Officer, Lieutenant Colonel A. Jolly. (Regimental History)

HOLLAND AND THE ARDENNES

Cunliffe's own account of the advance, through a countryside which was then sandy heathland, makes light of his 'somewhat alarming' experience.

> 24 hours in which a lot has happened to me, yet which I can't describe in anything but the barest terms. This morning I took part in a recce. We advanced about 3 miles, in the course of which we liberated a village. We ended up by occupying an objective for which the infantry had expected to fight. As we reached our final report line, my apprehensions ebbed away. First I felt immensely happy. Then the Honey commander in front of me caught sight of a few Germans to our front, several hundred yards away among some dunes. He opened fire upon them – tracer bounded across the heath – everyone grew excited – the leading scout car backed into cover. The Sherman troop leader behind me, persuaded by his gunner that there were Germans moving about in a dark little copse a hundred yards to our right, suddenly blasted at the copse with H.E. After a few minutes of intermittent firing, without any reply from a coy enemy, it became apparent that we had found some sort of rearguard position. The tension eased; the Honey stopped firing; the sun came out. All at once the dark forbidding waste became friendly, as shades of monochromes warmed into soft greens and browns. It seemed a fitting end to our adventure – sunlight, an inoffensive enemy, a fairly rapid progress. Everyone was pleased with life. I resisted a strong temptation to boast when I got back into Roggel (the village we had liberated), and an equally strong desire to be mock-modest. As the famous author said to the young one, 'what the hell have you got to be modest about?'
>
> Back in Roggel, I billeted my troop and all was sweet. As usual – one develops a drill in these things – RHQ was established in a pubcafé. Pubs for HQs, schools for billeting men, because neither of these is in operation in a newly-liberated place.

The action ended in farce:

> a strange figure . . . blundered in upon us. A herald of confusion: an elderly captain in a British warm and Glengarry, who blinked at us from a round, unhappy, face, and then said – 'I'm looking for

some Kangaroos.' Everyone was politely rude; they got rid of him by murmuring that they'd gone on up the road. I, being essentially unmilitary, stripped the word Kangaroo of its army significance. A fantastic picture came to my mind, of large brown animals hopping away over the Dutch landscape in all directions.[18]

The Ardennes

In late November the Regiment moved to Helvoirt, near s'Hertogenbosch. The British were preparing for a major battle for the Rhineland which would start with a breakout from the salient around Nijmegen. Hitler, however, had other ideas. On 16 December he launched the Ardennes offensive, subsequently known to the Allies as the 'Battle of the Bulge'. The German intention was to split the Allied armies and cut off the northern armies' supply route by driving west to Antwerp.

However fanciful the ultimate aim of the attack, the initial thrust, through the snowy Ardennes, met with a degree of success. The subsequent story is well known. The German advance was hampered by increasing American resistance, particularly in Bastogne which formed an undefeated pocket. As a result of that, of Allied air attacks and of limited German fuel supplies, the attack ran out of steam by late December. Nevertheless, while the Germans were still advancing the situation seemed serious. There were relatively few Allied units along the Meuse (as the Maas was called in French-speaking Belgium) and reinforcements were urgently needed.

Like practically everyone else, 144th RAC at first knew little. Cunliffe wrote in his diary on the 17 December that there was news of 'a bold German counter-attack on the American First Army which has apparently made several miles progress and got into Belgium'; but he did not single it out as of special importance. Even Montgomery was not, at first, greatly concerned.[19] By 19 December, however, the Allies realised that they were confronted with a major problem. The 33rd Armoured Brigade and other units were summoned south. Ironically, the Regiment, supported by the younger female population of the village, had just persuaded the local priest to allow a dance: 'the music pulsed through the hall while a hundred couples stepped to its rhythm', Cunliffe recorded in his diary. Then 'Robert Thorne told me there was a "flap" on – the 2 i/c had been called away suddenly to the phone'. Cunliffe was reminded of Childe Harold and the ball before Waterloo. It was a prescient thought because the

Regiment moved the next day, the tanks on their tracks as transporters were not available, and by the 21st were in a blocking position to the east of Brussels, near Waterloo. It was a testimony to the reliability of Shermans that they could make a journey of 90 miles without problems.[20]

Over the next few days the situation became clearer. The German advance had been stopped, while Montgomery had been put in charge of American as well as British units to the north and west of the salient. In the New Year, the Allies began large-scale counter-attacks. By 2 January the Regiment was established in the Marche-Hotton area, supporting 158th Brigade of 53rd Welsh Division, all under Thirtieth British Corps. Their opponents were units of 116th Panzer Division, and also of the much less formidable 560th *Volksgrenadier* Division, which included Russian and Ukrainian conscripts. Before they arrived Hotton and the surrounding area had been the scene of a gallant defence by American forces, who had subsequently counter-attacked and driven the Germans out of Verdennne.[21] (Map 5.2.)

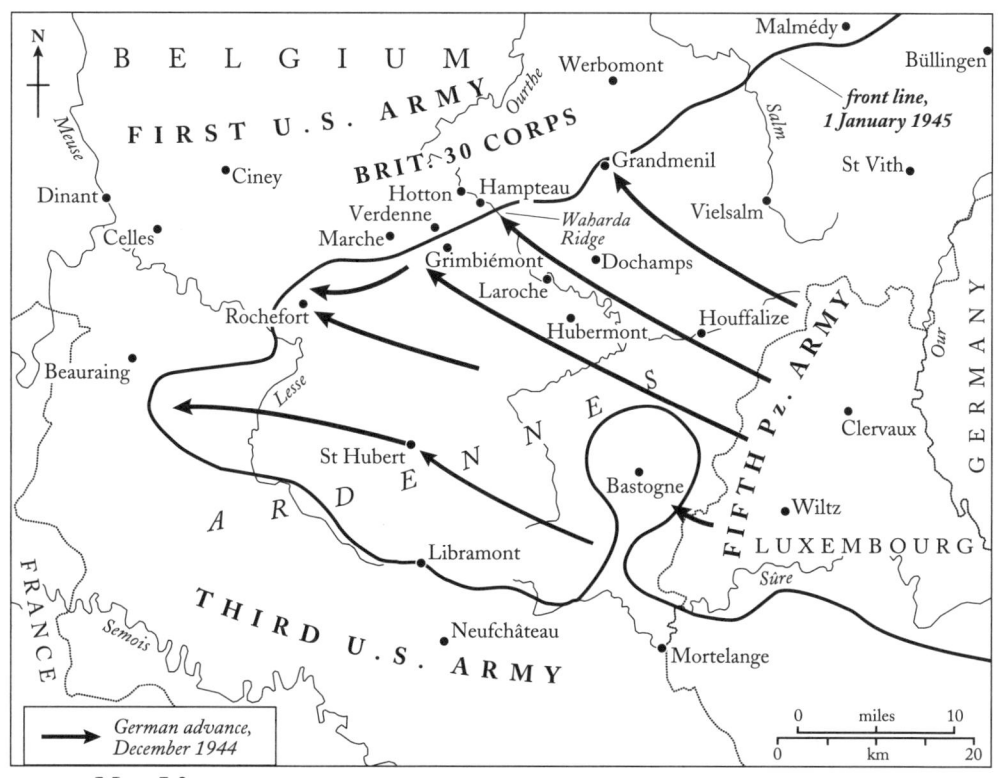

Map 5.2

Jolly described the position with a typically sardonic touch: the forest in front of them 'looked thoroughly unsuitable for tanks [and] . . . we therefore felt certain that we would have to attack it before long'. In the event, the attack started on 4 January. To the left of the British, the Americans had already started their assault, but apparently were having trouble with flanking fire and needed the British to clear the area. The next few days were a patchwork of actions, relatively small scale in themselves but in some cases very costly for the infantry, and fought in bitterly cold weather with frequent snowfalls. Although casualties for the Regiment were not on the scale of Noyers, the period in action cost it nine dead and twelve wounded.[22]

As with the fighting in Holland, only some aspects will be examined, allowing space for the testimony of one of the participants. On the first day, the Regiment supported all three battalions of 158th Brigade in a series of attacks between Verdenne and Hampteau. Only limited progress was made, and by agreement A and B Squadrons both stayed with the infantry that night for support. The weather was very cold but, 'the crews dug holes in the ground which, when lined with blankets, were tolerably warm'. Tanks carried blankets, which made them better off than the infantry. The infantry battalion most heavily engaged, coincidentally, was the 1st East Lancashires, which had supplied a number of 144th RAC's original personnel, including Bob Thorne.* Because of difficulties with transport it was not possible for them to get blankets or additional clothing up to the front line that night – although John Moore, the East Lancs' Quartermaster, personally carried a 'warming cargo of rum' up to the troops in the early morning of 5 January.[23]

The transport situation was dire because carriers shed their tracks easily on the ice, and even tanks found progress very difficult. Over the next few days the position was eased for both infantry and tanks by the provision of yet another vehicle in the Allies' armoury, the Weasel, a carrier-like vehicle of American origin, with wide tracks which made light of the conditions. It was also used to evacuate casualties.[24]

The attacks carried on with a pause for consolidation on 6 January. On the 7th a major artillery programme was laid on and the Waharda Ridge,

---

* Like most regional divisions, the 53rd Welsh incorporated a number of units from other parts of the United Kingdom.

the main obstacle, finally captured.* Further south C Squadron, with the East Lancs, had more difficulty and could only give peripheral help to the infantry, who nonetheless successfully reached their objective, Grimbiemont. C Squadron's vicissitudes are described in the first of the personal accounts which follow. It is a measure of the extreme difficulty of the conditions, as well as the fierce opposition, that the East Lancs suffered 243 casualties over the 4 days of fighting and subsequent 36 hours of line-holding. Most of these were wounded, or casualties of the extreme weather, rather than killed or missing, but it was nonetheless an appalling total.[25]

The two personal accounts below were both written by Lieutenant Hilary Phillips, commander of 1 troop in C Squadron. The footnote contains further details. Phillips was described by Cunliffe, when visiting C Squadron mess in November, as a 'rather callow boy', but judging from his description of events he was a competent and conscientious officer. The accounts are written in a less studied style than Cunliffe's, but one which is straightforward and effective. The interest of the accounts lies in the detail they contain of exactly how an operation would be organised and of what went on in a tank, and a tank troop, when the operation was under way. The first also describes an infantry attack from a tank commander's perspective. They are couched in the form of letters home, but are in The National Archives – see the footnote, and references there. A few silent corrections of spellings and punctuation have been made. The titles are as given by Phillips.[26]

'A Deliberate Attack and a Bog'

Phillips starts with the ideal conditions for a 'Deliberate Attack'. The unit of tanks involved needs a knowledge of the ground, preferably secured by personal reconnaissance. The ground conditions must be favourable, and the tank unit should have full information about supporting forces. All this should be passed to individual tank commanders, and the crews should have a good grasp of the situation as well. Troop leaders need to think about different scenarios and have solutions ready. Most important is coordination. 'It is essential that the tanks, the infantry and the artillery, together with any supporting arms, tie everything up in a complete spirit of cooperation. . . . everyone <u>must</u> know what everybody else is doing

---

* Jolly called this the Waharday Ridge; it is spelt without the 'y' on the *Carte Provinciale Luxembourg*.

and the exact time at which they are expected to do it'. Finally, the ideal attack should achieve complete surprise.

The subject is the attack of 7 January 1945 on Grimbiemont. The infantry battalion involved was the 1st East Lancashires.

> This is the story of an attack which was successful, but which could have met with considerably greater and speedier success had all the factors outlined above been fulfilled. Before anything else the weather holds pride of place in this affair, as it was the weather which was principally to blame for the trouble. Everywhere was covered in a thick white blanket of snow. Everywhere had been for some time, and by now we were quite used to all the normal disadvantages to which this snow subjected us.
>
> The squadron had harboured for the night in a large wood on the top of some high ground, captured from the enemy the day before. The wood stretched away to our front in the direction of the Germans and the ground gradually sloped away in the same direction, until the wood ended in a shallow valley. From the edge of the wood and across the valley one could see a long stretch of open snow, with the ground rising to a ridge in the rear.
>
> This was how the ground appeared to us when Cheese [the nickname for another of the troop leaders] and I went to have a look at it the day before the attack. The only way out of the wood for a tank was down a straight path and out into the open ground. Just where the path left the wood it crossed a stream. We went down there principally to see whether or not the stream would be a tank obstacle and, realising the importance of this question, were rather inclined to be conservatively minded in our views. However we decided that, taking it at speed, the tanks would cross the stream alright. Bob and the Major [Major R. Hill, C Squadron C/O] had also had a look at it before us.

The officers then discussed the tanks' planned movements when they had crossed the stream. The account continued:

> The whole of the forward edge of the wood was held by our infantry, who were dug in right down to the border of trees, from which Cheese and I had a look at the open ground. They were

living in small slit trenches and dug-outs, each holding one or two men. Cheese and I, not for the first time, thanked our lucky stars that we were not in the infantry. They had been there for two days and their blankets had only just come up. It was intensely cold and they seemed, justifiably, so we thought, not a little fed up.

We had a chat with one of their officers and with the artillery observation officer who was cooperating with us on the next day. Then we returned to the tanks, we told the Major of what we had seen and also of the infantry officer's report that a German S.P. was somewhere behind the open ridge in front of the wood, and had fired a shot the day before, which had fallen right in the middle of the avenue leading out into the open ground. He asked us if we thought the stream a tank obstacle and we told him no, that we would be able to cross it if we could take it at good speed.

That night we stayed where we were in the wood, and the Major gave the troop leaders a warning order about the operation for the next day. Our objective was a small village about half a mile beyond the ridge of open ground in front of the wood [this was Grimbiemont]. I remember that I set my map inside the turret that night and we brewed up some tea at about ten o'clock inside the turret. This is strictly against all rules and regulations and, of course, in England there is no smoking allowed within five yards of a vehicle.* We had some rum in our tea and it kept us warm for nearly an hour. It was abominably cold, however, so I decided to risk having to move in a hurry and unrolled my bed on the back of the tank. I took my zoot suit off but got into bed fully dressed otherwise except, of course, for my wellingtons. I slept pretty well, and when I woke up I found I had six inches of snow on top of me. However my bed was quite dry, owing to the tank sheet, and the only result was that my crew didn't know where I was, not realising that I was hidden beneath the snow on the engine deck.

---

* Jolly took a relaxed attitude to this. In *Blue Flash*, p. 35, he notes that cooking in or under a tank was strictly forbidden but, 'when a welcome cup of steaming tea was handed up to the tank commander during the chilly "stand-to" at dawn . . . he was not disposed to enquire too closely about its origin. "Such excellent stuff, this self-heating tea", as one officer is reported to have remarked.'

FROM ARROMANCHES TO THE ELBE

> The morning was a busy one. A troop leaders' 'O' group was arranged for nine o'clock, and owing to some trouble we had with our tank cooker, I had to turn up for it with breakfast in my hand. Cheese turned up without having set his map and received a rocket.

Phillips then described the planning of the operation, including the artillery support which included the laying down of smoke to mask the tanks' movements. The plans were detailed but a warning was given that they might have to change, as Phillips went on to describe.

> At the same time, however, the Major impressed upon us that circumstances might alter the position and we might find ourselves forced to support different groups of infantry from those we had planned to support. How right he was.
>
> After the major had given us these instructions, we all went over to the infantry battalion HQ and met our respective company commanders, whom we were to support. They had some very good aerial photographs. H Hour was fixed to be 1200 hours, and the final 'O' group for all tank commanders at, I think, 1100 hours.
>
> I returned to my tank and explained to the crew what the plan was. I also had a shave and a very good cup of tea. Then I found I just had time to put the other crews in the picture. At the tank commanders 'O' group orders were given for us to start up at H -25, and move off to the last piece of wood which was hidden from the enemy, at H -20. We had to allow this time, although it was only half a mile to the end of the wood, to keep the noise down. It is always necessary to travel very slowly.
>
> Order of march was to be 2 troop (Cheese), 1 troop (myself), and then, I think, HQ, 4 (David), 3 (Harry). [David must have been Lieutenant Wells – see note 26 of this chapter]. As soon as we reached the open ground, Cheese was swinging left to the tongue of wood and I was swinging left and then right to a hull down position on the ridge in front of the wood. So as to leave the avenue clear for us the infantry were forming up in the wood and coming out of it to the left of the avenue.
>
> The arrangements for this show were rather rushed, and there were several details about which I was not too happy. Nor were any of us, I think, though nobody said so. At H -25 we started up

and began to get formed up in our correct order of march. I was just getting my tank out onto the track behind Cheese's last tank, when a heavy stonk came down right on our forming up area, causing casualties among the infantry positions which were nearby. I heard my troop sergeant call up and report a casualty, so as soon as the stonking stopped, I ran up to his tank and found him bringing it out himself, the driver having been wounded. Luckily the M.O.'s half track was very handy, and the driver had been put straight into it within less than a minute of being hit. I then returned to my own tank and told the co-driver to move sharp and take over as driver on my sergeant's tank. [Presumably the sergeant's tank had no co-driver]. I didn't even give the poor fellow time to get his cigarettes out of his greatcoat pocket. Despite the fact that we had been as quick as possible, we had held up the rear of the column, although Cheese had carried on without us. However, we then moved off as quickly as possible to try and make up for lost time and arrive at the top of the avenue on time. The going was extremely bad. We had to follow the track through the wood where the branches of the trees were very low and it was impossible for me to get my head out of the turret. The snow was being shaken off the branches down my neck, and I remember Leach, my operator, grinning as he watched me wrathfully ducking up and down.

However the lead troop, Cheese's, got badly stuck, with only one tank remaining a runner. David's troop took over the lead, but by then the tanks were behind schedule and the smoke would be finished.

We came down the final avenue at about H + 10 and David's four tanks went across the stream and swung left according to plan. But only David reached his expected position, and he only made it because he had plenty of speed on, being the leading tank. As soon as he crossed the stream he sunk right down into a bog which had been completely hidden by the snow, and just managed to drag himself through. Of his other tanks, one managed to get through about thirty yards, and the other two got stuck ten yards beyond the stream.

I was in the next tank and, naturally, was a little depressed by what I saw. I told the driver to go flat out and swing hard right. He did so and we managed to get just over a hundred yards. My other two tanks followed on and got bogged behind me [the troop must have been one tank short]. We were all three broadside on to the high ridge, and it was a good thing that a good stonk had been put down on to it. Had the German S.P. reported the day before been there, we would have made three sitting targets.

I called up the Major and told him that it was impossible to go right or left. He decided to make a large detour to the right with what tanks he had left – HQ troop, Cheese's tank, and Harry's troop.

Meanwhile the infantry had gone on without any support from us. There was not much we could have done anyway as the only opposition from the enemy, bar a few odds and ends, was mortar and artillery fire. Their artillery fire, however, was accurate, and the infantry were going through hell. Obviously the Germans had their guns laid on the ridge ready for when we came over it, much as they had them laid on our forming up area ready for when they could hear the engines being started up. One was bound to feel tremendous admiration for the way in which the infantry went on, despite the stonk. They disappeared over the ridge in front and we could see no more.

Sometimes sheltering from intermittent stonks, David Wells and he decided to extract some of the bogged tanks by towing them with Wells' tank, which was still a runner.

The stonking stopped again, and I returned to my tank. On the way back I helped a wounded infantryman across the stream and he told me there was a German armoured car by a house beyond the ridge. I managed to get the rough position from him and reported it on the air and the map reference. With their usual efficiency the enemy had whitewashed this car.

Bob, who is our recce officer, then called me back on the air to know if I could find out what had happened to the infantry, as their colonel was quite out of touch with them and did not know how they were doing at all. Meanwhile, our squadron was still valiantly battling away through the wood, knocking down trees and trying to find a way round. I was glad of a job, as it was very sickening to be stuck back where we were and to be completely useless. I took my sten gun and started to run over towards the ridge in front. My two bogged tanks covered me and I ran fairly fast, in case there were any odd snipers about on the right flank. Unfortunately the stonking began again and I had to fall flat for a while.

I eventually got to the top of the ridge and made for a hayrick which stood on the top, so that it would act as some cover; it was also in a very good position as an O.P. Round the back of the rick was a very cunningly concealed slit trench, semi built into the rick. I had been on the look out for this, and we had all been told to destroy all ricks as they [were?] believed to have snipers in them or under them. The trench was deserted here, however.

From my position I could see a reserve company lying down on the forward slope of the ridge, and one of the forward companies doubling on to the second ridge – the high ground in the distance which looked down over the village. The reserve company were under heavy shell fire and had no cover at all. I felt for them, indeed.

It was down the hill all the way back to my tank, and I ran, or stumbled and ran, all the way. I fell down twice, much to the horror of my troop sergeant, who was watching from his turret. Far from being hurt, however, I was merely very much out of breath. What with my zuit suit and my wellingtons and the snow, running was extremely difficult, not to say exhausting. Not in my line at all. When I had got my breath back, I gave them the report over the air which they had asked for, and they were pleased to hear how well the infantry were doing.

The squadron, following the persistent attempts of the Major to find a detour, had at last extricated itself from the wood and hoped to catch the infantry up within five or ten minutes. They had come out on a road on our right and were having difficulty in climbing it, due to the usual frozen surface. But they made it alright, and I saw them appear on our right side soon after, slipping and sliding from side to side, but making progress all the same.

By now, too, David had extracted one of my tanks and all of his. He then decided that he had better push on cross country with his troop, plus my corporal's tank, and I wirelessed to the Major to verify this: he told David to carry on and be as quick as he could, so David went over the ridge.

So there we were, with two tanks stuck in an utterly useless position. However, if there should be a counter-attack, we decided that we were in a good position to get the first shot in and, with this possibility in mind, we had all round observation within the tanks, the drivers looking to the right, as the tanks were facing that way, and the operators to the left, with the gunners and commanders to the front.

I had wirelessed for the A. R. V. [Armoured Recovery Vehicle], to come and pull us out, and there was nothing left but to sit and listen to the battle and wait.*

There was no stonking at all. Everything was very quiet. By about two in the afternoon the infantry were down in the village and the squadron was with them, consolidating.

Finally two ARVs appeared and pulled his tanks out.

That was the end of that operation. I have given a . . . description of a deliberate attack in which the supporting tanks were thrown out of gear. The reason being, as I said before, the weather. If the ground had not been boggy, we should have got through. If there had not been snow everywhere, we should have seen the bog. And the result of the time table when things go out of gear is also shown only too well. But the infantry carried on with such complete certainty and steadfastness that the attack was a complete success. They deserved every praise that words can give them.

1 Troop has a Night Out
It was during the interlude between the capture of the Waharda Ridge and the Regiment's next spell of action in the area that Cunliffe and Jolly went on the trip to find a brigadier described in the Introduction. The Regiment was not finished with the Ardennes yet. It rejoined 51st Highland Division, which had relieved the 53rd, at a point where the country got even more difficult. The Division was advancing from Laroche, a town in a picturesque gorge. (Map 5.2) The rivers ran north-west through deep

---

* The next two sentences make it clear that he meant listen to the reports on the battle coming through on the radio.

ravines and the hills were almost impassable, meaning that movement could only take place on a 'one-tank front' along the roads following the rivers; once, in Jolly's words, 'it was accepted that tanks should be in the lead at all'. Clearly, Jolly thought that they should not but, during an advance along the River Hermeux towards Hubermont, a troop leader of C Squadron had been overruled by an infantry commander. The result was that one of the tanks, an easy target and lacking support from other tanks, was knocked out. It is the subsequent 'night out' which is described in Phillips' account.

The account refers to the night of 12/13 January 1945. The events as described in *Blue Flash* more or less correspond with the more extended description here.[27] By now, C Squadron was supporting 5th Black Watch of 153rd Brigade. Phillips introduced the account by pointing out that it was an occasion when only a limited number of tanks were involved, primarily for defence, in contrast to the operation described previously.

> This is an account of how my troop spent a night once, when we were wanted for a job of the kind which I have outlined, a consolidating job. Incidental to the story are a number of red herrings which have little to do with the main theme. But then, I am only writing about what happened, and not about what should have happened. In warfare the two are seldom exactly alike. In training they are. In training one makes few allowances for the intelligence of the enemy, for lack of information, for mechanical difficulties, road blocks, counter attacks, or, indeed, for very many of the interferences which one actually encounters.
>
> My troop had been detached from the squadron for the afternoon, but at five o'clock the rest of the squadron joined us. We were, much as usual, at the top of a high hill surrounded on three sides by thick woodland. To our front, and between us and the enemy, was a regiment of infantry, which was slowly feeling its way forward along its main axis of advance, a road which wound with difficulty to the summit of the hill where we were harbouring and then to the open country beyond the woods to our front.* Further along the road, camping in the wood for the night,

---

* He meant a battalion of infantry.

was David's troop. He had been detached from us early in the morning and had advanced with the infantry along this road. Suffice to say that he had lost a tank, knocked out by a Panther, and had remained in his position unable to advance any further until either darkness, or the supporting infantry on our right, made this practicable.[28]

The troop had been advancing in line ahead along a narrow road which at first had a thick wood on either side, limiting observation.

> I have not mentioned the snow. Partly, I suppose, because at the time these events took place, the snow was more or less part of our existence – a primary consideration of more importance even than the German military defence. It was, indeed, with the country, the strongest German defence.
>
> Further on, the road emerged from the wood and ran along in a straight line, with the open ground rising to the left, beyond the ditch by the road side, and with a big spur flanking the valley on the right. Anything travelling along the road was a perfect target from this spur, and it was from somewhere here that the Panther fired and knocked out David's second tank. His own tank, which was leading, the enemy did not fire at first. They waited, as is their custom often, for a tank with a 17 pounder gun. Then, when David tried to take evasive action his own tank had become firmly bogged in the ditch on the left, and he had, wisely, bailed out with his crew.
>
> This, then, was the position when the squadron arrived in the harbour, at dusk. To our front and on our right flank the enemy, we thought, also to our left. I had already made a foot reconnaissance with my troop sergeant, and we had decided that the only route by which we could advance any further was up the road.
>
> The Major had a quick 'O' group when he returned from Brigade, where he had been for the last couple of hours. He was very upset about David's tank. It had brewed up instantly and the driver had been wounded badly in the legs. Two of the crew had been badly burned. He looked as tired that night as I saw him all the time during this period. We were told what he knew of the tactical position, and also he warned me that if the infantry called for tanks in the night my troop would be moving out. Then he had

HOLLAND AND THE ARDENNES

to go away to RHQ and Nigel was left in command of the Squadron.

Each troop was responsible for its own guard, so I decided that of my four tanks two were to have a man watching from the turret, while the other two remained closed down to keep some warmth inside. I learned afterwards that there were thirty-five degrees of frost this night [presumably Fahrenheit, equal to about -20 ºC]. I kept my tank on wireless watch, hoping the batteries would stand it, so that I could be in the picture at the earliest possible moment if there was the likelihood of a quick move. I explained the tactical picture to my commanders and lent them my map so that they could show it to the men in their crews. It was rather a hazy picture, built up on not very reliable information, and I was not very happy about it.

Then I returned to my own tank. We were pretty cold, but we still had some tea in a thermos flask which was a good job and which we enjoyed. I wrote a very sketchy note home, resting my map case on my knee as a desk – a use to which I have put it often now. I also explained the tactical situation to my crew – with a little more conviction than I felt, I hope.

Not long afterwards – about half past eight, I suppose, the quartermaster sergeant came up with the rations and mail, also the petrol and water and ammunition. The water was of no use, however, as we found that it had all frozen solid inside the jerricans. It had been a tremendous feat for the QMS to get through at all, however, and we certainly didn't grumble. I gave him my letter and a few others which I had censored. I had three parcels that night, I remember, one of them contained a scarf, which came in handy later on.

It was very cold and there seemed to be nothing happening, so I decided to unroll my bed on the back of the tank and get into it. I had to take my zuit suit and my wellingtons off to do this, but otherwise I remained fully dressed.

As a matter of fact I slept very well and was wakened soon after midnight by the sound of Nigel's voice shouting for me. He waited down by my tank while I climbed out of bed and groped for my glasses and my wellingtons in the blanket bin.

An urgent call for a troop of tanks had come through from the infantry. We were to move at once up the road, passing David's troop, to the position held by the infantry. They had, apparently, heard the sound of enemy tanks forming up for a counter attack, and, owing to the snow, had not been able to get any anti-tank guns up to their position.

It took very little time to warn my tank commanders, and within less than five minutes all were on the road. We moved off as soon as I saw they were all on the road, and while we went along, Nigel rode on my tank and explained to me what he knew of the situation, which was remarkably little. I dropped him off and we moved on.

Soon we passed a little knot of men sleeping in the trees on the left of the road, with a couple of tanks backed in off the verge. This was David's troop. Then I looked ahead and saw David's knocked out tank blocking the road. There was a deep ditch on the right hand side of the road. I asked my driver if he thought we could get past without going into the ditch and he said yes, we could. We passed it alright, but we were the only one. My second tank slid sideways, due to the frozen surface of the road, and got completely stuck in the ditch.

It was obvious that, unless the road was cleared somehow, nobody else could get through. Sergeant Carr's tank was so hopelessly stuck that I knew we could never move that. I had a hope that we might move David's knocked-out tank. We backed my tank up to his and, after a lot of difficulty, due to shortage of shackles, managed to get the two tanks hitched up.

Meantime, in between watching this business, I had been trying to get Nigel on the air. I was in a raging temper with the operator at the other end because he didn't know where Nigel was. I told him to send out runners in any number he liked, but that it was important that I spoke to Nigel – or 'Sunray Minor' – as he termed it on the air. Eventually I got him but not until my question had been answered. I was going to ask him if he wanted me to continue by myself and, if he did, to send reinforcements through as soon as he could get the road clear. Also, to do this, I realised that an A.R.V. would be necessary.

However, while I had been yelling over the wireless, the crew had been working like hell and had got the two tanks coupled up and ready to move. David's tank was still on fire, although not seriously so.

HOLLAND AND THE ARDENNES

With some branches placed under the left-hand track, it was towed until it swerved off the road.

All this had taken about twenty minutes, and when I finally arrived with my remaining three tanks, having left Sgt Carr behind in the ditch, at the map reference where I was to be met by the infantry, it was nearly forty minutes since we had left the harbour. There I was met by the Adjutant of the infantry, and he showed me a road block two hundred yards up the road and asked if I could clear it.

It was a large beech tree right across the road, and I told my driver to have a go at pushing it out of the way. While he was climbing in to try, Major Hill arrived in a scout car, and together we went off to find the infantry colonel.

There was a certain amount of stonking going on here, and I found the C.O. in the ditch by the roadside together with a subaltern and a wireless operator. There was a wrecked jeep not far away, which looked to have been blown up on a mine. While we were here we heard tanks starting up their engines and changing into a higher gear. The noise faded away and the major and I were almost certain it was the German tanks pulling out. The infantry were held up on the slope and crest of a low hill, and were still nervous of a counter-attack with tanks. Therefore the major said he would go and get Harry to come and take up positions on the left flank and, until then, I was to position myself hull down in firing positions along the rise in front of me.

I returned to my troop to find that they had managed to clear the road block, but that only my tank was still in action. The second tank had flat batteries and could not start and the third had a badly slipping clutch. I called up the major and told him the situation and he said that I must get them into position somehow. So we hitched up to the first tank and towed it off the road. Fortunately, he managed to get his engine going, with the aid of the auxiliary charging motor, and I told him to get into the position which I had shown him. I then left my tank and returned to Sgt Parkin and we found that in bottom gear, on maximum revs, we could just move.

Eventually we were all three in position. One tank fired its machine guns once during the night at a suspicious looking place in the edge of the front, but apart from that, we never fired a single shot all night, and I never heard a sound of the enemy tanks. About four o'clock in the morning I heard Harry's voice on the air, getting his troop into position over on my left. By then, however, I felt fairly confident that we were not going to be attacked. All the same, it was good to know he was there at last.

It was jolly cold and I couldn't keep my feet warm at all. I then remembered the scarf which had come in the parcel earlier that night, and fished it out from where I had stuffed it, over the wireless set. I took off my wellingtons and wrapped my feet up in it like a parcel. It would have been unfortunate if I'd have to move in a hurry, but it was a good way of warming up my feet. One man in my crew felt the cold very badly during this period and I remember he was in a bad way that night. He had slight frostbite in the feet the following day.

The dawn came eventually, a fine sunny day, and in every way the anti-climax to the anxieties of the night before. My bed was still unrolled on the back of the tank, unharmed, and all complete. I was pleasantly surprised at this, as there had been some stonking during the night and one shell had landed less than ten yards from our tank.

Phillips finished by pointing out that: 'Often . . . if only he knew, the enemy has missed the most wonderful chances of catching us on the hop'. If 1 Troop had been attacked, his tank would have been the only mobile vehicle in the troop.

Conclusion

In *Blue Flash* Jolly produced a familiar criticism of the initial series of attacks on 4 January – they took place on too wide a front and thus were not concentrated. He admitted, however, that the necessity to immediately support the Americans dictated the possibly premature attacks.[29]

Apart from Jolly's tactical criticisms, another and more serious point could be made about the British contribution. Jolly's explanation, that they were attacking to protect the flanks of the Americans, was no doubt the one passed on to subordinate formations at the time. The American Official History, which seems admirably balanced, does not directly contradict this but does not give it much support either. It implies that the British attack increased pressure on the Germans but did not have any particular tactical rationale. Peter Caddick-Adams suggests that Montgomery favoured an attack from the north and west as he was concerned that striking at the base of the salient, the obvious solution, might be too ambitious. But whether it was really worth attacking the very nose of the salient when assaults further down would eventually drive the Germans back still seems an open question.[30]

There seems little doubt that the rationale for the British part of the operation was as much political as military. Eisenhower had temporarily appointed Montgomery as commander of all forces to the north of the salient, including American ones. Even a man with Monty's deficient perception of others' point of view could work out that, as he was giving the orders, some British involvement in the fighting would be tactful.

It would be wrong to conclude from this that the sacrifices of the British infantry, and the more limited sacrifices of the tank regiments, were unnecessary. Politics, especially given the sometimes fraught relations between the Americans and the British, were a necessary factor in the decisions made. It was unfortunate, however, that Montgomery then infuriated the American high command with an ill-judged press conference on 7 January, in which he seemed to claim responsibility for the stabilisation of the front and give only grudging credit to American forces.[31]

Chapter 6

The Rhine to the Elbe

With the defeat of the Ardennes offensive, the stage was almost set for the final attack on Germany. The climactic scene, in which 144th RAC would play an important part, was to be the crossing of the Rhine. But before that could take place, the west bank of the river had to be cleared. The German offensive had disrupted the timetable for this for both the Americans and the British, who had diverted XXX Corps to help in the Ardennes. When the Allies resumed their planned series of attacks, the main contribution of the British and Canadian forces was to clear the Reichswald Forest and then advance south-east, utilising the bridgehead across the Maas established at Nijmegen as a result of the Arnhem operation. This operation started in February and by early March the west bank of the Rhine down to Wesel had been cleared of German forces, while further south American forces were doing the same thing.[1]

The Allies could now make their preparations for the Rhine crossing virtually unobserved by the Germans, who by this time had little air reconnaissance capability. If the crossing could be accomplished successfully, the Ruhr, Germany's major industrial region only a few miles away, would be enveloped by British and Canadian troops to the north, and American to the south.

The Regiment's part in this was to ferry troops across the river. To do this, they converted to become operators of Buffaloes, yet another of the numerous specialised vehicles in the Allied armoury. Buffaloes had been developed in the USA in the early 1940s and were widely used by American forces in the Pacific theatre as well as the Allies in Europe. They were amphibious tracked vehicles (DUKWs, still seen on London streets as novelty tour vehicles, are wheeled) the tracks making them highly effective for river crossings where they could crawl up steep banks. Buffaloes were giant vehicles, wider and taller than Shermans, and could carry guns or jeeps, although in the initial stages of an assault they would

THE RHINE TO THE ELBE

mainly act as troop carriers. They were armed, with machine guns and rapid-firing Polsten cannon.[2]

It is an interesting sidelight on the wealth of equipment now available to the Allies that 144th RAC's Shermans were stored pending their return when the Buffaloes were relinquished. It is hard to believe that the German Army by that time would have been able to spare sixty tanks in good condition. Once equipped with Buffaloes in late January the training started, initially on part of the River Maas well away from the front line in a Flemish-speaking part of Belgium. The welcome given to the Regiment in the Belgian villages where they were billeted is described in Chapter 7. Three weeks of training on Buffaloes on land and water was followed by a similar time spent practising loading, crossing a river and discharging troops quickly on the other side.[3]

It was during this period that 144th RAC changed its name, and in doing so moved up the military pecking order. On 1 March it became the 4th Battalion Royal Tank Regiment, taking the name of a historic tank battalion whose origins went back to the first use of tanks in 1916.* The original had been virtually wiped out at Tobruk in June 1942, and most of its personnel captured, and the unit was effectively in suspense until its resuscitation. The background to the Regiment's promotion is described in Chapter 8. The change of name involved a rare ceremonial parade. The Guard of Honour was commanded by Bob Thorne – perhaps because, as a Regular Army sergeant before the war, he knew rather more about parades than most wartime officers.[4]

Important although the change of name and status was to the Regiment's future, a far more significant event was about to unfold. The Allies were at last ready to embark on crossing the Rhine. Planning had been going on since the autumn of 1944. One reason for the lengthy build-up was Montgomery's caution: he 'was determined that everything that could be put in place was put in place, risks were to be eliminated as far as possible, and thus casualties reduced to a minimum'. How this was realised at the level of the individual unit is well illustrated in the accounts, which follow shortly, of 4th RTR's crossing and the preparations for it.[5]

---

* For the remainder of this chapter the title '4th RTR' will be used, but the unit, although technically it had become a battalion, will still be referred to as 'The Regiment' to preserve continuity. They now carried a blue shoulder flash and the regimental news-sheet became *Blue Flash* – the name of the book.

FROM ARROMANCHES TO THE ELBE

In truth, the preparations were probably rather overdone. By now the German Army was shattered after a series of hammer-blows from the Western Allies and the Russians. The former's contribution culminated in their counter-attack in the Ardennes and the losses subsequently inflicted on the Germans in the offensives on the west bank of the Rhine. As a result German defences on the east bank were seriously undermanned. Furthermore, the Americans had already seized a bridgehead on the east side without the trouble or drama of a contested crossing. This was a result of the capture of the famous 'Bridge at Remagen', the Ludendorff railway bridge, to the south of the Ruhr. The Germans had blown up most Rhine bridges but not this one, and on 7 March it was captured by quick-thinking troops of the US 9th Armoured Division. To rub salt into the injury to Montgomery's pride, Patton also crossed the Rhine at Oppenheim, further south still, the night before the main Allied assault.[6]

Nevertheless, a large portion of the Allied armies, and their main supply route through Antwerp, was in the north and so crossing there was still essential. Montgomery's caution was also partially justified by the Germans' apparent ability to conjure resistance out of nowhere, as the Ardennes offensive and then the fierce resistance in the Reichswald demonstrated. One other reason for delay was that he could build up his stockpile of supplies and the extensive kit needed for bridge-building unhindered on the west bank, ready for a major development of the offensive as soon as the Rhine was crossed.[7]

Whatever the merits or demerits of his plan, it was a stupendous logistical and administrative feat: in support of the crossing the British and Canadians used 32,000 vehicles, amassed 118,000 tons of stores and lined up 3,500 guns to provide artillery support.[8] Again, the 4th RTR account shows how this manifested itself at the level of the unit.

The British attack on the night of 23/24 March 1945, Operation Plunder, was spearheaded by the 51st Highland Division of XXX Corps on either side of the town of Rees and 15th Division of XII Corps between Rees and Wesel. (Map 6.1) The 4th RTR was again in support of 51st Highland Division, although now in a different role. Further south the US Ninth Army also attacked as part of the same offensive. The next day a large-scale air assault was launched. As it happened, one of the few areas where the Germans put up a serious defence was Rees. So although the initial crossing went well, as described below, 51st Highland Division suffered quite significant casualties in fighting for the town itself. One of those was its commanding officer, the popular and effective Tom Rennie. The Regiment's casualties, in contrast, were relatively low. Three men drowned when a Buffalo hit a submerged cable on 26 March, while one shell killed two more men and wounded twelve; only one other man was wounded in the operation. It is a tribute to the effective Allied suppression of German fire, and a reflection of the role of chance, that there were so few casualties, and that most of them were caused by this one shell.[9]

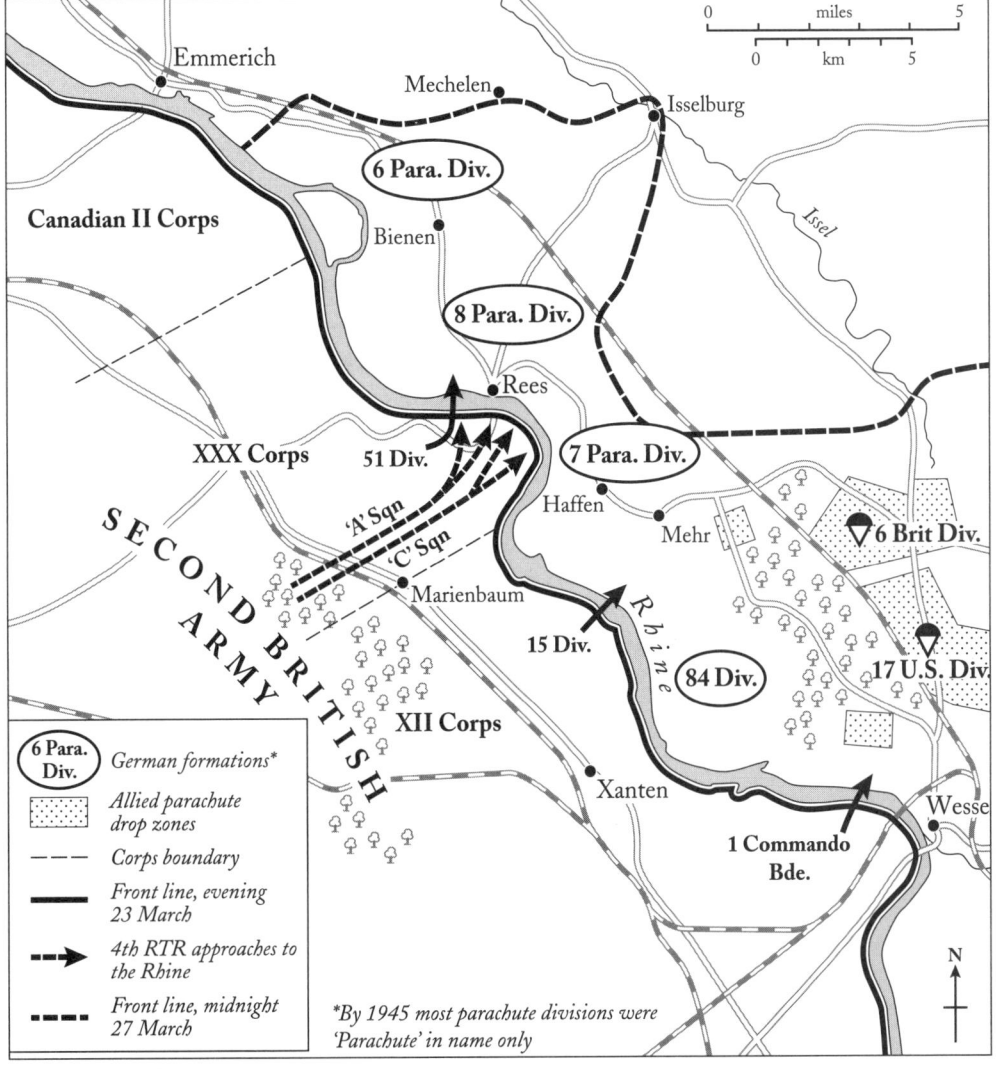

Map 6.1

One task before the crossing was to ensure that 'The Flag' would be in the van of the attack, carried in a Buffalo and accompanied by Alan Jolly himself. No doubt his usual instinct for publicity was behind this. The Flag was 'an old tattered flag in the colours of the Royal Tank Regiment', usually kept at Bovington, the headquarters of the RTR. Its colours were brown, red and green ('Through mud and blood to the green fields beyond') and the material used for it had also been used for a flag flown in November 1917 at the Battle of Cambrai, famous as the first large-scale tank attack, and another which was carried to Berlin by 1st RTR in 1945. The one Jolly accompanied had been carried across Cologne's Hohenzollern Bridge by an armoured car leading the first Allied troops to cross the Rhine after the end of the First World War. According to Jolly's account, 'The flag was so tattered that it threatened to disintegrate in the breeze, so it was only unfurled for the last part of the journey'.[10]

Carrying the flag was a neat gesture, although Jolly ruefully admitted that it failed as publicity, at least for the Regiment, since the press report on the operation mistakenly credited 5th RTR.[11]

Many details, both of the crossing and the Regiment's preparations for it, are contained in the two accounts, written by participating officers, which are reproduced below. One was by Lieutenant Phillips, already familiar as the author of the two accounts of operations in the Ardennes reproduced in the previous chapter. This is complete save a few omissions, replaced by commentary or, if unimportant, shown by ellipsis. The other was by Lieutenant David Wells, also of C Squadron – the 'David' mentioned in Phillips' earlier accounts. A few excerpts only from this have been used to supplement Phillips' account.[12]

Over the Rhine*

> [Phillips] It is difficult to know where to begin. If I were writing the script for a film I would begin with a description of a day not so long ago in the Ardennes, when we first learned we were to lose our beloved tanks and take over some extraordinary new amphibious vehicle, about which we knew nothing and cared still

---

* The title of Phillips' account. As before, a few misspellings and minor matters of punctuation have been silently altered.

less. I would go on telling about the days and nights of training which we had, on a river where the currents were strong and the banks often boggy. Of the hours we spent at lectures and discussions, learning all about Buffaloes and the best way in which we could use them. Of the re-arranging of crews, the re-establishment of the squadron organisation, of the navigation and the gunnery, of the loading and unloading of infantry and vehicles by day and, later, by night. There was certainly a lot to be learnt.

But now I have only time to talk of the few days covering the one operation for which we were working, and in particular of the night of the initial assault, when we crossed the river at nine o'clock on a Friday night. The papers have printed so much about us now that I think I can say quite a lot without breaking security.

Phillips described the journey to their destination, a few miles from the Rhine, and continued.

As soon as we had unloaded off the transporters we went into the wood which had been allotted to the squadron. For the next hour or two we were all very busy digging slit trenches and camouflaging the craft. It was essential that, even if we were spotted in the wood, the enemy should not realise the type of vehicle which we were hiding. We were at this time about three miles from the river. The next two days were spent in putting the finishing touches to our craft, cleaning the guns and making certain that all the special equipment was in working order.

All German civilians had been evacuated from the area used to prepare for the crossing, while smoke was continually discharged to shield it from prying eyes. The Regiment was harboured in a wood near the village of Marienbaum. It had been divided into two squadrons, A and C, with B (Cunliffe's squadron) divided between the two. A would carry the 5th Black Watch and land to the west of Rees, C with the 5/7 Gordons would land to the east. Later A Squadron would carry over the 1st Gordons to assault the town itself. In the initial journey to the river, both squadrons would leave the wood together, as the distances they were to travel were more or less identical, and diverge after about 3,000yd. Phillips calls this the Regimental Dispersal Point. Nearer the river, the two leading troops of each squadron would diverge again to two different launching points. Phillips refers to this divergence point as the junction point (JP). With each Buffalo carrying roughly a platoon, a troop could deliver a company of infantry.[13]

> [Phillips] Two days before D-Day, all the troop leaders went out with Bob Secretan, who was Major commanding C Squadron in place of Major Hill, and we walked right up from the wood to the junction point where the two assaulting troops swung left and right respectively. It was a longish walk to this point and we were all boiling hot when we reached it. The smoke which was being put down about a mile behind the river bank all along the shore made our throats very sore but was a big help in allowing us to get well forward. We were not able to go further forward than the J.P., due to the lack of cover. The J.P. was a T junction just behind a small group of farm buildings, and it was arranged that 1 troop (my troop) should swing left and then bear right down the river bank, and that 3 troop should carry straight on and down to the water. Bob Osbourn – the recce officer – had not had a chance to pace the distance on the ground, although we were hoping that he would manage it that night. However, he reckoned that it would take my troop 14 minutes to reach the bank from the J.P. and Harry's troop 8 minutes. This calculation was one of great importance to us, as it was essential that we should hit the water dead on H Hour. Not a minute too soon, or we would have to sit on the bank or go forward into our own barrage. Not a minute late, or the enemy would have had a chance to recover from the effects of the barrage.

Phillips then explained that the Buffaloes were essentially transports, and that the troop leaders' next destination was the area where the Buffaloes would be reloaded after the initial assault.

> This business of transporting vehicles and supplies was, in our case, to be the all important one. The river is pretty wide and we knew it would be some time before it could be bridged. During the last few weeks we had worked out (by making mistakes in exercises) a system of running our ferry service, in which everything down to the smallest detail was planned with the greatest of care. . . .

THE RHINE TO THE ELBE

After we had got it all firmly into our heads where everything was, from the command post to the latrine, we returned to a barn a few hundred yards back on the route we had come, to await the darkness. The whole of the three mile journey from the wood to the J.P. was clearly marked with posts and white tape and later would be lighted with lights. Further back, near the wood where we began, was the Regimental Dispersal Point, where the squadrons each went their own way. Our squadron was on the right. Altogether probably 20,000 yards or more of white tape was used to mark out routes and areas for the operation, together with hundreds of coloured lights. A great deal of this was done by Bob, who had to work like hell to get through it all, often held up by enemy shell fire.

As soon as it was dark we went up to the group of farm buildings by the J.P., where the infantry holding the line at this point had their Company H.Q. They were leading a terrible life, and almost every day two or three were forced to go sick and be temporarily evacuated. This, thanks to the Smoke Screen. It made us all cough and our throats were very sore after an hour of it. How the infantry stuck it, living in it day after day for a week, I don't know. It was just like poison gas. The whole area was one thick blanket of smoke. It must have kept the Germans very jittery, especially in view of the length of frontage which was being smoked. [Martin Lindsay put this at 60 miles.[14]]

That night ten Germans had been captured patrolling on our side of the river and there had been quite a fierce fight. So that we decided that to recce the banks, which it was essential to do, we should go out as a fighting patrol, in case we bumped into anything. We therefore went out with two infantry sections under a sergeant major, and ourselves made up the third section. Bob led the way, having already recced the area the night before. We only had our pistols, but personally I found it was all to the good not to have too much ourselves, as we had a lot of crawling to do and the infantry was fully armed. First of all we went down Harry's route. It was impossible to see far in the dark, and although they had stopped smoking [discharging smoke] there was a lot of it hanging about close to the ground. We had an awful job to stop ourselves from coughing – particularly the infantry who had been in it for so long.

However, we slowly got near the bank and managed to get right down to the water without any disturbance at all. We found that the banks were, as we had been told, ideal for the job. They were just like the shore at the seaside.

They then looked at Phillips' setting off point and the landing points, which were also satisfactory. Phillips continued:

From [the landing point] we intended to return by the direct route to the centre of the Ferry Service area, but owing to the smoke Bob lost his bearings slightly and we returned by a roundabout route. However, we all had a goodish idea of the correct way back and Kelvin guaranteed to have it taped out by the time we were on the home shore after the assault. Luckily transport was waiting to take us back, as we were all pretty tired. We got back to the wood at 11.30 p.m. and did an assault on the cookhouse, having had nothing to eat since breakfast. We all managed to find something and then we retired to bed. We were shelled during the night, but it was inaccurate and none of it quite close enough to make me get up and shiver in the slit trench we had dug. On the whole I think we all slept very well, despite the stonking.

The next day the troop leaders took their craft commanders all round the course, to show them the layout. We finished work fairly early and everybody was in bed by nine o'clock.

Then came D-Day. In the morning we had an O group [Orders group] with the major (Bob Secretan) which lasted until after eleven o'clock. There were one or two final things to tie up with Bob – lights, timings, route marking etc. Not long before we had an exercise in thick fog and it had been so chaotic that we were all insistent on the route being marked really clearly. During the morning I showed my commanders the detailed air photos which we had with all the routes we needed to know. After this, the Colonel gave an excellent talk to the whole regiment, finishing just before lunch. First, he gave us the general war situation, forecasting a good deal of what has since happened. Then he told the troops that their troop leaders doubtless had everything tied up and would be giving them their final orders themselves. Then he wished us the best of luck.

THE RHINE TO THE ELBE

Wells also commented favourably on Jolly's talk. Of course, they were both writing for the regimental archives, but Phillips' account at least seems to have started life as a private letter and one can probably assume that, if they said that Jolly spoke well, he did.

> After this I gave my troop their orders. I had the whole troop together for this O group, as I always do for the final one if it is at all possible. For the commanders it is usually just a repetition of what they have already been told. My orders took me an hour and then the issuing of codes took me nearly half an hour.
>
> Then we took it easy, after we had removed all camouflage from the vehicles and had them ready to move out instantly. Our squadron was due to move out first and my troop was leading the squadron out, so it was essential that we should be able to get out quickly so as to be out of the way. Timings were all very carefully worked out, and I had all mine chalked on my map board together with code names, bearings, back-bearings, and all sorts of other things which I knew I would never remember in my head.

Meanwhile, Wells' troop was loading the ammunition carriers of the 5/7 Gordons. Wells commented that, 'The most difficult job of all was that of Bob Osbourn, the Recce Officer, who had the most hazardous task of setting out the small green lamps marking the Buffalo routes from the flood bank to the water's edge. [The flood bank was roughly at the junction point.]' Osbourn had an hour to complete this task, since it could only be done after dark; he and the other squadron reconnaissance officer achieved it with the help of military police.[15]

Wells described some of the details of the barrage, which had started while they were loading. The numerous German positions around Rees, and the German artillery, had been pinpointed by air reconnaissance:

> the whole lot were to receive special attention from the artillery as soon as the barrage opened. On our own particular sector of the front we had in support an immense number of guns of all calibres from 25 pdr. field guns to rocket batteries. Also we were using 4 captured 88 mm. guns. It seemed only fair and just that the Germans should have at least this opportunity to sample their own medicine! The fire plan was due to start at 1700 hrs. – 4 hours

before H hour – and the intensity of fire would be gradually stepped up so that by the time we assaulted something like 400 shells per minute would be going over. At H hour the barrage would lift inland simultaneously with our entry into the water. Additional close support would be provided by what the gunners termed a 'pepper pot' – a miscellaneous collection of tanks and mortars which would plaster the enemy bank from a position on the flood bank. The knowledge that this great weight of artillery was to be used in support of the operation gave the troops great confidence . . .

Phillips takes up the story:

By 6 o'clock [pm] the infantry were all here and at the appointed time my troop moved out. The weather had been perfect all day, but there was a sign of mist, which made me somewhat apprehensive. I was worried more than anything else that I would not be able to find my way to the exact spot where we would go into the water. Going across water is different from going across land, if you start wrong it takes you a long time to get right again, because of all the errors which the current causes. Similarly, control of a group of craft is not easy in the water if they once get out of formation. It was essential that we should all land in as close an area as possible, and I had instructed my commanders that if the attack caused a thick fog they were to stick right close to my tail and land wherever I landed even if it was not the exact place.

After a few words about the barrage, he continued:

As we lumbered forward in the twilight, the whole sky was lit up with the flashes and tracer shells. Every kind of gun was pressed into service to add to the general weight of shells being hurled across to the other side. The route up to the J.P. was beautifully marked with coloured lights and a stranger to the course could hardly have got lost. The mist cleared away as we moved on our way and I found myself far less apprehensive than I had been before we moved off.

THE RHINE TO THE ELBE

At a halt on the way we loaded all guns – we can produce a very effective fire power. Slowly the barrage increased in force, and slowly we blundered on, nose to tail. I was worried because I could not get Control at all on the air; it later turned out that several people were having difficulty, so I realised that it must be something wrong with their set. Of course Nigel, in the command post, was very worried as he had no means of telling what had happened to us at all. Luckily my wireless within the troop was working well and I had first class communication with my other commanders.

We left our last piece of cover and fanned out. It was beautifully clear and I could see my furthest vehicle with ease. I misjudged the last [illegible] 14 minutes slightly, though I maintained afterwards that 14 minutes was an over-estimate of the time it would take us to reach the bank from the J.P. In any event we had the uncomfortable experience of sitting a few yards back from the home bank, with two and three quarter minutes to go. I was expecting an 88 or something to fire at us at any minute. But all was well and we entered the water at H hour and drove straight across. When we were about a hundred yards from the enemy bank a Spandau opened up at us, firing very high over our heads. None the less he made us duck involuntarily.

I was too busy watching my other craft to think of firing, until Buggy shouted to me to know if he was to fire. I nodded and at the same time opened up with my own guns. Of course I was miles out as usual. But between the two of us we scared the Spandau man and I saw him scramble to his feet and go haring off into the darkness. It seems silly writing this at much length because, of course, it all happened within a few seconds. The next seconds were the most worrying of all. Would we be able to touch down or not? We had been told that the banks were the same on this side as they were on the home side, but not having seen them ourselves and being confirmed sceptics after past experiences of the army, we were all worried about the landing.

In actual fact when we were 20 yards or so from the bank, I realised that it was touch and go whether or not we would be able to touch down and keep a grip while the infantry piled out over the front. The bank was steep and faced with cobble stones. It could hardly have been worse. We charged it and, holding my breath, I told the driver to change to bottom. We hit it at just the right angle and swung round. I thought we were coming off but one track gripped and we stayed there listing at a terrific angle.

The Jocks were beginning to scramble out and Buggy and I gave them a hand by pushing them up their backsides. I told Fisher the bearing we wanted to drive back on and called up the other craft to know if they were all in.* They all reported in and close to me – I could see two of them myself. It could not have gone better, and we were tremendously excited and longing to get home and tell them how well we had done. I was most annoyed that I could not get Nigel on the air, as I had looked forward so much to reporting that I was in position dead on time.

Wells wrote that 1 and 3 Troops – the latter being the other lead troop which had deviated from Phillips at the junction point – 'earned for themselves the distinction of being the first troops of the first regiment to cross the Rhine. This may possibly be disputed by A Squadron but most competent judges agree that C Squadron won the race by several minutes'. On the other hand, at 21.04 – only 4 minutes after H hour – Horrocks, the commander of XXX Corps, received a message that the Black Watch had landed. The Black Watch was carried by A Squadron, along with Jolly and the Flag, so the landings must have been very close together. According to an unnamed newspaper account, it was Lieutenant Campbell, a Canadian officer in the Black Watch, who was actually first on shore, 'As British shells screamed across the Rhine just prior to the assault', Lieutenant Campbell's troops sang 'Doon the Watter', 'Loch Lomond' and 'I Belong to Glasgow' (as a number of them did) before singing 'Onward Christian Soldiers' on the crossing.[16]

[Phillips] My craft was the first unloaded and, as soon as the Jocks were all out, we slid back into the water and steered for home. I managed to pick the landing point without any difficulty as soon

---

* George Fisher was Phillips' regular driver; his first name was mentioned in one of the latter's Ardennes accounts.

as Fisher was on the bearing and in three minutes we were back on the home bank again. We went over the rise near the water and hit the dead ground beyond, where I waited for the others to join me. One by one they reported they were on their way, and a moment later I heard some of Harry's troop on my B set too, talking to him.

All the way across our only opposition had been a Spandau. But the Germans were now beginning to recover a little from the numbness to which our barrage had reduced them and the stonking was beginning. Fairly heavy shelling was falling all round the home bank, so we did not waste any more time, but started for home. On the way home I passed Kelvin and Sgt. Lord marking out the route home with white tape for subsequent journeys and for the other troops which had not yet followed on. It cannot have been at all a pleasant job, and every now and then they had to fall flat on their faces.

It was not long before we were passing through the trees on our way to the command post, and as soon as we arrived in the area the sergeant major was dashing up and asked me to report to Nigel at once. We were the first craft to return and my troop was the first complete troop back. And we had been the first to cross the Rhine and had landed at the place. And so of course we felt on top of the world.

Phillips reported to the command post, and then 'began an all-round-the-clock ferry service taking over all that was wanted until the bridges could be built. For the first few hours we were shelled pretty heavily, but it did not interfere with the service at all.'

As Phillips implied, 4th RTR continued ferrying at full pace all night and into the next day. Bridging in the vicinity was difficult because of the continued resistance in Rees, although other ferries were established. These included a Class 9 raft service, carrying up to 100 men per raft; according to Lindsay, one was hit by a shell on 24 March. While 4th RTR's ferry service was in operation the tracks of the Buffaloes were frequently damaged by the stone facing of the banks, so the recovery teams and fitters were working continually. Eventually, a bridge was built and the Regiment's involvement effectively ceased on 26 March.[17]

Fortunately for 4th RTR it did not get involved in the bitter fighting for Rees which took place after the crossing. The 1st Gordons, for example, who crossed in the Regiment's Buffaloes in the second wave, suffered no casualties during the crossing, but fifty in fighting for the town's outskirts in the afternoon and evening of 24 March, and more subsequently. The 51st Division's best-known casualty was General Rennie. He had transformed them from a division which, in its first weeks in Normandy, had been seen as failing, to one of the most respected in the British Army. Rennie, a tall, impressive, saturnine figure, 'always wore one of those naval duffle coats with the hood hanging down at the back, his hands in the two large front pockets, and on his head always a tam o'shanter with the red hackle of his old regiment, the Black Watch.... No wonder the Jocks loved him.' Another of the inspirational British commanders of the Second World War was Brian Horrocks of XXX Corps. Like Rennie, Horrocks frequently visited his troops. Martin Lindsay met him on 26 March, when Rees had finally been cleared: 'he took the trouble to explain the situation to the company commanders whom we'd picked up in the course of our wandering, with his big map placed on the bonnet of his car'. Lindsay also noted that, after the first day, German shelling virtually ceased. Horrocks told him that the Allies were constantly taking air photos and, 'as soon as a new battery is spotted about sixty guns open up on it'.[18]

Meanwhile, 4th RTR was, in a modest way, enjoying the fleshpots.

> The inhabitants had fled, leaving us comfortable accommodation and not a little livestock. Being one of the first units in the area we were able to 'liberate' a good many pigs which would otherwise have starved to death (or, more probably, been eaten by the Jocks). . . . A fat sow with a maternal look in her eye was preserved for posterity, together with a selection of young porkers. A 3-ton lorry was misappropriated and special ramps constructed so that the pigs could be rapidly embussed, when we had sudden orders to leave. But Sergeant Berry found that pig discipline was not all that it should have been and moving the livestock was always apt to be fraught with a certain amount of excitement.[19]

Early in April the Regiment returned to Holland, to Gorssel near Deventer where the Canadians were in the process of breaking out northwards from the Nijmegen bridgehead which had been established so many months ago. At Gorssel, 'we harboured once more in pleasant, clean pine woods, the more fortunate ones being established in the bright and attractive modern houses which are such a feature of this part of Holland'. Starting on 11 April, by the next morning the Regiment had ferried practically the whole of the 1st Canadian Infantry Division over the Ijssel, by which time a bridge had been built. Jolly explained how the process, perfected at the Rhine crossing, worked. 'The infantry had been given blocks of serial numbers which they could allot to their vehicles in the order in which they wanted them to cross the river. They told our officers at the ferries which serial numbers were required and the vehicles bearing those numbers were sent forward.' The Regiment had officers at the Vehicle Waiting Area and the loading areas. The ease of the crossing was helped by the limited opposition – one 'elusive' self-propelled gun, which was knocked out on the 12 April.[20]

Over the next three weeks, as the war dragged to a close, the Regiment assisted at two more water crossings. Before these had occurred, Alan Jolly moved on to a senior staff appointment at 79th Armoured Division. His replacement was Lieutenant Colonel F. Wetherell; in practice Wetherell seems to have done relatively little during the last weeks of the war. He was on leave for the first few days and Bob Reid, the long-standing commander of A Squadron, carried out the planning for the next operation. This was south of Bremen, where 4th RTR carried troops of 3rd Division across flooded ground south of the city in the small hours of 25 April, less than two weeks before the final German surrender. A Squadron plus a troop of C carried the 2nd Royal Warwicks of 185th Brigade, and B Squadron plus another troop of C carried the 2nd Royal Ulster Rifles of 9 Brigade.[21]

The shallowness of the water to be crossed – most of which was usually pasture – led to some Buffaloes becoming grounded. Nevertheless, there were independent witnesses who paid tribute to the Regiment's part in the operation, although the complete dominance the Allies had now established obviously helped in its success. The Warwicks' wrote that, 'the barrage drove [the enemy] all into their shelters, and the Buffaloes took them completely by surprise . . . Great credit must go to the Buffalo Regiment . . .'.[22]

B Squadron's task was, according to 3rd Division's historian, technically the most difficult which 4th RTR had accomplished, since it was the longest water crossing they made. Like the Warwicks, the 'Ulster Rifles were full of admiration for the 4th Royal Tanks. Not a Buffalo was either lost or permanently bogged. And after a 2000 yards night-crossing, they touched down exactly at the assigned "crook in the bund" – the bend in the bank of the Ochtum which the leading company (C) was to take and consolidate.' Unlike the Rhine crossing, where there was little initial opposition, C Company men, 'rushed from their Buffaloes as soon as they landed, and found German gunners just bringing into action two Flak guns [presumably 88mm]. The gunners were dealt with . . .'; the guns were then fired by the Ulstermen at another German position which was holding out. The Rifles took over 100 prisoners who, 'boggled at the *Schwimm-Panzer* [the Buffaloes] in astonishment'.[23]

There was only one more wartime task for the Regiment. A Squadron had moved to the Lüneburg area. They were then ordered to support the US 82nd Airborne Division, loaned to British Second Army with the rest of the US XVIII Airborne Corps, which was to cross the Elbe at Bleckede, about 30 miles upriver from Hamburg.[24] Jolly personally brought A Squadron's orders from 79th Armoured Division and helped Reid plan the operation. It must have been difficult to resist the opportunity to play a part in a final action with his old regiment. The actual assault, at 01.00 on 1 May, was carried out by assault boats, with the Buffaloes then ferrying replacements and supplies. Apart from shelling, the Germans managed, remarkably, some air attacks and Trooper C. Tanner was killed 'in the hour of victory'.[25]

It was, indeed, the hour of victory, and the fighting was over for 4th RTR. A Squadron remained near Bleckede, and the other two a few miles from Bremen. Cunliffe's account of B Squadron's muted celebrations on the night of 4/5 May, after the announcement that German forces in north-western Europe would surrender the next morning, is in Chapter 8. The regimental celebrations took place on 9 May, after the war in Europe had been formally brought to an end at midnight on the 8th. Jolly commented, 'did they seem a little forced?' For those who had fought, rejoicing at victory must have been mixed with regret at those who had not come through, as it was with Cunliffe. Eighty-four men of the Regiment had died during the campaign. It was a lighter toll than that suffered by most infantry battalions; nevertheless it was over 10 per cent of the Regiment's initial complement.

Chapter 7

The Experience of War

The most important part of most wars is the fighting, for it is that which determines who wins and loses. In the Second World War, few would deny that the result was of vital importance not just to the nations concerned, but to the future of mankind.

But much else occurs in a war. A great deal of that is a side effect of the fighting, but important enough to the people concerned. Men are killed, wounded or taken prisoner; civilians suffer, or sometimes enjoy, the presence of the military; possessions change hands by force; buildings are destroyed or damaged. Marcus Cunliffe's diary, and the selection of episodes in Normandy which he wrote about later in 'The Other Side', contain material which tells us something, often vividly, about those side effects. Other sources have contributed at times. The first section deals with something which, for the troops, was one of the abiding memories of war: waiting.

Waiting
There was less waiting for British troops in the Allied campaign from Normandy to the Baltic than in most earlier wars. Even in the First World War, spells at rest or in reserve were interspersed with spells on 'quiet' sectors of the front; periods of intense fighting were relatively short. The final Allied offensive, from August to November 1918, involved more continuous action; but even that, as its semi-official name 'The Hundred Days' indicates, was only a little over three months long.

By comparison, the campaign of 1944–5 lasted eleven months, or a little less for the majority of units which landed after D-Day. During that time there were rest periods, but for many units action was almost daily for considerable stretches of time. The 144th RAC were fortunate to have almost a month after landing to acclimatise. From the start of the Battle of Noyers on 16 July until the beginning of September, however, action was almost continuous. After a few days' rest the Regiment prepared for and carried out the attack on Le Havre, in mid-September. There followed a longer rest period until mid-October and the move to Holland. From then on, with short gaps, the Regiment was engaged in the series of small-scale operations contingent on clearing the Germans from Holland. Early and mid-December saw training, until the 20th when the Regiment moved to become one of the Allied backstops against the developing Ardennes offensive. At the end of December it moved again before becoming involved in the counter-attacks which pushed the Germans back.

After relief by the Americans in mid-January there followed the longest period without action, lasting until the Rhine crossing in late March. However, there was considerable activity as the Regiment retrained following its conversion to Buffaloes. A brief period of rest after the crossing was followed by other river crossings before A Squadron crossed the Elbe and finished the Regiment's part in the war.

So there was plenty of activity for 144th RAC. In spite of that, there was also plenty of waiting, not just in the periods between operations but during them too: the waiting while an advance was planned and then called off; the waiting during the evenings and nights during a period of continuous action; the waiting for a major operation. Waiting, as the extracts suggest, could shred the nerves as much as the more violent forms of action. But at times, when men were together and some relaxation was possible, waiting might be a form of recuperation. Cunliffe writes quite a lot about waiting. It was, after all, a chance for him to catch up with his diary.

By October, 144th RAC was supporting 153rd Infantry Brigade as they cleared the area around s'Hertogenbosch. It was slow work, fighting at one river line after another. Cunliffe was commanding the Reconnaissance Troop.

> The morning is quiet. All sounds are deadened by the mist. The nearest sound is the crackle from the wireless beside me, in the scout car. Other sounds are intermittent, and the ear too accustomed to notice them particularly. They are an occasional burst of M.G. fire, the crump [?] of a shell, the whine of a truck going up the road through the woods.'[1]
>
> Am I a coward? I'm inclined to think that I am. At any rate, I dread the summons to action. Once we are committed, I lose the greater part of the dread, and before anything begins, I am

fortunately able to conceal my feelings under a pretence of imbecilic cheerfulness.

Subsequently he received orders for an attack the next morning, and passed them on to his troop. The anticipation of action is well described.

I made out my own orders and gave them out to a fascinated group of [scout] car and tank commanders. Seven of them. Each knew what the others were thinking. We had all seen too many burnt out vehicles not too appreciate the risks that the leading vehicles would take. I felt that I ought to put myself in the lead, but that wouldn't be any use. Besides (I felt that it eased all sorts of personal dilemmas for me) the Colonel had forbidden me to lead. I felt that I sounded too cheerful, too confident, too brave – how to strike the appropriate note? I realised there probably wasn't one.

The night went uncomfortably. I slept in a slit-trench, because of shelling. It was a singularly beautiful night, lit by a young moon and ornamented by stars. At intervals shells came whining over, to crump among the nearby trees, while our own artillery kept up their purposeful din through most of the night. When it came to my turn to do an hour's watch, I was glad to get up. I heard heavy trucks pass down the road towards the enemy, and wondered how the bridge-building had gone. We were to pass over it at first light.

He set off with the troop, to be told that the bridge was not yet completed due to shelling and mortaring. 'The mists dissipated slowly, the morning wore away in thuds and bangs, while we brewed tea and I read a stupid novel for distraction.' In the afternoon they set off again. 'Again we lined up, to be halted by the spectacle of another column lined up for the same job. The two colonels argued with each other.'

The Regiment was then stood down. 'After so much "mucking about" my nerves were not perfect. I swore at my driver as we about-turned.' The incident is described further in Chapter 5; in the end, the Reconnaissance Troop was not involved in the operations.

In mid-November the Regiment still continued the wearisome sequence. On the 14th, it supported 153rd Brigade in crossing the Wessem Canal. Operations were to carry on the next day and Cunliffe describes the evening of the 14th, when his troop was billeted in a farmhouse close to the Canal.

> Scene now: a whitewashed farm-kitchen, crowded with my recce troop. A light has been fixed up from a tank, and a welfare wireless set plugged into another tank sounds incongruously sweet. Outside, the world is very different. It is night-time, turned into a weird twilight by searchlight beams. [The troop listens to a French song on the wireless.] The men whistle soulfully in support of the tune, so soulfully and so shrilly that the music is quite drowned.²
>
> A group of them play cards with an ancient, begrimed pack. One of them sits on a jerrican, another on an upturned milk churn. Others stand round, commenting upon the play. E. – solid E. from the linoleum works at Lancaster – is cooking in one corner. The cooker roars steadily.
>
> There's an estaminet atmosphere about the kitchen. Music, soldiers, cards, conversation, laughter, good-humoured argument, swearing in the usual harmlessly monotonous fashion; lights and shadows, a restless *va-et-vient* [toing and froing]. It's the usual impersonal atmosphere; everyone is needlessly noisy to show his contempt for the shells and bursts of fire that can be heard above the uproar.

Apart from the wireless and the sound of shelling, it is a scene which could have been written throughout history about detachments of soldiers waiting for battle.

Towards the end of the war, Cunliffe struck a reflective note about waiting. It was 18 March, and the Regiment had been training for the crossing of the Rhine.

> We are living under the shadow of an operation – operation 'Plunder'. This means, in plain language, an assault across the Rhine. It's a familiar feeling, this sense of – I won't call it dedication; rather commitment. We've known it before, especially before 'D' day. To be set apart from the rest of the world, to carry knowledge in one's head that is as dangerous as an explosive, and as exciting, to know that danger lies across the path of the future like a wall: all this breeds a curious outlook. The only pre-war

parallel I can think of – an inexact one – is going to the dentist, after you have made an appointment. The diary note catches your eye insistently: it says, 'your journey brings you nearer to me. Me you must pass; there is no other way you can take'.[3]

Civilians

The men of the Regiment had little chance to get to know French families in the way they later did Dutch and Belgian ones, since in Normandy they were so often in action, or preparing for it. Marcus Cunliffe wrote one vivid piece on French civilians, reproduced below in 'The Costs of War', but it was about an exceptional incident. Many soldiers' experience of French civilians, in fact, must have been one in which the costs of war were paramount, as a letter of George Pearson's suggests. Writing to his mother, he started by wishing he was home, for 'You see, Ma, I have seen that you people back home just could not realise'. He explains that he is not thinking about the fighting so much as 'the civilians, the refugees, I mean, whole families with their only belongings being a small bundle on their backs. No wonder our lads nearly giving their everything to them [*sic*].' He goes on to describe a young boy, 'not unlike Tony [his younger brother] only much younger', who had been wandering for days in the front line. Picked up by Pearson's detachment, 'He was practically naked, blue with cold. We brought him back to our camp in the truck and from then on I bet the poor little "b" thought he was in heaven.' The boy was fed, given sweets and chocolate and a cut down shirt and battledress and taken to the nearest refugee camp. Pearson was very complimentary about the latter, run by the Red Cross.[4]

There is a little more from various sources about Dutch and Belgian civilians. By mid-October the Regiment was billeted in St Oedenrode, a town in southern Holland. The regimental HQ was in a cafe; in the words of *Blue Flash*, 'The first of many occupied by our Regimental Headquarters'. *Blue Flash* goes on to describe the set-up.

> The proprietress and her family were still living in that part of the café which we were not using. She was a stern-faced woman who gave the impression that she had no time for soldiers, of whatever nationality, and that we were definitely there on sufferance. While the 'O' Group was in progress she twice pushed her way in and rummaged for tradesmen's bills, quite unconcerned at the blight

she had cast on the C.O.'s eloquence. We debated whether she was a spy but decided that she probably considered her business more important than ours and that it was her café anyway.[5]

Cunliffe tells us some more about the town. The tanks were parked 'in a sort of "place" round a bandstand. . . . Chestnut leaves fall on our vehicles; the methodical inhabitants sweep the leaves from cobbled pavements each morning'. Life in the town focused on the Town Hall:

> a sort of administrative beehive. Outside it youths with orange armbands stand on guard, rifles slung across their shoulders. Local police in elegant black uniforms stride in and out; dilapidated vehicles drive up and spill out more excited Orangemen with rifles and orange armbands. A large red-white-blue Netherlands flag droops over the building.[6]
>
> Nearby is the burgomaster's house. It is a worthy house, appropriate to everything connected with the word 'burgomaster'. It is broad and prosperous and symmetrical; and so is the burgomaster. When the broad green front door opens upon him, a wide hallway hung with stuffed animals becomes visible.

The troops lived in billets, 'in the quiet homes of solidly affable burghers'.*

A few weeks later, having moved on from St Oedenrode, Cunliffe noted the civilian reaction as the Regiment's tanks set off towards the front. This was the journey to support the crossing at Weert described in Chapter 5.

> At each village the inhabitants, realising from the volume of traffic that something was on, had gathered in knots to wave and smile. Girls, standing by themselves, were pleasurably affected by the soldiers' interest, smiled intimately at the passing tanks. Married women, thinking of their husbands perhaps, waved energetically. Old men took their pipes from their mouths, awed by the thunder of the tanks and yet anxious to appear knowledgeable. They

---

* St Oedenrode's bandstand is still there, as is the Town Hall, although at the time of visiting (March 2018) the latter was for sale.

pointed out to one another how the tracks went round the bogies. Small boys, many of them wearing berets, jerseys or rank stripes, cheered indiscriminately.'[7]

In late November and early December the Regiment had moved to Helvoirt, in North Brabant, where their tasks were primarily defensive and training.

> The possibility of holding a dance in Helvoirt was even mooted, but the problem was to find partners. The local priest ruled that dancing was wicked and in such matters the clergy's word is still law in the country districts of Holland. There were signs of open mutiny among the girls of Helvoirt towards the end of our stay and the priest was forced to issue a stern rebuke from the pulpit. . . . During the occupation, the girls would have nothing to do with German soldiers so he had no need to worry about their morals. Now we had brought gaiety and laughter back to the village for the first time in four years – perhaps the first time ever, for Helvoirt can never have been a very exciting place . . . At last the girls could joke, talk to soldiers and sing *Lili Marlene* with them without being dubbed collaborators.[8]

A dance was finally allowed but, as related in Chapter 5, while it was in full swing news was bought that the Regiment had to move to counter the Ardennes offensive.

Later, having given up its tanks to train on Buffaloes, the Regiment moved to eastern Belgium, on the Meuse facing Holland's 'Maastricht Appendix'. They were billeted in three villages, Boorsheim, Uykhoven and Cothem.

> These villages, with their cobbled streets and red brick houses, were not particularly attractive but their rather unprepossessing exteriors belied the warm hearts of the inhabitants. The welcome and hospitality extended to us will always be remembered by the regiment and, before long, everyone had his feet firmly "under the table". And if it was against the regulations to share one's rations with the family as one sat round the communal stove in the evening, who cared about that? So popular did the troops become

that a letter was received from the Mayor of Uykhoven after the Rhine had been crossed asking that the Regiment should be allowed to return to the area as soon as the war was over.⁹

Finally, there are some brief glimpses from Cunliffe's diary about German civilians, as well as some post-war reflections on Germany and the Germans. By July the Regiment was stationed in Mettingen, near Osnabruck in Lower Saxony.¹⁰ The gardener of the house where they were billeted was wearing a black tie. The tie was for his son, killed only ten weeks before – almost at the end of the war – fighting against the Americans. The gardener had only just received a message about the death.

> He came to see me, agitated and respectful, to know whether by any means he could visit his son's grave. Because he had helped us a good deal with flowers (which he arranges superbly) and food, I risked trouble and got one of our trucks to take him there, on the pretext of buying foodstuffs. [The son had been killed about 40 miles away.] He thanked me, on his return, for the kindness, mumbling in German interspersed with bits of English. He was buried with two others – the grave was 'schön, oh schön' – he had taken a photograph, which would soon be ready – it was very good of us . . . He tried to tell me of the beastliness of Germany, and of the war: of the coercion that pushed you into an organisation for murder. The Wehrmacht: finished, he said: there were three graves. One man was forty-four. His son was twenty; the third was sixteen. That was the German Army; dead, defeated. The barrel had been scraped until nothing came from the sides but shavings of wood.

Cunliffe continues with reflections on Germany.

> Am I being deluded into a false pity for him, and for Germany? I don't think so. I'd do as much for anyone who was not a Nazi or a vile creature. I don't feel 'sorry' for Germans as one pitied the French, or Dutch or Belgians. I feel irritated that they were such blind idiots, when their nation had so much promise; I feel weary for the misery they have occasioned everywhere. The adolescent German males I dislike and distrust. They are sullen, determined

and dangerous. The older people are broken and they know it. It's hard to generalise about Germany when so many of its men are away and prisoners: their return may provoke a more violent reaction. But I am certain that Germany will never cause another war in Europe. She's too licked. And I'm certain there are many many good Germans. Towards them I have no animosity. I ought to have more, perhaps.

Prisoners

A tank regiment such as 144th RAC was not likely to take many prisoners because it was usually advancing in tandem with an infantry brigade and the infantry would be the ones doing the mopping up. When the Germans cracked completely at the Battle of the Falaise Pocket, however, the Allied advance speeded up. Consequently, the Regiment was at times more or less on its own and was the only unit to which prisoners could surrender – as, it was clear, they often wanted to do. Cunliffe's account below is entitled 'Flotsam and Jetsam'. It starts with the reflection that it was very easy for people to lose all rootedness in a community as they were pushed hither and thither by the winds of war. Cunliffe is thinking in particular of Eastern Europeans or Russians who, more or less involuntarily, fought in the German Army.

> In Normandy we found hundreds and hundreds of men who were so much cannon-fodder. I suppose they had fathers, mothers, wives and children in some corner of Europe or Asia. But over such distances, these links were tenuous in the extreme. They were nearly all soldiers in the German army, whom we captured or who had deserted. They could usually speak some German, but none spoke English. They were lucky to be captured intact, but what would their future be, in all the bedlam of war?[11]
>
> I remember two or three men who emerged thus from the ranks of the *Wehrmacht*. The first was one of a batch of about thirty prisoners whom we captured in a village on top of a hill, about twenty miles south-east of Caen.[12] Of these thirty, twenty-five sat in one group, and the remaining few sat a few yards away in segregation. Had there been a quarrel? The minority did not look very different from the others: all wore uniform, all were dirty and smelly and unshaven.

FROM ARROMANCHES TO THE ELBE

Prisoners would normally be sent back to division or direct to a prisoner-of-war cage where interrogation might take place. If there was someone who spoke German in the British unit which captured them, no doubt it was common practice to have a preliminary talk with prisoners to see whether any useful information could be gained about other enemy in the locality. As Intelligence Officer, this role would naturally have fallen to Cunliffe, who had some German apart from his excellent French.

> I interrogated them in pidgin-German, and found that the four or five were all Poles (and all anxious that I should realise this). One, a man of thirty-five, pulled some photographs from an inner pocket of his wallet. Most of them were of Warsaw, his home-city; they showed damage and ruin. Then there was another photo. It was small and distinct: a glossy little print, like a 'still' from a Hollywood film. It was a picture of an execution. There stood the firing-squad, rifles levelled; how smart they looked! Their German helmets gleamed; their long greatcoats were neatly pressed; their jackboots shone with polish. Two or three despondent little figures stood before them, in tattered clothing: the victims. 1944: would you like to see my photos? Here's one of Warsaw University – in ruins. Or here's a nice one of an execution: it's come up very clearly, hasn't it? The Pole pointed to the victims on the print, and said 'my friends'.
>
> Next to him was a fair-haired boy, with tears in his eyes. I looked at his paybook; he was a Pole, sixteen and a half years old. I tried to ask him why he was in the German Army, but could not frame the question properly. However he seemed to understand, for he explained the alternative: 'the salt-mines or the Army. Salt-mines: dead in six months. The Army: maybe die, maybe live . . . '.
>
> The boy also pulled a photo from his wallet. It showed a soldier's grave, the name cut on a wooden cross, the cross surmounted by a helmet of an unfamiliar shape. The name on the cross was the same as his own: the date September '39. His father, killed in Poland by the Germans, in the first months of the war.
>
> No wonder the Poles sat apart from the Germans.
>
> A little while after we took these prisoners somebody began to shell us with high-velocity H.E. It sounds like an S.P. gun – crack-woomf! – the two sounds almost merged in one another. None of

the tanks were hit, mercifully, as we were filling up with petrol; but some of the prisoners were. One had most of his head blown off. It was the sixteen year old boy. The Germans had killed the second generation. His blood went all over some of the German prisoners who were crouched nearby, in terror. In fact, it went all over eighty million Germans.

There was another figure, this time a deserter. We found him in a barn, quite near to the Seine, still dressed in German uniform, but without any arms. He was a little, wizened man, clearly of peasant stock. His build was slight but sturdy; his face was brown and wizened, so that it was impossible to guess his age – he might have been anywhere between twenty and fifty.

His papers showed him to be a Russian, in the late thirties. He came from a village near Odessa, where he had been a wagon-driver. He was not frightened, only bewildered and very stupid. He spoke only a few words of German; he had no idea where he was, or what was happening in the war, except that his own unit had gone back. He, tired of the moving and the frightening sounds, had simply rolled under the hay in a barn and let them go without him. It was too easy, at a time when men were being killed, wounded and taken prisoner in such quantities.

We could not converse with him, having no common tongue. We could not keep him. We did not quite know how to dispose of him, as a Russian and as a deserter. Finally, we got the map-reference of a prisoner-cage and sent him down to that. The cage swore at us, because they were just on the move, and in any case didn't want to carry odd cases about with them. So they sent him somewhere else. I thought the affair must be quite familiar to him. He had been captured by the Germans in the first place, bandied among innumerable prison-camps, sent on marches, taken in trains, 'enlisted' in the German army, given a horse and a wagon (with which he was probably quite happy), sent across Europe to this strange country, suddenly mixed up in another war . . . and all the time among strangers who did not understand his tongue, confronted by a thousand sights that lay too far outside his experience for him to understand, and that were too difficult for his stunted peasant imagination to register. It's probable that a Russian from, say, Leningrad or Kiev could not converse with him.

He had a wife's name in his paybook, but no wallet even, no photographs (what is a photograph? You need something called a camera for that, surely?). How long since he had seen his wife? Did he still think of her? Or she of him? The way back to her was such a long one that I shuddered to contemplate it.

What fate for the Pole with the execution-snapshot, or for this Russian? For the Pole, little alternative but to enlist in the Allied Polish Army. Two months training in England, then back to Europe again. That wasn't so bad: at least he was on the winning side now, and would have good food, and tobacco to smoke. Afterwards, when the winning side had won? That was another matter.

There are two, more light-hearted, codas to these stories: one about other Polish soldiers serving with the Germans, the other about Russian soldiers.

A little after the Polish soldiers were captured, on the final part of the Regiment's advance towards the Seine, 'B' Squadron went ahead in order to assist with a river crossing, although the Germans were now so weakened that they were not needed. They returned to join the rest of the Regiment in harbour, 'bringing with them their latest recruit, a Pole, who said that he had resigned from the *Wehrmacht* three days before and now wanted to join 'B' Squadron'.[13]

The other story originates with a German soldier captured by a unit of XXX Corps, probably just before 144th RAC's Noyers operation. At Noyers itself, Russian soldiers serving in a German unit were captured and their motivation – or lack of it – was no doubt similar to the ones described below, who were perhaps more typical than the benighted wagon-driver. XXX Corps' report described the German, named Dietrich, as indoctrinated with Nazi propaganda about the dangers of Bolshevism and the eventual need for the Western Allies and Germany to confront it.

The report went on to outline Dietrich's opinion of the Hiwis, as the Russian soldiers were called. They had agreed to serve in the German Army 'mainly because of the better rations they thus obtain' – quite a likely reason. He described them as of 'almost sub-human intelligence'. The report continued:

> those employed by 988 Grenadier Regiment appear to have been at pains to cause their masters as much inconvenience as possible.

THE EXPERIENCE OF WAR

> Dietrich was employed in a battalion armoury in Bayonne for a time and his stories of how Russian drivers and fatigue men consistently drove the wrong way, delivered the wrong ammunition to the wrong units, perpetually got lost in the town, forgot to deliver messages etc, are too circumstantial to be described as the actions of other than men with a reasonable intelligence quota and a well developed sense of humour.

To the writer of the report, it was clear that the Hiwis, far from failing in the simplest task because of stupidity, did so in order to inconvenience the Germans. According to Dietrich, the Russians had not been armed previously but had been on fatigue duties and suchlike; now their unit was in action, they had been issued with rifles and a small quantity of ammunition. The desperate straits of the German Army are shown by its use of men of such unreliability – perhaps from stupidity, as Dietrich thought, but more likely from malice – as fighting soldiers.[14]

Sadly, although the Russians seem to have done their best to help the Allies, their fate was not likely to be a happy one. After discussing the likely outcome for the captured Poles, Cunliffe concluded with some reflections on the Russian wagon-driver:

> And the poor, stupid, Russian? Prison-camps, more incomprehensible journeys . . . And when the winners had won? I don't know. But I don't think he will be welcome back in Russia. I think they will call him a traitor. I think they will quite probably shoot him. Perhaps it's just as well he is so stupid; it's not always a comfort to have a vivid imagination, or be clever enough to foresee your own future.

Sadly, his conclusion was probably correct.

Once into Germany, Cunliffe writes very little about contacts with Germans until after the war had ended, although there is a reference to the 'crowds of refugees'. *Blue Flash* also has a brief glimpse, when the war was almost over. After 'A' Squadron had done its work ferrying American troops across the Elbe, and returning with prisoners, on 1 and 2 May, 'The fields across the river were choked with dejected German soldiers, and it was clearly only a matter of days before the final surrender'.[15]

FROM ARROMANCHES TO THE ELBE

The Costs of War

The sections on 'Prisoners' and 'Civilians' both illustrated the costs of war in one form or another. The episode related below described a different kind of cost. It occurred a few days after the capture of the Poles. The British had taken Lisieux and were now advancing rapidly; the episode, whose context is explained in Chapter 4, took place soon afterwards. At this point the Regiment was supporting the 7th Duke of Wellington's Regiment, from 49th Division.

The advance from Lisieux started promisingly. Jolly wrote in *Blue Flash*:

> We felt again the exhilaration of pursuit and the thrill of liberation. No longer was the countryside deserted. From every farm people came running to greet us, young and old, often with tears streaming down their faces. Flowers and apples were showered upon us, and at every halt we were offered their potent cider and calvados, until forced to protest that we really did have a job of work to do.[16]

Cunliffe takes up the story.

> Between Caen and the Seine, by the route we took, a number of rivers flow northwards to the sea. Dives, Touques, Risle – they cut the landscape into deep wooded valleys, each a formidable obstacle. Each river-line was a natural defence-line, on which we could have been held up for days, if the enemy had been strong enough. Instead, he blew the bridges and left rearguards of infantry, with Spandaus and the odd anti-tank gun. Each time the infantry had to get across somehow, and make a bridgehead on the far bank while the sappers put across a Bailey bridge. Then the tanks got over again, cleaned up the enemy if any remained, and again pushed on.[17]
>
> One of our squadrons reached a river line.* On the map it looked obvious enough: a river, a valley, a bridge-site. On the ground it

---

* The location as identified by *Blue Flash* (p. 74) was La Vallette, on a small river named the Calonne; this must actually have been a house and mill named La Vallette, in the little village of St Jean D'Asnières.

was much more uncomfortable. The tanks dropped down by a farm-track to the valley-floor. The river itself, narrow and swift, was the great obstacle. On the far bank the valleyside rose up like a green wall. It was very steep and deuced wooded. It towered above the stream, so that standing down in the valley-bottom you felt tiny and helpless, at the mercy of whatever lay hidden above you in the thick tree-growth.

This was the scene when I came there with the Colonel, mapreading for him without a great deal of confidence down the steep tracks to the valley: 'B' Squadron's tanks hidden in orchards, beside it a blown bridge across a swift little stream, a tank blown up on a mine just short of the bridge, beyond the stream a little water-meadow, turning after a few yards into a densely treed slope, even steeper than the one we had descended. A green, sunny canyon of a place – but made sinister by the bridge, the mines, the silent slope, the tanks.

There were mines everywhere, all round the approach to the bridge: Tellers buried clumsily in the road, with their top plates showing, S-mines along the grass verge, with their little prongs sticking up.

There were infantry too, brown, lean, undersized, with the dogged grumbling air of men who are tired of achievement and would rather have twenty-four hours sleep than anything. They had just arrived and were about to go across the stream, up into the thick hill-wood. A patrol had already gone up and was firing one or two shots.

There was the house, a flimsy, charming place. We peeped in through the open doors at old furniture, portraits, a gleaming kitchen. Houseproud, evidently.

And there were the people of the house, just two of them. An old, trembling, bewildered lady, and a misshapen, dwarfish girl who was evidently her servant. She had very black eyes and very red lips and a curiously wicked air. There was also an Alsatian, a splendid animal but chained up in the sad French way.

My Colonel conferred with the Infantry Colonel. Two fierce, competent men, intensely interested in their occupation. The Infantry Colonel said he would like a few tanks over the stream if it could be managed. My Colonel said it could be managed. How?

He had a quick look with me, then decided that tanks could ford the stream, but only at one place. They would have to turn into the yard round which the parts of the house were built, then slew between the kitchen and another building, through an eight-foot gap, down into the stream, up on to the tiny meadow. In getting through the gap, the tanks were bound to damage the house, although quite how much I couldn't estimate.

'Tell the old woman', my Colonel said to me, 'that we'll have to take the tanks through her yard and we may damage her house.' She was cowering near to us, scared, bewildered and lonely. That morning, German soldiers and the explosion under the bridge; then the English and all these tanks and infantry, this noise, this violence. It was all overwhelming her quiet backwater in a flood of horror. Why should war's spotlight fall on her home, in her old age?

I explained as nicely as I could what must be. When she understood she wept; she told me her husband had been taken away, her son was a prisoner of war; there was no-one. Would there be a battle here? – there were still Germans in the woods across the stream. Could we not cross the stream elsewhere? – impossible, I said, wondering how much consideration we ought to give to civilians in planning this sort of thing. There was probably another place, a hundred yards up or downstream. Still, there was no time to lose, and the Colonel had decided.

Meanwhile, the first tank was manoeuvring into her yard. Its commander did not look too happy. He had to slew round near the chained Alsatian, which leapt away to the length of its chain, howling and whining. The old woman heard and wept afresh . . . But her maid, the dwarfish girl, wasted no tears. She had on her own initiative got a jug of wine, and was pouring it out to some of the infantry. She smiled at them boldly, nodding her black head in approval as they drank (they drank avidly, as though the red wine was some panacea) and gazing in glad awe at the tank in the yard.

A tank in her yard: the universe had gone mad for the old woman. She stood by herself, knees a little bent, hands clasping a handkerchief with which she dabbed at her red eyes.

The tank was now fully in the yard, and reversing and turning to line itself up for the gap. In turning, one of its tracks tore up the thin paving of the yard, and the tank dropped into a pipe-way, crunching the porcelain pipes. In reversing, it went back a little too far. It hit the main wall of the house, bearing steadily back against it with thirty tons of force. Going forward again, the tank made more inroads into the yard's drainage system. Moreover it had cracked the wall of the house, and had broken a pipe along the wall, from which there poured out water in a steady jet.

The tank-commander prepared to break his way between the buildings. One, on his left – the kitchen – was almost as high as the tank; the other towered fifteen feet above him. He got his tank lined up, then closed down his hatches and told the driver to advance.

The tank rumbled forward, a Juggernaut, across the yard (how the dwarf-girl's eyes glittered at the spectacle!), slow but utterly unstoppable. It reached the buildings, disputed with them a moment, had its way, broke through them. The kitchen wall was sliced away like a sliding door to disclose a sink, a table, a large white refrigerator. The other wall, of tougher material, disintegrated into sturdy beams and lumps of stone, that fell all over the turret of the tank, belabouring it like a policeman's cudgel in a Punch-and-Judy show.

Dust hung in the air. The tank, rolling blindly on, crashed down into the stream, bit into the far bank and heaved upwards out of the water. On to the meadow. The Alsatian cried like a banshee; the old woman was numb with horror; the dwarf girl smiled and smiled with lunatic gaiety; the bricks and mortar continued to tumble slowly from the broken walls. The water still gushed from the broken pipe. The first tank had been through the yard. Its commander opened up his turret to survey the world.

'Oh, good show, good show!' cried the Colonel, almost dancing for happiness. 'A <u>jolly</u> good show. Now we'll have the rest of the troop, eh?' Trying to avoid the old woman's eye I said, 'Yes, sir'.

The story is heartbreaking. The progress of the war and the time of its final end was probably not speeded up by one minute because 144th RAC got some of its tanks across the Calonne in a timely fashion. On the other hand, according to *Blue Flash*, 'The troop did good work later in the evening and the enemy withdrew during the night. His withdrawal may have been hastened by the unexpected appearance of tanks east of the river as a German ration party arrived in the middle of the night looking for their forward companies. They were duly "put in the bag".[18] So British lives may have been saved, while the Germans retreated that much faster. Given that it was important to chase the Germans to the Seine as quickly as possible, in order to prevent them and their equipment crossing, Jolly's haste seems more reasonable.

It was a pinprick in the overall war effort, but most of the war effort consisted of such pinpricks. If the Allies had never caused collateral damage they would have advanced more slowly. And arguably commanders during an advance do not have time to debate ethical questions.

The material costs of war were, of course, as nothing compared with the human. Many British families suffered these, and far more in Russia and in Germany itself. Immediately after the war the Regiment was billeted in Sottrum, a village near Bremen.

> It's a village peopled by women, children and old men. Where are the youths, the men? You'll find part of your answer in the village church. It's a cool, squat old building, red-tiled-roofed with a big, squat, low tower. A few tiles are missing and some glass is broken, from the explosion of the charge that demolished the bridge nearby. [It had been blown by retreating German troops.] Inside, all along the gallery, are pinned silver-paper crosses, Melkse-pattern, each about a foot square. On each is printed a soldier's name, the date of his death, the place where he was killed. A few are Westfront deaths, a few North Africa or hospital. But the great, overwhelming majority say 'Russland'. And there are 151 crosses. 151 men killed, in a village that cannot have more than 2,000 people in it. 151 dead, not counting the wounded, the missing and the prisoners. That's where some of the men are – underground.[19]

The Spoils of War

A victorious army has plenty of opportunities to seize loot or, as British soldiers sometimes called it, booty: the enemy leaves material behind; or, as an army marches forward, buildings vacated by civilians are tempting targets. On several occasions Cunliffe wrote about these spoils of war. One reference was made in passing, and has already been quoted in Chapter 1. This was to the seizure of prisoners' watches by the Jocks –

the 1st Gordons – after the capture of Cramesnil at the end of the Totalize night attack. Cunliffe recorded this in a matter-of-fact way, and the same kind of pilfering was actually encouraged by Martin Lindsay after the capture of prisoners at Le Havre (see Chapter 4). Similarly, in Holland Lindsay records with amusement an NCO's comments as his company marched up ready for an attack: 'Noo then, nae indiscriminate shootin'. Mind thur watches and founten pens'.[20] The comment was made to relieve tension but, again, suggests that appropriating small personal possessions from prisoners was taken for granted.

On other occasions, however, Cunliffe obviously felt quite strongly about, and deprecated, the habit of seizing other people's possessions, although admitting that he had occasionally done it himself. As he points out in the passage quoted below, however, there was a distinction between personal items and those belonging to the opposing army, with more justification for taking the latter. He entitled this account, appropriately, 'Loot'.[21]

'All the acquisitive fevers in mankind are unpleasant. The prospect of getting something for nothing blinds men to any other consideration. They abandon decency, honesty, unselfishness.' He follows this with a few more reflections in the same vein, comparing the 'Loot Trail' of Northern Europe to the Alaskan gold rush, before returning to individual instances. 'The bearded miner in Alaska pegs out a claim without telling his friends, wearing the same shame-faced, excited expression as a British lieutenant-colonel whom I saw steal some linen napkins from a wrecked Belgian house in the Ardennes.'

> Anything got for nothing tends to corrupt humanity. But in the matter of loot we may draw a distinction between loot taken from houses or from civilians, and loot taken from the opposing army. Both tend to make soldiers behave abominably, yet there is some justification – and much more satisfaction – in the latter. At least one is depriving a nation, not an individual; and at least one may claim that the loot is a just reward for danger endured in conflict with the victims. I should be both a liar and a hypocrite if I claimed never to have done any looting; and indeed, I enjoyed my first opportunity to gain 'booty' on a large scale.
>
> The opportunity came when, after a period of ugly contest in the Bridgehead, followed by a fortnight of pursuit, we reached the

Seine. All its bridges between Paris and the sea had been destroyed by bombing; and in consequence the Germans had to abandon any material that they could not manage to take with them on the few inadequate ferries in operation.

The first big collection of loot I saw was at Quilleboeuf, almost at the mouth of the Seine. My Colonel and I were both anxious to get our first glimpse of the river, which had been our Jordan for so many weeks. There had always been one more river – Dives, Touques, Risle and others I've forgotten, one after the other – and now we had got up to the Seine.

The incident he is about to relate occurred on 27 August. The Regiment had just crossed the Risle, the final river before the Seine, at Appeville. The war diary recorded that, 'The Colonel and IO [Cunliffe] drove up to the outskirts of Quilleboeuf, where they had their first and long-awaited view of the Seine.' They were considerably ahead of the rest of the Regiment, since even the more advanced units only reached Bourneville, about 7 miles short of Quilleboeuf, on that day.[22]

Cunliffe continues the story.

We came upon it suddenly, round a corner, moving circumspectly in a scout-car, uncertain whether any Germans still lingered on this seaward tongue of land. We saw the Seine below us, on our right, grey and majestic. Four hundred yards across. Yes – we agreed – this was a river. On the far side we could see several miles of open ground, studded with round trees and square farms. The far bank was deserted.

Then we met three Frenchmen, who were riding some superb horses down the road towards us. They waved and shouted as they went by 'Vive les Anglais! Boche sont tous partis – tous!'

No wonder it was vive les Anglais. The horses all bore German Army markings, and military saddles. These peasants were making off with them as souvenirs of the liberation; good tangible souvenirs. A little further down the road we saw where the horses had come from. Down on the river was a landing-stage, on the far bank another jetty to which two or three small waterlogged ferryboats were tied. This was the Quilleboeuf ferry, and in the fields above it the retreating Wehrmacht had peeled off its equipment. Half a dozen fields were covered in material. Waggons were drawn up all along the hedges: fifty or sixty horses roamed at large, some still in harness. There were half a dozen broken old ambulances along the roadside. Helmets, rifles, stick grenades, egg grenades, cartridges, leather belts and pouches, bayonets, respirators, boots, packs, greatcoats, suitcases, packing-cases, wicker shell-cases lay everywhere in monotonous profusion. The first French peasants were rummaging eagerly among the wagons and the limbers. We saw more, hastening up the road towards the plunder.

My Colonel and I eyed the scene in some bewilderment. We picked up a few items, then put them down again. There was so much . . . then he saw a fine chestnut, still saddled, mounted it and cantered round the field. I found a medical wagon and took some kit from it for Neil, our M.O. Beautiful stuff. I found another wagon and took some writing paper . . . It was hopeless: there was so much. My Colonel stood now stroking the horse's handsome neck, with a wistful query in his eye? We debated whether or not we could take a few horses for riding, and keep them in the regiment. It was a magnificent notion, but we both knew it to be impracticable. Meanwhile I was chasing echoes round my head. Quilleboeuf? The name? This sort of scene? Months later I discovered what my brain had tried to remember, in the opening paragraphs of Maupassant's *Boule de Suif*: 'Les derniers soldats francais venaient enfin de traverser la Seine pour gagner Pont-Audemer par Saint-Sever et Bourg-Achard; et marchant après tous, le general, desespere, ne pouvant rien tenter avec ces logues, disparates . . . s'en allait a pied, entre deux officiers d'ordonnance . . .'*

Then, in 1870, it had been the French who tumbled across the broad sliding Seine. In 1940 there were probably others. [There were: thousands of the British Expeditionary Force who had been trapped south of the Somme, and who escaped via French ports on the west coast; they included Robert Thorne.] In 1944 it was the

---

* The last of the French Army had just crossed the Seine, making for Pont-Audemer by way of St Sever and Bourg-Achard. The rear was brought up by the General marching on foot between two orderly officers. In despair, unable to attempt anything with this medley of broken units . . .' (Guy de Maupassant, *Boule de Suif and Other Stories*, trans. Marjorie Laurie (London, J. Werner Laurie, 1926)).

Germans who had left behind even their cartridges, even their coats; even the little Bakelite containers in which they kept their butter... now, the French peasants scrabbled for booty, and dragged away as much as their strength would allow; brought carts for the job. German letters and German underwear and German bottles of lotion covered half a dozen acres. Soon the soldiery arrived to share in the frantic pillage, arguing and boasting in hordes. Perhaps Maupassant would have found even less dignity and more vulgarity in this victory than in the defeat of which he wrote.

By 30 August the British had more or less completed their work on the south bank of the Seine and had a chance to get to grips with the abandoned enemy equipment, at Quilleboeuf and elsewhere. *Blue Flash* recorded the result.

There is a great attraction about the enemy's equipment, even though one's own may be better. This particularly applies to transport and we yielded to the temptation of appropriating a varied assortment of German vehicles, although possessing ample of our own. They miraculously changed colour overnight from German buff to British 'olive green' in order not to draw attention to the fact that we were disobeying orders by not handing them in. Eventually, through lack of drivers, maintenance and spare parts, they all broke down and were abandoned in various parts of Europe during the next few months.

The only regret was a 'sumptuously appointed' caravan, the property of a German general. C Squadron had been seen taking it to present to Jolly, and 'orders soon came from Divisional Headquarters to hand it in'. A little later, however, while the Regiment was resting near Le Havre, they found in the German coastal defences some pianos, 'which henceforward accompanied us on our travels'.[23]

Back on the banks of the Seine, members of the Regiment had managed to collect numerous personal keepsakes such as pistols, binoculars and briefcases. While this was going on, one of the captured lorries was 'driven back to harbour with an undiscovered demolition charge under the bonnet. The igniter was attached to the choke but fortunately the engine had started at once so the driver had no cause to pull it.'[24]

THE EXPERIENCE OF WAR

Much later, soon after the end of the war, Cunliffe made more references to looting, recording a run in 'our [possibly the Regiment's, possibly the Squadron's]' sports car 'Wolfgang', an Auto-Union and 'very beautiful if you like that sort of thing'. It had been acquired, or 'stolen' as Cunliffe censoriously put it, in Lüneburg.[25] This was a prelude to a longer passage a few days later when he vented his anger at looting rather more explicitly. He and another officer were inspecting buildings in Sottrum, the village in which they were billeted, with a view to using them for various purposes. One building was to be used for a recreation room. The ground floor consisted of some offices; each had been used by a firm from Bremen, presumably evacuated to Sottrum.

The other officer, senior to Cunliffe,

> began to root around in the desks, looking at photos, exclaiming in delight at novelties he saw and wanted. The loot-fever gripped him. I said 'are you coming down to the school with me?'
> (Drawers being pushed open and shut).
> 'Wha . . .?'
> 'Are you coming down to the school?'
> 'Not just yet . . . Oo, we could do with one of these . . .'[26]
> I left him. Rubbish to say in defence of oneself that the Germans looted all Europe. True enough, but the retribution has got to be on a government level; no individual has the right to steal for his own profit as 'revenge' or 'punishment'. Looting is a nasty contagion; it catches even the best of men.

Cunliffe then expanded on the story of the colonel in the Ardennes which he mentioned in 'Loot':

> I saw a cultivated, well-to-do artillery colonel steal some linen table-napkins from a Belgian house. American bombs had already smashed the house and most of its furniture; and he couldn't even leave the owners their small personal possessions. It made me sick at heart: the more so as I had noticed the napkins, coveted them and then, realising what a meanness I was contemplating, left them in a drawer where I hoped no-one could find them. The Colonel found them. When you go to dinner with him, these same napkins may grace his table. And they are stolen, filched, looted. You are sitting at table with a charming – thief.

Cunliffe did, however, go on to admit that he looted books, felt little compunction, and had no defence, except that he prized them and had no intention of selling them for gain. So his admirable dislike of wholesale looting was a little equivocal.

Chapter 8

Regimental Ins and Outs

The previous chapter dealt with experiences common to most soldiers, and with the way war spilt over into civilian life. This chapter is more focused on issues specific to 144th RAC. It does not pretend to be a comprehensive social history of the Regiment. Much of it is based on Cunliffe's diary, and to that extent it reflects some of his idiosyncrasies. Later in the chapter, however, the subject matter extends to questions of wider interest: morale in the Regiment and in the army at large; and what the Regiment's records tell us about training, a vexed question in the history of the British Army in the Second World War.

Cunliffe's diary has much of interest about relationships within the Regiment, although sometimes this is because of what he did not write rather than what he did. And what he did write needs to be read through a particular lens, that of Cunliffe himself.

No one was a typical officer in the British Army of the Second World War, but Cunliffe was perhaps less typical than most. One segment of the officer corps was clearly differentiated from the rest – those who came from the pre-war army. There was a distinction here between those who had entered as officers and those promoted from the ranks, such as Bob Thorne and Major Bill Marsden, O/C Headquarters Squadron. However, although Cunliffe occasionally refers to this distinction, he never makes a significant comment about it. It seems likely that the shared experience of pre-war soldiering, encompassing service in a variety of units, in many cases overseas, appeared more important to him than the class distinctions which, usually, were the reason why some men started their careers as officers, and most as 'other ranks'. In addition, a recently formed and technically orientated regiment such as 144th RAC was less likely to attach importance to the traditions which played a considerable part in many infantry regiments, and which often revolved around the officer's mess. In the latter, whether someone started as an officer before the war or was promoted from the ranks may have played more of a part.

FROM ARROMANCHES TO THE ELBE

Although university education was still reserved for a minority, even of the middle classes who still comprised the bulk of officer recruits, a number of the Regiment's young officers had been to university, if only for the two years which Cunliffe enjoyed before he was called up. Lieutenant Phillips, whose accounts of various operations were reproduced earlier, was one. We can guess that Douglas Draycott, Cunliffe's best friend in the Regiment until he left, was also a graduate or undergraduate.* Occasional references by Cunliffe suggest that there were others. But not all undergraduates or graduates were necessarily intellectuals, and Cunliffe unquestionably was – not something which could have been said of many young British males of that period (or perhaps any period), graduates or not. Apart from the evidence supplied by his omnivorous reading, and his later career, this is clear from his tastes in conversation, and his leisure pursuits. So it is not very surprising that, in the privacy of his diary, he revealed that he found the company of some of his fellow officers either irritating, or boring, or both. However, apart from Draycott there were a few officers with whom he was able to discuss books, the theatre and current affairs, in spite of his occasional complaints to the contrary.

Officers

A passage written at the end of the war, in which Cunliffe reflects on the men of the Regiment who had died, shows that that there were a number, both officers and other ranks, about whose loss he felt real sadness, although at the same time it reveals his rather jaundiced attitude towards others.

'I suppose this is a solemn moment', the diary entry on 4 May 1945 began. 'On the nine o'clock news we have just heard that all German forces in Holland, Denmark and northern Germany will surrender to 21 Army Group (Montgomery) at eight o'clock tomorrow morning, 5 May 45. Victory, in bits and pieces, is now almost complete.' He went on the next morning to write about the celebrations of the night.

> We were not particularly jubilant. In fact, we were rather flat. It rained, our tent was crowded with beds and chairs, we shivered,

---

* Given his relatively unusual name, it seems likely that he was the Douglas Draycott who later became a barrister.

the wind banged the canvas. Along the column Verey lights climbed into the dark sky – red, green, white – and fell glaring among the trees. We fired off some great German cartridges from a twin-barrelled Verey pistol. But it was flat, flat. We cursed Kelvin [the temporary squadron commander] for turning us into a field on this night of all nights. After so long, why must the moment come among these people, in this place. Only with Leslie do I have anything in common: and we both glowered at the world. I thought of Eric Jones, of Will MacGregor, of Charles Veall, Tom Lovibond, Bill Pickering, Mike Barnes, Sergeant Skeer, Cpl. Callwood – those I had liked, who were now dead. One hasn't always time to remember them, engrossed among the living. I wondered what Keith would be thinking, my father, my mother. Now that danger no longer faced us (at least, not for some time to come), we fell back among the humdrum hordes of the rest of the army, the L of C [Lines of Communication] troops, Light Ack-Ack, Pioneer Corps. It seemed almost a commonplace thing to be still alive.

Of the first six names, all but Will MacGregor, a friend from Oxford, were 144th RAC officers who had lost their lives in the 1944–5 campaign.[1] And the penultimate sentence quoted above suggests that Cunliffe had his own pride in having been a member of an armoured regiment, rather than of the various other units mentioned which, by implication, he considered rather inferior.

In spite of these more upbeat feelings about the Regiment and about some of his fellow officers, when he makes positive references to other officers there are often reservations attached. Thus, in late November in Holland he recorded a rather rare 'perfect morning'. Perhaps the sunny weather improved his mood and the following note was the result.

Robert Reid has just burst in upon us. He was wounded in the Caen night attack [Operation Totalize], evacuated to England, and has been knocking around Newmarket for a long while. He met K [Keith, Cunliffe's brother] on the train from Cambridge. Everyone is delighted to see him; the Colonel insists on a gin; there are some new faces but nothing has changed.

FROM ARROMANCHES TO THE ELBE

Positive though the passage is, the last phrase may reflect Cunliffe's view that there were few other officers with whom he had much in common. Later in the diary entry on the same date he noted: 'Now that D [Douglas] has gone I feel quite alone here. There is not a single person in the mess that shares my tastes. Some of them are excellent in their way, but none can talk of the things that interest me most. None is fascinated by peoples and places, books and ideas, as D and I were.'[2]

Soon afterwards, however, he had a much more favourable impression, although of a squadron rather than RHQ mess.

> Spent last night a few miles forward in Helden. It was a good evening and a blessed relief from RHQ. I visited C Sqn for five minutes, on the way home from a call at Bde HQ. They invited me in for tea, then for dinner, then to spend the night. I called up over the air for permission; permission granted. So simple. Forgot the tired atmosphere of our mess. New faces – the fascination of studying new people in order to understand them. Roland Hill I don't yet fully understand – an interesting person. Colin Fraine came to dinner from Bde [Brigade]. A tired, cynical, talented man, journalist before the war. I believe he has written a few good poems.
>
> We discussed almost everything, in an airy way. Books – war books, Evelyn Waugh, A. G. Macdonell, Siegfried Sassoon, Ernst Juenger. We were all civilian soldiers, all talking from the same viewpoint. I picture the Colonel and Sandshoes [Cunliffe's nickname for an officer at RHQ whom he disliked] embroiled in such a conversation.
>
> The curtains were drawn, the room softly lit by a bulb from a battery. Round the white tablecloth the young faces gleamed. Everyone felt that it was a little occasion; Bennett and Cameron, the two servants, bought in the dinner in the friendly yet polite way of squadron messes – in RHQ one always feels that the batmen are hostile. That they air their grievances as soon as the door closes behind them. The dinner was not spectacularly good, but enjoyable. Colin had brought some red wine with him, Bert Humphreys produced a packet of 'Adkins' Whiffs' is lieu of cigars, there was coffee. Puffing at these acrid substitutes, we felt mature and experienced. We told stories, recollect anecdotes that had long lain submerged in the brain, and that now – at this moment –

mysteriously came to the surface. Hilary Phillips, a rather callow boy not unlike George Brown in appearance ['callow' was a favourite Cunliffe word, used on other occasions], spoke of Oxford (he was at Merton) and of the News Chronicle (in which his father features as Dogbery).* John French, a sturdy young artillery captain, grinned from the other end of the table, without saying very much. From time to time the windows shook as our guns opened up: otherwise it was strangely silent.[3]

In February Cunliffe finally moved out of RHQ, having joined a squadron of Buffaloes. At that point his impression of other officers, once he was away from the RHQ mess, was still favourable. 'As a Buffalo troop leader, I have finally discovered the big consolation – perhaps the only consolation – in this way of life: I mean People. People with a capital P.' He follows with a sketch of some of the 'other ranks' in his troop, before coming to the officers in the Squadron.

> Then there are the people in the mess. I have never before lived in such amity and comradeship. In the RHQ mess this spirit was lacking for many causes; here it flourishes. There is no malice, in spite of large differences in temperament. The highest spirits prevail. This morning, after finishing work, we all piled into a truck and went to RAQ for a bath. Greenhalgh, grimacing through his spectacles, was busy at the infernal machine; loveable Greenhalgh, who used to be a sales-manager in a Manchester shop (Lewis's, I think), and who employs his £1500-a-year energy and singleness of purpose in seeing that the regiment is supplied with water, and that the Mobile Bath operates correctly . . .
> In the bath, under the stinging, miraculous hot spray, we sang and bellowed any song that came into anybody's head. Nigel appeared suddenly out of the steam to tell us that he had written a counterblast to Herbert Farjeon, a 9-page article on the Ideal Theatre. He is going to give me a copy.[4]

---

* 'Dogbery' was the pseudonym of Hubert Phillips, an economist and leader writer on the *News Chronicle*, but perhaps best known for compiling puzzles – as Dogbery – and as a writer on bridge and other card games. Phillips junior wrote the accounts reproduced in Chapters 5 and 6.

FROM ARROMANCHES TO THE ELBE

The mobile 'shower bath' – it was evidently what we would describe as a shower, albeit a communal one – is described further in *Blue Flash*. Showers were, apparently, usually provided by the infantry division to which the regiment was attached but, 'this was somewhat uncertain and usually meant a long, cold drive in a lorry before and after bathing'. In a rest period after the Le Havre operation, therefore, the unit fitters built 144th RAC's own shower bath: a 'misappropriated' 3-ton lorry housed a 'liberated' German boiler. The boiler must have been found among the equipment the Germans left behind on their retreat. The lorry also carried the shower apparatus which, with canvas screens, could be set up alongside the lorry and fed from the boiler. The description in *Blue Flash* concludes: 'The mobile bath also served a valuable though subsidiary purpose as a diversion for visiting generals. Usually they were delighted with it, but on one occasion we merely received a rocket for misappropriating a three-ton lorry. After that we were more careful in the choice of general to whom we showed it.'[5]

After the shower, Cunliffe continued his upbeat diary entry.

> Coming back, along the bumpy cobbled road, in the gloom of first darkness, we continued to sing – Lili Marleen, Jerusalem, the Harlot of Jerusalem, My Bonny Lies over the Ocean, Roll Me Over . . . military melange. In the little house we still sang, sprawling round the stove with glasses of whisky or red wine. Everyone was happy, and everyone at peace with his neighbour. At dinner we argued over music and over James Joyce. I found myself explaining James Joyce with exceptional lucidity – as I thought – to a sympathetic but slightly scornful audience.[6]

Even this positive perception of the fellow officers in his squadron did not last, or some of the dramatis personae had changed. By 4 May, in a continuation of the diary entry cited earlier in which he listed fallen friends and comrades, he went on to a series of critical character sketches of the other Squadron officers. Some were accorded a few good qualities, but only Leslie Gomme, 'a capable, pleasant and admirably disenchanted public-school type. . . . intelligent and endowed with a discriminating sense of humour', got high marks; others were severely criticised. The end of the war perhaps produced in Cunliffe a reaction against military life in general because two days later, while waiting at RHQ for Alan

Jolly, he observed of the various officers present, 'Mediocrities and bores all of them . . .', before various opprobrious references to individuals. To complete this spleen-ridden series of entries, on 8 May he noted 'A thick night in the mess, God save us'.

The most intriguing of Cunliffe's references to fellow officers and to RHQ are those relating to Alan Jolly. On the face of it, Cunliffe seemed to dislike Jolly, and believed that Jolly disliked him. In one passage Cunliffe, while still at RHQ as commander of the reconnaissance troop, deprecated Jolly's inattention to the social life of the RHQ mess.

> The bar is the same appalling clutter of maps and papers and clothes. The Colonel, with no sense of social life, uses what should be a mess, and is styled as a mess, for an office. Here he holds conferences: if they are secret the officers not meant to be present must stay away. A mess, indeed! It's infuriating when one sees the happy little rooms in which squadrons live and feed together.[7]

The entry is unintentionally amusing: Cunliffe, the embodiment of a type of young, educated man whom one would imagine criticising the crustiness of the British Army, hankering after a degree of tradition in the conduct of regimental life. At this remove it is pointless to consider whether he or Jolly were right or wrong. But maybe Cunliffe should have been a little bit more grateful for Jolly's scouting of the niceties of a mess. German generals after the war, and many historians since, have had fun at the expense of the British Army's amateurishness. Jolly's weakness, if Cunliffe is to be believed, is not that he was amateurish but rather the opposite – he spent too much time planning operations and not enough on social chit-chat. The chances of his men surviving may have been enhanced by his attention to business.

In April 1945, a diary entry related Cunliffe's hope of being chosen to write a book on 79th Armoured Division, the division in which served all sorts of special purpose armoured vehicles, such as flail tanks for exploding mines and the Buffaloes for crossing water. The 144th RAC was part of the Division while it had the Buffaloes. Cunliffe's initial information had come from his friend Douglas Draycott, by then serving with the Division, who told him: 'You've got a job. You're our new Historical Writer – mugging up the history of the division for the Old

Man [presumably Percy Hobart, the GOC of 79th Armoured]'. However, the job did not transpire, as Alan Jolly refused to release Cunliffe. Cunliffe went on to say that Jolly 'may have said I was lazy and erratic and therefore not to be recommended'. Presumably this was just a guess and, since most commanding officers would have leapt at a chance to get rid of an officer they thought was less than efficient, it seems unlikely that Jolly would have stood in Cunliffe's way for the reasons Cunliffe thought. On the other hand, it was quite likely that Jolly, with his single-minded pursuit of winning the war, would have been reluctant to lose any reasonably efficient officer while the war was actually being fought, whatever the cost to that officer's convenience or *amour propre*. It also seems unlikely that Cunliffe would have been given the responsible job of leading the reconnaissance troop if Jolly had really thought that he was lazy and erratic. Once the war had ended, no obstacle seems to have been put in the way of Cunliffe working on his quasi-official book on 21 Army Group.[8]*

We have no direct evidence of what Jolly really thought of Cunliffe, with the exception of Bob Thorne's's recollection that Jolly considered Cunliffe's hair too long. One suspects that, if this memory was accurate, Jolly's remark was a convenient way of making a short-hand comment with which other senior officers could sympathise, without having to reveal his real feelings. Of these, there is evidence in both directions. On the one hand, Jolly seems to have treated Cunliffe less than generously in the acknowledgments to *Blue Flash*. Cunliffe, it is clear, wrote a large portion of the summaries of various actions in Normandy which Jolly had caused to be compiled during the war, some of which have ended up in The National Archives.[9] Jolly based the relevant parts of *Blue Flash* on these. In turn they are partly based on the war diaries, again written by Cunliffe, in a reasonable degree of detail, from landing at Arromanches up to 17 September. Captain R.E. Bowyer then took over and wrote the war diaries, in stupendous but not very interesting detail, until the end of the war. Bowyer is named in the acknowledgments to *Blue Flash*, but not Cunliffe, although Cunliffe's contribution must have been as great or greater.[10]

---

* The book on 79th Armoured was written and published in 1945 as the *Story of the 79th Armoured Division* (author unknown). Not surprisingly, it is quite rare. Presumably Hobart was eager to start the book before the war was over because he knew that the division would be wound up when it was no longer needed, as happened in August 1945.

REGIMENTAL INS AND OUTS

Whether Jolly had some grievance against Cunliffe which was vented by not naming him, whether he just forgot, or whether he felt that, as he had mentioned Cunliffe several times in the body of the text, that was enough, is unknowable. However, one cannot help feel that there was some bond between these two men in spite of their differences in rank, age and interests. Various lengthy rides in scout cars which Cunliffe took with Jolly are mentioned elsewhere. These might have been just a matter of a senior officer taking with him the nearest junior officer, which was likely to be Cunliffe while he was attached to RHQ. But if Jolly actively disliked Cunliffe, it is hard to see why the latter was kept on at RHQ, first as Intelligence Officer and then commanding the recce troop, for so long. And there is one intriguing entry in Cunliffe's diary which suggests that he had considerable respect for Jolly of a sort that he clearly did not feel for many of his fellow officers, and which may have been reciprocated.

The Regiment was in Holland, training for the Rhine crossing. Jolly had gone to Eindhoven, the HQ of 79th Armoured Division to which the Regiment was then attached, and Cunliffe had gone with him. He was included in the invitation 'through Douglas [Draycott's] good graces'. Jolly could presumably have easily got out of taking Cunliffe with him if he had wished to. On both the outward and the return journeys: 'I talked ceaselessly with the Colonel; neither of us knew enough to argue well, but – though I thought my own notions better than his – I was unable to support them (apropos the future of Europe, the future of the Army etc etc). I vowed to improve my general knowledge, and my conversational powers.' All this was part of a longer reflective passage by Cunliffe – one of quite a few in the diary – in which he made various good resolutions as well as those mentioned. What had stimulated them were the conversations he had had with Jolly, as well as seeing Douglas whose 'belief in me lifts me out of my normal torpor, dissatisfies me with my present existence etc'. As a result, in the course of the visit, 'nothing happened, and yet everything happened to my mind. It came alive; it became more aware of its limitations, its [indecipherable] staleness.'[11]

All this was, in a way, a tribute to Jolly. Cunliffe may have disagreed with him or thought that Jolly didn't know enough to argue well, but most of Cunliffe's fellow officers would have received a far sharper treatment in the diary after expressing their views (and a number did). It also suggests that Jolly saw something in Cunliffe. One can hardly imagine an impatient senior officer voluntarily subjecting himself to lengthy conversations with a junior, with many of whose views he disagreed, unless he had some respect, and perhaps even a fondness, for that officer.

Other Ranks
When Cunliffe named various men in the Regiment who had been killed, and whom he had liked and missed, he included two 'other ranks'. Sergeant Skeer was a troop leader in a squadron (most troop leaders were officers, but there were a few NCOs) who was killed early in the campaign, at the Battle of Noyers.* The other was Corporal Callwood, who was the member of Cunliffe's crew killed while he and Cunliffe were taking shelter from German shelling beneath their tank in August. In spite of the inclusion of these two, Cunliffe otherwise showed no particular tendency to single out other ranks for mention. He records a few conversations with drivers or other members of his crew, but usually because the conversations had some quirky feature rather than because he wanted to record a deep insight. With the exception of Callwood, no members of his crew are singled out in the diary. In spite of his frequent irritation with his brother officers, on the whole he seems to have looked to them, or to books, for company.

Similarly, in the uncharacteristically positive diary entry on 5 February in which he eulogised his discovery of 'People', there followed a fairly low key description of various other ranks in his Buffalo troop: one was described as 'steady, serious, admirable', but the next as 'well-built, slightly evasive, conceited'; one was 'cheerful, youthful', but another 'self-conscious, withdrawn'; an 'ex-gents outfitters' assistant' was 'regarded as a man of learning by his fellows and inordinately proud of this'; another man was described as an 'arrogant cockney, thick-built and a singer'; a Glaswegian was described as 'blinking out at a hateful world through steel-rimmed spectacles'. One gets the impression of an incipient novelist setting out his cast of supporting characters rather than someone with a lot of sympathy for the 'People' he had just discovered.

This is not to criticise Cunliffe or to suggest that he neglected the men of whom he was in charge. For a long time, as Intelligence Officer, he

---

* Sergeant Skeer was Cunliffe's troop sergeant when Cunliffe was a troop leader, before he became Intelligence Officer. There is a reference to him in Cunliffe's diary of 5 April 1944, when Cunliffe was reminiscing about his practice in LCTs in Inverarary the previous year.

would not have been directly responsible for any men except his tank crew. Later, as Reconnaissance Troop commander and subsequently as commander of a Buffalo troop, rather more men would have come under his command. In this role he was confronted with a problem of personnel management to which he seems to have responded in a compassionate but pragmatic manner.

On 15 November 1944, the day after he described an evening in a farmhouse with the reconnaissance troop ('Waiting'), they were still in the same farmhouse – and still waiting. Cunliffe described how a crew member of one of the tanks – not Cunliffe's own – had asked to see him that morning. He was a Scot,

> honest and intensely reserved. When I saw him he was almost hysterical; his normally impassive face quivered and he did not trust his composure enough to look squarely at me. It was a simple enough story. [He] didn't get on with his crew; he blamed himself profusely, but said he'd rather be away from them. No, nothing he could explain – just that he knew he was a misfit in that particular crew. Could he be put with others? I talked gently about the necessity of getting on with one's comrades in these trying conditions . . . although naturally I respected his point of view. While I talked, trying to ease him, I thought of the misery of the misfit.

After some musing on that subject, Cunliffe continued,

> I can't put him in another crew; they're all indissolubly close now. I suppose he'll have to leave the [illegible; possibly an abbreviation referring to the troop]. His tank-commander said it was true they didn't hit it off . . . [He] was a silent chap – sometimes didn't speak to them all day – got on their nerves a bit.

There was no further mention until 5 February 1945, when a man with the same name was mentioned in the diary entry quoted earlier, which sketched the characteristics of various Buffalo troop members. He was the one described as self-conscious and withdrawn, and must have been the same individual. By then the Reconnaissance Troop personnel had been allocated to Buffalo squadrons, so it is impossible to know exactly what had occurred in the intervening period. At any rate it seems that the problem of the misfit had been resolved in some way.

I have devoted some attention to the story because it was the only one related by Cunliffe about the problems of an individual soldier. In a diary covering over six months of the war, written at some length, this is worth noting. It seems that such problems were few. What light Cunliffe's diary and other 144th RAC sources throw on wider problems of morale is the subject of the next section.

That most officers of the British Army felt a strong duty of care to their men is also suggested by another story. George Pearson, the young – he was 20 – A Echelon driver whose letters have been cited before, was wounded on 14 July. Having recovered, he returned to Normandy in early September but as a Royal Army Service Corps driver. And there, tragically, he was killed in a road accident on 11 September. Meanwhile, his C/O in A Echelon, not knowing of his death, had written to his home address enquiring whether he was now fit enough to return. Evidently his mother replied because the officer then wrote her a letter of condolence in which he praised Pearson both for his abilities and as an individual. The officer was Bob Thorne, my father-in-law. Mrs Pearson must then have asked him to find her son's grave. This cannot have been easy when 144th RAC was continuously on the move in Holland, but Bob Thorne did so and wrote again to Mrs Pearson in late November. Evidently, she wrote once more to thank him, enclosing the ubiquitous cigarettes and a photograph of her son, and his final letter acknowledges these. That photograph, identical to one reproduced in the memoir of George Pearson in the Imperial War Museum, is in an album of my father-in-law's, although until I saw the memoir no one in the family knew who it was.[12]

Morale

A fair amount has been written about morale in the British Army during the Second World War. One influential argument has been that morale was never the strongest point of the British Army; but, by 1944, the Allies had a massive material superiority, in armour, in the air and particularly in artillery, and used this to achieve by brute force what they could not achieve through high morale or by tactical sophistication.[13] The argument has often been applied to armoured troops, with reference particularly to various less than successful actions in the earlier part of the Normandy campaign. John Buckley has cogently retorted that there is little hard

REGIMENTAL INS AND OUTS

evidence for low morale among British armoured troops. When such evidence is examined, it suggests the opposite conclusion. Analysing, by brigade, convictions for AWOL, desertion, insubordination and drunkenness – four offences which between them would strongly suggest a correlation with morale – indicates that the infantry had a much higher rate than armoured troops from June to September 1944. However, even among the infantry the rate was not actually that high, and was inflated by relatively high levels for brigades in 50th Division. The 144th RAC and the two other tank regiments in 33rd Brigade had the lowest rate of all – precisely one conviction between them for the whole of July, August and September.[14]

Undoubtedly there were issues of morale among the infantry at times. These were evident in Normandy and reappeared in the bleak, cold, slogging campaign in Holland and Germany from the autumn of 1944 into the winter of 1944–5. There is a good discussion of them in Norman Scarfe's *Assault Division*, a history of 3rd Division.[15] Scarfe shows that, while such problems were inevitable given the situation of the troops, they could be mitigated. The issues he highlighted are very similar to those mentioned in the one sustained discussion about morale recorded by Cunliffe, between an infantry major and Alan Jolly. While this casts most light on infantry problems, its relevance to armour lies in Jolly's conviction that the problems did not apply to 144th RAC.

The discussion took place in late November 1944, after a lengthy period of exactly the sort of fighting that caused morale and motivation problems in 3rd Division. In this case, it was 51st Highland Division, 144th RAC's regular partners, who were the infantry concerned.

> Morale. The B.M. [Brigade Major] from 153 Bde (Highland Div) came to dinner the other evening. An able man, with a face of hereditary ugliness and importance: black, flat hair, closeset black eyes, a long beaked nose, prominent teeth. M.C. and bar, Africa Star, a disarmingly easy manner. He ventured the remark that the British soldier was going down the nick [presumably this means losing the will to fight, or perhaps deteriorating generally]. The Colonel disagreed hotly. The B.M. explained: 'The way I look at it is this. Almost any man will crack if enough happens to him. You put pressure on them from the top. As the pressure increases, they begin to peel off. The worst go first, naturally; then, as the pressure

grows, even the better chaps peel off. The pressure takes different forms, but for our chaps it means rain, cold slit trenches, shelling and mortaring, the death of your pals.'

The Colonel was impatient – 'Yes, I know that, but I can't believe that the chaps are not streets ahead of the Germans. I have every faith in my chaps – I know I can rely upon them.'

'Yes: it's a question of the amount of pressure exerted, isn't it? One of our battalions has 27 men attending court-martial for desertion. There are 5 due for court-martial on mutiny charges. This is the way it takes them. After a few days fighting a truck gets bogged, with an officer and some blokes in the back. The officer jumps out, and – because he's an officer and also a good chap – he says "Come on, chaps: let's shove this out." And not a man will move. They'll all sit in the back; they'll say "These f—ing officers – what the f— do they think we are." And it's all a matter of pressure – sleepless nights, discomfort, danger, fear.'

Still the CO was incredulous. I thought of the infantry I had seen so often, digging slit trenches when we moved back, helpless under mortar-fire, helpless against Spandaus. I pity them with all my heart. In the advance up to the Seine, the HD [Highland Division] companies were nearly all down to platoon strength. The 1st Gordons have only 2 of the officers left with them when they came over – the QM and the BTO [Quartermaster and Battalion Transport Officer; neither a post involving frequent front-line duty].*

During the last phases of fighting – the canal crossings and perhaps 15 miles of country gained – we have suffered no casualties. Each infantry battalion has had perhaps 40 or 50. Whilst we have lived here (minus one squadron) for several days, in warmth and a reasonable degree of comfort, the wretched infantry have been mopping up towards the banks of the Maas. They have lived in the open, with a blanket and a greatcoat (if they were lucky).[16]

Jolly was an intelligent man, who was frequently close to or on the front line – in Totalize, in Stonk Wood, on his scout car rides with Cunliffe

---

* Martin Lindsay did not join the battalion until mid-July.

REGIMENTAL INS AND OUTS

in Normandy and, later, crossing the Rhine. He would hardly have been likely to completely misread the mood of his men and so, when he expressed confidence in their morale, we should take him seriously. Cunliffe's contribution to the debate lies in what his diary does not say. He makes no comment on Jolly's remarks, which he surely would have done if he had significantly disagreed with them. Instead, he empathises with the infantry. And indeed, apart from relating the story of the individual misfit, which was not really a morale problem in the ordinary sense of the word, the diary does not otherwise mention morale. Again, it seems very unlikely that he would have ignored it if it had been an issue.

It is true that 144th RAC was more fortunate in its active service career than many units. It had quite lengthy spells without fighting: between D-Day and Noyers, after Le Havre, and while training with Buffaloes. So it had not gone through the sort of experiences which many infantry battalions had. On the other hand, its casualties at times were severe – Noyers alone cost sixty men killed or wounded – so it was by no means unblooded. It was clearly going to be less likely to suffer from morale problems than infantry battalions, but its apparent immunity from them lends support to Buckley's contention that they have been overstressed as a factor in British armoured troops' performance.

Training

What actually went on when British soldiers trained in the Second World War? The question is infuriatingly difficult to unravel. One way of approaching it is via an analysis of battle performance. If this was inadequate, it suggests that training might also have been, although obviously other factors might be involved. In Chapter 1 the debate about battle performance was sketched out, and some detail about tank tactics was added in Chapter 2. To some extent, Chapters 3–6 all contribute to the debate, but the focus in them is on 144th RAC's actions, rather than on analysing its performance relative to the enemy. That will be left to the conclusion, but it will clearly help if we can grasp how thorough the Regiment's training was.

Suggestions that training was inadequate sometimes tend to rely on individuals' post-war memory. This is hardly a dependable source but it has been used by historians because of the difficulty of working out what went on from contemporary records. Even Timothy Harrison-Place, who has written a book on the subject, admits that the content of training in individual units is something of a black box (my phrase not his). In one of his examples a troop of the 2nd Armoured Irish Guards was training as if coming under fire from an anti-tank gun. But the war diary only recorded this because General Alexander was visiting that day. On most days the Irish Guards and other units, in his words, 'merely recorded "troop training" or some such'.[17]

For the most part, the 144th RAC diaries are not much more forthcoming. Taken over a period, however, there are some details and, overall, a fair amount of information about training. If we do not know the full contents of the box, we can get a number of peeps inside. The material they contain, from the beginning of 1943 until D-Day, is reviewed below. That mentioned is a considerable proportion of the total, although not all.[18]

In January 1943 there was a Corps Exercise from the 16th to the 19th. The Regiment split up, with one squadron to each infantry brigade, and 'mock battles' took place. Presumably, although it is not stated, there were opportunities here to practise tactics with the infantry. In February there was a lengthy spell of tank gunnery practice – eleven days in all, although it may be that squadrons practised separately at different times. In March two squadrons practised troop training, that is training involving individual tank troops. As with Harrison-Place's example, one has to infer what such training entailed. It seems likely that it would include, for instance, manoeuvring in the face of enemy tanks and anti-tank guns, as in the Irish Guards' example above. In Marcus Cunliffe's account of Totalize cited in Chapter 1 he wrote about: 'the training in England, where someone waved a flag to represent an anti-tank gun. When you saw it you rushed off into cover.' Artificial this sort of thing might be, but it meant that habits were learned which would be valuable on the battlefield, while tank commanders, drivers and gunners would practise reacting to stimuli. In April there was specific training as each squadron was detached and sent to Inveraray for practice with LCTs.

Here Cunliffe's diary provides additional evidence. The pre-D-Day portion does not have much to say about training, but in April 1944 he reminisced about the time in Inveraray a year earlier.[19]

> All day my LCT had been chugging up and down the loch in the rain. . . . Now and again we would turn and swing bluntly into some beach. Then the routine . . . the LCT crept in slowly, with the

second officer watching on the bow and members of the crew ready at the winches. Finally, the first faint sound of gravel under the boat – 'down Kedge' – 'down Door' – the bow fell abruptly away to disclose (through the [tank's] periscope) a stretch of shingle – 'Driver advance – keep going – straight up the beach'. [The other two tanks – it was a Churchill troop with three tanks only – would steer left and right of the commander once clear of the LCT]. The tank-engines thundered within the boat's hollow walls, their tracks clanged on the steel decks – up the incline, out through the bows . . . through the saltwater to the beach . . .

We did this three or four times, each time returning lamely to the boat and re-embarking. Each time something went wrong to mar the performance: either my driver missed his gear, or somebody didn't come out straight and had to reverse and swing his tracks again.

The next day entailed a squadron landing under cover of a smoke screen, although no further details are given; nor do we know how long the training went on. The point to note is the considerable amount of repetition – enough to mean that drivers and commanders had the opportunity to discover the pitfalls and problems of landing from an LCT.*

The sequence of events after Inveraray becomes a little hard to follow, as Shermans were recorded arriving in April – the Regiment had previously had Churchills – but there is also a mention of them being received throughout June, and by 26 June there was a full complement.†There was a divisional exercise on 15 and 16 June and liaison with infantry brigades in 61st Division throughout the second half of the

---

* The training, presumably, took place because 144th RAC was then destined for Sicily. From the description it was training for an assault, not just for driving off the LCTs. It does not seem to have repeated the practice in preparation for Normandy. Given the need to train the many other units landing there, the existing landing practice may have been thought adequate. The Regiment, also, was landing some time after D-Day, and likely to meet relatively peaceful conditions – as it did.

† It may be that this was the period when the Regiment reverted to Churchills before ending with Shermans. Jolly, *Blue Flash*, p. 2, says that the switch back to Churchills occurred when the Regiment was at Lesmahagow, in Scotland (see below) but there is no mention of this in the war diary. Jolly was not C/O at the time and must have garnered the information at second-hand.

month. In July B and C Squadrons demonstrated the use of tanks for infantry cooperation, in conjunction with 182nd Brigade, part of 61st Division, before going to Orford Ranges for 'firing 75 mm guns and Brownings'. There was also a regimental exercise on the control and formation of echelons, concerned with maintenance and supply. This highlights a point which can be forgotten – that all parts of a unit had to be trained, not just those at the sharp end, because all parts were vital to its smooth operation.

In August rather more detail was given. The Regiment had moved to Lesmahagow, in Lanarkshire in Scotland, although the squadrons were scattered in different places. The first week of the month saw a divisional wireless exercise. Also during the month 'the Recce Tp. and D.R.s [Despatch Riders] have put in some intensive training, the latter have done a number of night schemes'. B Squadron was cooperating with 49th Infantry Division at Blackford Assault School in Perthshire, while A and C Squadrons undertook several three-day tank marches which included troop training, harbouring and moves at night into alternative harbour locations. There was also individual training consisting of classes in 'Wireless, D & M [presumably Driving and Maintenance] & Gunnery with a view to trade testing early in September'. However, training was restricted by a lack of training areas, the diary observing that the county 'has a record proportion of bogland'.

In September training was 'chiefly' concerned with infantry cooperation, each squadron working with an infantry brigade. Unfortunately, there is no detail about this, but there is more about other training that month. Squadrons also ran their own training programmes, to include night marches (in spite of the bogland), attacks on harbour areas at night – presumably the training was in defence against attack, rather than the other way round – 36-hour troop marches and a period on a range firing 75mm HE. When more detail is given, as here, it is evident that a lot was packed in.

In October parts of the unit participated in a corps exercise and there was more range firing, followed at the end of the month by a move to Warcop Range in Westmoreland, where practice extended until November. The move was en route to Bury St Edmunds, where they had been stationed before. Later there was a Recce Troop exercise and then Exercise Bridgepoint in the Stanford Battle Area, near Thetford in Norfolk, where the Regiment had trained earlier in the summer. The intention of this was to train the Regiment in a 'quick counter-attack role', and also to give the men some idea of the infantry's part in an attack. To that end men from 144th RAC made up, temporarily, an infantry company – an imaginative attempt to give tank men some insight into the infantry point of view. It is worth noting that live ammunition was used. In December the level of detail given in the diary declined but it noted that particular attention was paid to trade test classes.

In early 1944, however, plenty of activity was recorded. In January, 'Training on similar lines to last month' apparently included small arms firing, including PIATs – the British equivalent of the *Ofenrohre* or the American bazooka. Since there was no mention of this in December's diary, it is clear that lack of detail in a war diary does not mean that little was happening. It also reminds us that tank men, if dismounted for whatever reason, might have to defend themselves, while maintenance and supply areas might have to defend against an enemy tank attack – hence, presumably, the training on PIATs – and tank commanders might need to fire a Sten gun or similar while standing in the turret. Tank gunnery was practised between the 10 and 23 January, and more briefly in February when it took the form of 'firing by Squadrons' – possibly meaning that collective fire, rather than individual gunnery, was being practised. Exercises included one practising regimental battle procedures and a 'full B Echelon' administrative exercise. In addition, there was more practice in small arms firing, mines training and waterproofing classes for B Echelon drivers. The latter would be connected with preparation of the lorries for landing from LCTs on beaches. In March, by contrast, activity dried up, or more probably the diary writer thought that much going on was routine and not worth recording.[20] Various TEWTs – 'Tactical Exercises Without Troops' – were mentioned from March onwards. These had occurred before but the numbers stepped up, especially in May, as D-Day plans advanced. One of the later ones was on issues involved in landing. TEWTs were useful in enabling officers and, where appropriate, other ranks, to mutually discuss tactical and administrative questions. Thus, another in May, on tanks' cooperation with infantry in an advance, involved all tank commanders. This particular TEWT was extended outdoors the next day, in order to apply the lessons 'to actual ground'. Other training in April and May included several days of gunnery practice, including practice for the Firefly gunners and the AA troop, and various exercises testing administrative procedures.

FROM ARROMANCHES TO THE ELBE

Finally, there was some intensive training in April 1944 in case 33rd Armoured Brigade was needed in an armoured division, to replace a brigade which had suffered heavy losses. Since much of the training so far had focused on the infantry tank role, the Regiment had to 'learn a new trick', in Jolly's phrase. Much of April was devoted to this, and it culminated in an exercise near Thetford in which 'we had the exhilarating experience of being allowed, for once, to take our tanks across country and manoeuvre tactically as we should shortly be doing in real earnest, instead of being confined to roads, tracks and well-worn training areas'. The last reference highlights some limitations of 144th RAC's previous training, although relatively confined spaces would not have affected training in the sort of close infantry cooperation which, in practice, the Regiment spent most of its time doing in Normandy, Holland and Belgium.[21]

As has been seen, a considerable amount of time was devoted to such infantry cooperation training: some time, certainly, in the early part of 1943 and a great deal of time in the summer and autumn of that year. We still do not know, however, much about what went on during that training. The diaries do make it clear that there were a number of other priorities in training, and a moment's thought shows that these were as necessary as training in infantry cooperation, even if that was the ultimate reason for the Regiment's existence. Much time was devoted to individual tasks – driving, maintenance, wireless operation and so forth. Gunnery practice was extremely important. And there were a variety of exercises testing administrative procedures, signals and movement. It is difficult not to conclude that training was thorough, although of course 144th RAC benefitted from its long spell in Britain.[22]

A little more light is shed by the letters from George Pearson, the A Echelon truck driver. Those preserved only start in April 1944 but they show not only that training really was intensive during the period, but that, whatever their occupation, soldiers would undergo all-round training. 'We are doing some intensive training just now – commando stuff, forced marches, plenty of assault courses etc. . . . We are on the ranges today when I won the individual rifle competition.' In addition, 'Andy and I led the way in the light and heavy machine gun team . . .'. And in May they were 'still kept hard at it . . .'.[23]

Once in Europe, training was often impossible because the Regiment was in action; and action, of course, was the best form of training so long as it did not involve too many casualties and the correct lessons were drawn and disseminated. Jolly's post-battle report on Noyers suggests that 144th RAC made every effort to do this. In the gaps between action, or during periods in defensive positions, some training did take place. On 5 August 1944 the Regiment, with the 7th Argyll and Sutherland Highlanders, practised for Totalize, both in daylight and then at night. This went well, but it was over a much shorter distance than involved in the real thing, and there was little dust. As a result, the practice was no doubt useful but did not prepare for the reality of the operation. Interestingly, it was followed by 'fraternisation parties' between tank crews and the Jocks on the evening of 6 August, the day before Totalize got under way and the first time 33rd Armoured Brigade and the 51st Highland Division had worked together.[24]

Later there was shooting practice when the Regiment rested after the Le Havre operation. This was mentioned in Chapter 4 where it was noted that, according to Jolly, shooting had deteriorated in Normandy. The Regiment's most sustained period of training between landing in Normandy and the end of the war took place when it converted to Buffaloes. The training lasted for around five weeks, from late January until 10 March, with an interlude, mentioned in Chapter 6, for the ceremonial parade on renaming. There were final rehearsals for the crossing after 10 March. Each crew was allocated 28 'water training hours': drivers and co-drivers would receive 3 hours training each in a canal, then drivers 15 hours training in a river, and co-drivers 7. Since the river was the large and fast-flowing Meuse, substituting for the Rhine, preliminary practice in a canal was wise. In the middle of February the Regiment was affiliated to an infantry battalion, the 1st Norfolks, for training in loading; there was also training at night. Jolly describes how 'the detailed method of carrying out the operation was demonstrated diagrammatically on a model until all officers and senior N.C.O.'s knew the correct drill. This was followed by full-scale exercises in which the theoretical technique, worked out on the model, was put into practice'.[25]

Cunliffe's diary entries confirm that training was intensive. Early on, for instance, he wrote: 'I'm tired again after a day on the river, in the rain', followed after a couple of days by 'another wet, wearying day on the Maas'.[26] And in March:

> Tomorrow is a working day (Sunday), and so the day after that, and the day after that: so on until – the operation? Our festivities are over [presumably those connected with the Regimental change of name]; training tricks out each day . . . Tonight, in our Buffaloes, we shall cross the Maas into Holland for the hundred and fiftieth time, run three hundred yards among trees, turn back into the current and make for Belgium again.[27]

It was, no doubt, tedious. But it meant that 144th RAC's crossing of the Rhine went smoothly, as did most of the crossings by other Buffalo regiments. So did subsequent crossings by the Regiment such as the one near Bremen mentioned by 3rd Division's historian and cited in Chapter 6, where the Ulster Rifles exited at exactly the spot where they were meant to land in time to overpower two enemy 88mm guns.[28]

Becoming 4th RTR

It was during its training on Buffaloes that 144th RAC became 4th RTR. As such the Regiment inherited a tradition going back to the First World War. The Battalion, as it now was, continued until 1993, having subsumed 7th RTR in 1959. In 1993 it amalgamated with 1st RTR and the new regiment took the latter's number. The Battalion's independent existence was at an end. The renaming of 144th RAC in 1945, therefore, elevated it to a senior position within the Royal Armoured Corps and ensured its future for almost fifty years.

The detailed steps by which this happened are untraceable or, at least, I have not traced them.[29] However, they are likely to owe something to Alan Jolly's lobbying. In September 1944, just after the Le Havre operation, Jolly sent a memo round to squadrons, attaching a draft of an account of operations between 7 and 31 August written by him. He wanted squadrons, in consultation with troop leaders, to fill in details and amend or alter the draft.[30] The much fuller account which found its way into The National Archives was clearly developed by Cunliffe from Jolly's draft and the subsequent additions (see Chapter 1, note 6, and also 'Sources and Bibliography').

Jolly's motives, apart from the laudable one of providing a fuller and more analytical record than that available in the war diary, were clarified in the memo: 'Not only will these accounts form a valuable basis for a regimental history after the war but, by judicious publicity of the

REGIMENTAL INS AND OUTS

Regiment's achievements, they may help us to survive as a unit when further disbandment of RAC Regts. takes place.'[31] The disbandment of 148th RAC and other units, mentioned in Chapter 4, had taken place only a month earlier and must have been fresh in his mind.

Presumably Jolly then put together a file which contained the Regimental account and other material written by officers, such as Cunliffe's Totalize account and Phillips' accounts of the Ardennes. The latter's account of the Rhine operation and another by Lieutenant Wells were added to it, although by then, of course, the Regiment had already become 4th RTR. The fact that the file ended up in a Twenty-First Army Group class, mainly consisting of accounts of operations submitted by divisions and corps rather than other regiments or battalions, is telling and is perhaps a testimony to Jolly's lobbying skills. But the Regiment also had a fine record and lobbying alone cannot have been the only factor in its promotion.

Chapter 9

Conclusion

There have been two leading characters in this book: 144th Royal Armoured Corps and Marcus Cunliffe. Their stories contain drama, pathos and human interest, as would the stories of most fighting units and personnel of the British Army. But in many cases the documentation is not there to tell these stories in any detail. The stories of the Regiment, and of Marcus Cunliffe, are worth telling because the wealth of documents enables us to learn much about the fighting, and about the life of a Regiment, which usually remains concealed or obscured. And these hidden details also cast light on aspects of the campaign which interest professional historians.

Historians like to aggregate and to compare, so what interests them are general questions. The central one is how the British Army compared with other armies: the friendly and, most importantly, the hostile – the German Army. An important subsidiary question, given the subject matter of the book, is how British tank units compared with those of their enemy. Matters for comparison include specific qualities and procedures such as morale and training and, crucially, the overall performance of units in battle. They also include that often debated topic, the merits and demerits of the Sherman tank. Beyond these topics, which are directly or indirectly about fighting, are others: for instance, relations with civilians and the treatment of prisoners.

Many of the diary excerpts and accounts reproduced in the book relate to the Regiment as an entity and therefore to these questions. Others, however, are more personal to Cunliffe himself. They tell us something about his and other men's attitudes, towards each other and towards the Regiment but also, from time to time, towards the wider world: a world in which, while a global war was raging, men and women had to live their lives and think about the future.

CONCLUSION

The Regiment and the Campaign in North-West Europe

Chapter 1 treated the campaign and 144th RAC separately but, once the Regiment landed in Normandy on 14 June 1944, it became a part of the campaign. So here the two will be treated together, since the insights gained from a study of the Regiment will apply to some extent to the whole of the British Army in Europe between 1944 and 1945.

Morale in the Regiment, discussed in the previous chapter, seems to have been good. The evidence for this is not so much positive statements as the absence of any indication to the contrary. Nevertheless this evidence is quite persuasive. Cunliffe would surely have mentioned morale in his diary, or in his other writings about the Regiment, if there had been problems; but the only significant reference is his résumé of the comments of 153rd Infantry Brigade's Brigade Major. This is focused entirely on the problems of the infantry. Neither does Cunliffe dissent in his diary from Alan Jolly's stout defence of morale in the Regiment, made at the same time. Bob Thorne, too, never mentioned morale as a problem in his talks with me.

John Buckley's wider survey has also discounted morale as a significant issue among tank or armoured regiments. (Tank regiments were equipped with Churchill infantry tanks and armoured regiments with Shermans or Cromwells.). Buckley does, however, devote a fair amount of time to discussing a question which frequently crops up elsewhere – the defects of Shermans and Cromwells. He discerns a problem which indirectly relates to morale: that these tanks' vulnerability to enemy tanks and anti-tank guns was perceived by their crews, making them cautious and defensive.[1]

The available evidence offers only a few clues, but those that exist suggest that the problem may be exaggerated. Shermans were not unique in their vulnerability as all British tanks, including the more heavily armoured Churchills, could be destroyed by enemy anti-tank guns and by the guns of Panthers and Tigers. Well-aimed shots from the standard German tank, the Mark IV, could also account for Shermans and Cromwells. But this vulnerability was not unique to Allied tanks; German tanks also had weaknesses. The Mark IV could be destroyed by all Allied tanks and the Panther and Tiger by Sherman Fireflys and Allied anti-tank guns. All tank men were at risk.

This was demonstrated at Noyers, when the Regiment knocked out a Panther. It was indicated even more strikingly on the day after the Totalize night attack when the Northamptonshire Yeomanry, the Sherbrooke Fusiliers and 144th RAC knocked out five Tigers between them, none at particularly close range. Later the Regiment knocked out another in Stonk Wood. A passage by a British tank officer describing the almost complete impossibility of stalking and knocking out a Tiger with a Churchill has been cited by various historians.[2] The passage is misleading, however, if taken as describing the situation for most British or Canadian regiments equipped with Shermans or Cromwells. Sherman regiments each had twelve Fireflys, and Cromwell regiments had some. It took time to build up the number of Fireflys after D-Day, but by the end of June 1944 there were almost 150. This compared with a total of 120 Tigers in the Normandy campaign – a number which was, of course, constantly diminishing.[3]

Jolly's careful analysis after the Battle of Noyers shows that he was well aware of the problems posed by enemy tanks and anti-tank guns, but also understood that they should be put into perspective. His answer to the dangers was that, if possible, British tanks should attack under the cover of artillery fire, which would suppress anti-tank guns and, at the least, disorientate enemy tanks until British tanks had closed the range. Of course artillery was not always going to be available but, given Allied resources, Jolly's preconditions must often have been met.[4] Whether or not the Regiment's personnel were nervous about going into battle in Shermans, in spite of Jolly's reassurances, is unknowable. There is no evidence that I have come across. But if there were fears, they seem to have been suppressed in the later stages of the Normandy campaign, given the Regiment's rapid advance after Totalize when it was often unsupported by artillery.

Training was also considered at length in the previous chapter. The Regiment's training seems to have been thorough. The war diaries suggest that lengthy periods were spent rehearsing infantry cooperation. When 144th RAC arrived in Normandy, it had clear ideas about tactics and there is no suggestion of uncertainty. At times a classic sandwich formation was used; this was a version of the tactic in which the front ranks of the infantry were close behind the front troop of tanks, rather than the tanks being some distance ahead. When buildings were attacked, tanks would stand off and provide fire support. If an advance took place in a mixed terrain of hedges and orchards, as was common in the *bocage*, the infantry would be in the lead when visibility was limited, but the tanks close

CONCLUSION

behind. The Regiment does not appear to have felt its way towards these tactics by trial and error. They seem to have been automatically adopted at its first full-scale battle, at Noyers. So for 144th RAC at least, British tactical doctrine was not inchoate but well understood and adapted to the terrain. The Regiment's account of Noyers, and *Blue Flash*, sometimes hint that the infantry was not fully prepared to play its part. If true, this may have been because of nerves, but maybe they simply lacked training. At other times during the Noyers battle tanks and infantry worked together well.

The Regiment, however, may not have been typical. Because it was originally equipped with Churchills, it had trained in the infantry tank role. Other armoured regiments may not have done so, or not so intensively. The ability of one regiment to effectively use a range of tactics does suggest, however, that historians need to spend more time on the prosaic task of digging down into war diaries covering the training period of 1943–4, and in analysing diaries and post-battle reports of units during the summer of 1944, in order to see how many others could do the same.

Training was undoubtedly thorough in all the technicalities of tank work. Driving, gunnery and the work of the fitters seem to have been thoroughly practised, judging by the war diaries. Jolly pays tribute from time to time to the ability of the fitters to get damaged tanks back into action quickly. Cunliffe's diary during his own training period was not studied, but Stuart Hills' memoir pays tribute to the intensive training in all aspects which recruits received, whether they became officers or not.[5] As a result positions could be swapped if necessary: Lieutenant Phillips' account of the Ardennes fighting mentions an instance where one of his tank commanders brought out a tank as the driver had been wounded.

After the close-infantry support needed for Noyers, 144th RAC played its part in a very different operation, Totalize, with complete success, bringing the accompanying infantry right on to the target with limited casualties. When the German front collapsed after Totalize, the Regiment, for the first time, had its chance to advance rapidly. At this stage it becomes difficult to make a judgment about its relative performance. Martin Lindsay's criticisms, mentioned in Chapter 4, might have something in them, but might equally be filed under that genre of military literature entitled 'moans about your fellow units'. Numerous other examples can be found in war diaries and post-war publications.[6] On the other side of the scorecard, the Regiment's advance to and capture of

FROM ARROMANCHES TO THE ELBE

St Pierre-sur-Dives was a minor coup, while its overall achievements in the advance to the Seine – the steady retreat of the Germans, the accumulation of prisoners – also suggest success. The context, however, was one in which the Germans were bound to retreat anyway under overwhelming Allied pressure. Jolly wrote thoughtfully and intelligently about this phase, and the next one in Holland in the autumn of 1944. While he did not make extravagant claims, he put a good face on the Regiment's performance. But because the circumstances of different units' advances, and of all the small-scale actions which took place, were so different, comparison is almost impossible.

There was tangible evidence of effectiveness, however, in the crossing of the Rhine and other subsequent river crossings. In these the Regiment achieved almost pin-point accuracy in arriving at its landing points, its performance at Bremen meriting a mention in 3rd Division's history. Cunliffe's diary gives some idea of the remorseless training which lay behind this. Most of the other Buffalo units involved seem to have carried out their Rhine landings with a similar degree of skill but, on a different part of the river, the East Riding Yeomanry landed several units of 15th Division seriously out of position. So achieving a perfect landing was not inevitable or easy.[7]

Where the Regiment's experience can throw valuable light is on the effectiveness of the British Army during a rapid advance. There is no question about the British ability to advance quickly when there was little or no opposition, as the armoured divisions' dash across northern France to Belgium at the beginning of September shows.[8] The problem was the sort of interrupted advance which 144th RAC made after Totalize when well-organised defensive positions would be encountered every few miles. These held up the British for a few hours or a day, allowing the enemy to prepare and fall back to the next position. In eastern Normandy during the Regiment's advance, and later in Holland, these positions were often located on a river or canal. But they could be on defensible higher ground or comprise a well-defended village.

On a number of occasions in *Blue Flash* Alan Jolly identified places where he thought that a better organisation of the attacking force would have led to quicker progress. The essential problem, as he saw it, was that British infantry divisions lacked the mindset and organisation which would have enabled a rapid advance to be made after a breakthrough. As a result the Germans had time to fall back or consolidate. This occurred,

CONCLUSION

for example, at Noyers where, although the British did not intend to make a breakthrough, Jolly thought one would have been possible after the successful attack by A Squadron and the 2/6th South Staffordshires on 16 July.[9] Later examples included slow exploitation after the capture of St Pierre-sur-Dives, and the incident in Holland where tanks belonging to the Regiment and to a regiment of 7th Armoured Division were double-banked along a road and Cunliffe witnessed Jolly and the other Colonel arguing.[10]

To Jolly, such delays could have been quite easily remedied, as all the ingredients for mobile operations were available without involving armoured divisions. The infantry divisions which were supported by armoured brigades had the infantry, and usually plenty of artillery. Later in the campaign, APCs were freely available to carry the infantry. Earlier this was not the case, but ad hoc measures such as using Bren gun carriers or tank riding were available. If the different arms had been brought together under one command, infantry divisions could have exploited opportunities such as those mentioned above. In some cases, as in Noyers and St Pierre, they could have seized opportunities which had not been foreseen by higher command. In others, the breakthrough had been envisaged but involved waiting for armoured divisions to be 'passed through', thus giving the enemy time to regroup. The key, in Jolly's view, would have been to keep an armoured regiment with some infantry and artillery in reserve. If a breakthrough occurred, this could have advanced under the command of the 'tank brigadier' – that is the C/O of the armoured brigade.[11]

Jolly's criticisms seem very specific, but actually add up to a rather fundamental rethinking of how the British might have fought the campaign. Although he does not press it that far, the logical implication is that armoured brigades could have become an organic part of infantry divisions. Two tank/armoured regiments from each brigade would still have been available to support the initial infantry attack on prepared German positions, leaving the third for the exploitation role envisaged by Jolly.

Although critics of the British Army in Western Europe in 1944–5 have seized on several aspects of its performance, Alan Jolly's criticism is not one that has usually been made. Indeed, so far I'm aware it has not strayed beyond the pages of *Blue Flash*. The neglect is surprising, as Jolly was someone who knew what he was talking about. But, judging by the paucity of references to it, the book has faded from historians' consciousness. Its neglect mirrors the neglect of the independent armoured brigades as a group. In most discussions of the campaign they hardly appear except as walk-on players in particular battles, when the focus is almost always on the infantry. When historians discuss armoured warfare, they usually devote most attention to the armoured divisions, even though there were in total more tanks in the independent brigades.

To summarise his analysis, Jolly focuses on the thinking and procedures of the infantry divisions, to which the armoured brigades were usually attached, as the major source of weakness. This, of course, reflects shortcomings in the doctrine of the British and Canadian Armies. They stuck to a demarcation in which infantry, assisted by independent armoured or tank brigades, broke through and armoured divisions exploited.

Alan Jolly's criticism, essentially, concerns the operational level. Comparisons of the battlefield performance of the Allied units with the Germans usually focus on tactics.

A number of these criticisms have been discussed in earlier chapters, although others are beyond the scope of this book. Historians have criticised infantry tactics and the lack of joint infantry training with independent armoured formations; in the case of 144th RAC the latter was not true, as has been seen. Infantry morale and its willingness to fight hard have also been called into question. British armoured divisions have come in for plenty of criticism, including the lack of integration of their own organic infantry with their armour, and their inability in battles such as Goodwood to break through successfully.[12]

The problem the Allies confronted in 1944, however, was not so much their own tactical defects as the fact that they met a well-organised and highly experienced opponent. The Allied advance was necessarily slow because the Germans had relatively strong forces within easy reach, while the Allies had to build up their forces over the beachheads. So the Germans had time to establish defensive lines inland, such as the concentric lines with which they defended Caen and the area south-east of Caen. The alleged superiority of individual German weapons in 1944 is something of a red herring, in my view, at least in the case of tanks, as has been explained in the course of the book. Much more important was how the weapons were used and here the Germans had plenty of experience, having been retreating on most fronts since late 1942. Tanks

CONCLUSION

were often dug in to act as artillery, effective in *bocage* country, while echeloned machine-gun positions made the best use of the high rate of fire of the German MG 34s and 42s. On the other hand the German penchant for immediate counter-attacks often told against them because of the weight of Allied artillery.

The Allies' slow advance has often been compared unfavourably to the *Blitzkrieg* of 1940 or the rapidity of the early German advances against Russia in 1941. In 1940, however, the Germans were confronting the demoralised and badly led French Army, and in 1941 the Russian Army which was, with some exceptions, equally badly led. Furthermore, both these armies had poor communication systems which were disrupted early on in the attack. When in 1940 German troops were confronted with reasonably well-organised opponents, they found the battle harder. The author has written elsewhere about such an episode, the Battle of the Ypres–Comines Canal, where the British put up two days of effective resistance in spite of occupying their defensive line only a few hours before the German attack.[13]

Back in 1940 and 1941 German emphasis on speed in the attack was a major factor in victory. The Allies in 1944–5 were much more deliberate. There were a variety of reasons for this, some good and some bad. Alan Jolly's criticism pinpointed one of the bad ones, which was a degree of organisational sclerosis, at least on the part of the British. But deliberateness played to Allied strengths in artillery and logistics and ultimately wore the Germans down. In other words, Allied methods were effective, and their effectiveness was more certain than trying to emulate German speed of action would have been. The proof of Allied tactics in the campaign from D-Day to the end of the war was that they worked. Furthermore, they worked in spite of a determined, well-equipped and skilful opponent. Comparing them with German tactics in the attack is not possible in any meaningful way, and historians who opine on the subject are essentially engaging in speculation rather than reasoned argument.

Certainly the total of casualties hardly suggests Allied tactical inferiority. Over the Normandy campaign, from 6 June to 30 August, German losses at over 400,000 were roughly double Allied losses of 209,000. Losses in dead and wounded were similar on each side, but large numbers of Germans became prisoners. As has been seen, most of 144th RAC's attacks resulted in the taking of numerous prisoners.

The discrepancy in losses conceals the cost to individual Allied units. The infantry suffered most, but even a tank unit such as 144th RAC, which lost fewer men later in the war because of its conversion to the relatively safe role of operating Buffaloes, recorded eighty-four dead from landing at Arromanches until 5 May 1945. There would have been more wounded than dead but not in the usual proportion for infantry casualties, which was around 2.5 or 3 to 1. For instance, at Noyers the Regiment lost twenty-five killed and thirty-six wounded.

Infantry casualties were appalling. Martin Lindsay's 1st Gordon Highlanders lost 75 officers and 986 other ranks; rather more than a quarter of these were killed, and the casualty rate was well above 100 per cent of the battalion's initial complement. The 1/7th Royal Warwickshires, whose history Cunliffe wrote, lost 38 officers and 513 other ranks killed and wounded in less than 6 weeks of fighting in Normandy.[14]

Beyond the tactics and weaponry which have inevitably absorbed much of the discussion, the treatment of prisoners is one of the aspects of war on which 144th RAC's experience sheds light. There have been suggestions that Allied forces shot SS prisoners 'routinely'.[15] The Regiment was only engaged against SS units on a few occasions, and the great majority of the prisoners it helped to take, at Noyers, in Totalize and on other occasions, were from *Wehrmacht* units. But for what it is worth I came across no evidence of significant maltreatment of prisoners, by 144th RAC or any of the infantry units with which it was associated, in the regimental records, in Cunliffe's diary, or in the vignettes he wrote later about Normandy. And a private diary such as that of Cunliffe, who obviously had views about some aspects of the conduct of the war (see below), would be a place where one might expect to find such things mentioned if he had experienced them.

Tank crews, for obvious reasons, were not always in a position to take prisoners. Bill Close wrote of his experience during the first stages of the Goodwood attack: 'Dazed and shaken figures rose from the nearest corn and attempted to give themselves up to the leading tanks. When I waved them to the rear they stumbled off with their hands over their ears'.[16] Often it was the infantry who would actually secure them. Nevertheless, there were plenty of operations where the tanks gave close support to the infantry and were at the scene of prisoner-taking; or, as in the drive through eastern Normandy, infantry were scarce and tank units had to take prisoners themselves.

CONCLUSION

The pattern suggested in Cunliffe's account of Totalize, cited in the Introduction, is replicated by other accounts such as those of Martin Lindsay, mentioned in Chapter 4. As the dazed Germans surrendered, according to Cunliffe, 'the Jocks [men of the 51st Highland Division] took their watches and told them to lie down'. In other words, there was a degree of bullying, which had functional advantages. Making prisoners lie or sit kept them in a position where any attempt at escape would be obvious; taking their valuables was a way of asserting the victor's superiority. It was also, of course, a safety-valve for the adrenaline built up by the attackers, not to mention their feelings of revenge for killed or wounded comrades.

Taking prisoners was an aspect of war which was only experienced in combat. As the Regiment moved through Europe it inevitably came into contact with another, and wider, world than the enclosed world of a military unit. One important component of the outside world were civilians, with whom relations generally seem to have been good. Early in the campaign, the humanity of most British soldiers is illustrated by George Pearson's story about the French boy his unit picked up, recounted in Chapter 7. But there is more in 144th RAC's records about Dutch and Belgian civilians than about French, and the Belgians in the villages on the Maas where 144th RAC trained on Buffaloes seem to have gained a particular place in the Regiment's heart.

Unfortunately, it is difficult to get a sense of the views held about contemporary events by either officers or other ranks, because Cunliffe was not particularly interested in recording this sort of thing. He launched occasional diatribes against the narrow-mindedness of the majority of other officers. But this, one feels, was because they did not share his interests in art and literature and not because of any political views they might hold. When Cunliffe wrote about contemporary events in his diary, the impression is of a man of sensibility but no strong political opinions.

Marcus Cunliffe and the Second World War

In actuality, Cunliffe did not write much about contemporary events, and when he did it was as often about the progress of the war as anything else.[17] Occasionally he made a moral judgment. Thus in late 1943 he noted the prevalence of heavy Allied air raids and added: 'These mass air raids are no doubt useful to us in beating Germany, but I detest them. By a simple inversion we gloat over the scenes we once wept over'. He returned to the subject in early 1944.[18] And in August 1945 he wrote a long entry after the dropping of the atomic bomb on Hiroshima.

> Is today the last of the 'Old World', the existence to which we are accustomed? Or rather, yesterday? For yesterday a bomb was dropped on Japan which obliterated an entire city. It was a bomb which we would have called Wellsian, ten years ago: an atomic bomb. Harold Nicolson wrote a fantastic novel about just such a bomb ('Public Faces'). What does it hold for the future? Everyone has been talking about it all day. But the majority only wonder 'will it end the Jap war much sooner? will it mean that we don't have to go to SEAC after all?'*
>
> They don't realise – yet – how much more is implied. Perhaps it's just as well that my brother officers, none of whom has shown any interest in the unleashing of sub-atomic energy on a scale violent enough to scatter a township, are at this moment in time grouped round our grand piano, where one of them plays 'Don't fence me in' and the others sing it . . .[19]

Although Cunliffe may have been annoyed at the incuriosity of his brother officers, his comments are hardly political, and such other comments as he makes about contemporary affairs are so vague as to offer few clues. Thus early in 1944 he recorded that 100,000 miners were on strike and added, 'What a country', which seems to indicate disapproval, although that was followed by, 'I cannot presume to blame them'. He hardly mentioned social reform, although in April 1944 he noted that 'Beveridge's scheme (now simply known as Beveridge) has disappeared', but with no further comment.† Perhaps most notably, he made no remark on the momentous result of the General Election of July 1945 when Labour won a large majority. He contented himself with an anecdote from Keith, his brother, about the family's gardener in Suffolk, who voted at 10 to 9 in the evening, not long before the polls closed: 'I wasn't having them thinking I were a-rushin' arter them'.[20]

---

* South-East Asia Command – at this time many British troops were wondering whether they would have to go to the Far East to fight.

† This was the Beveridge Report of November 1942 which had, of course, a great deal of influence on post-war welfare reforms. Presumably Cunliffe meant that it had disappeared from the news.

CONCLUSION

In an addendum to Cunliffe's obituary in *The Times*, Brian Holden Reid wrote, 'Like many of his generation, Cunliffe increasingly felt that his experience of frontline action in North-West Europe in 1944–5 was the formative experience of his life'.[21] And there can be no doubt that Cunliffe was marked by that experience. Anyone who served in that campaign would have been. Its direct influence on his interests and on his career, however, was limited.

Cunliffe respected many of the men with whom he served, but he maintained an intellectual distance from most of them. The life of the mind, and conversation about all the things that implied – art, plays, novels, ideas – were what interested him most. Even history does not seem to have been a major concern at that time. Neither was there much about the USA, the central interest of his later life, in his diaries for 1943–5. The exceptions were American writers: among others he mentioned James Branch Cabell, Henry James and Sinclair Lewis, and only a fraction of the books he read were recorded. Otherwise the USA is conspicuous by its absence. One of his few references to the American role in the war, apart from the dropping of the atomic bomb, was on Boxing Day 1944, when the Regiment was in a blocking position in the Waterloo area as a result of the Ardennes offensive. Cunliffe wrote: 'What are we doing here? Waiting for the Germans to come, if they succeed in pushing past a flimsy series of American defences.' It was hardly a vote of confidence in the American war effort and was in fact too pessimistic, since by then the Americans had stopped the German advance along most of the front.

Cunliffe must have been impressed by the cornucopia of American equipment, and in a passage cited by Holden Reid he referred, much later, to their contribution to the war: 'We had driven in American vehicles and fired American guns. I had seen Flying Fortresses spiral into formation at dawn over East Anglia . . . I had seen the American dead in Normandy, Holland and the Ardennes.' But in the same autobiographical piece he also said that the attraction of the Commonwealth Fellowship which first took him to the USA was, in part, that it was a good alternative to postwar Britain. He went to the USA almost by chance, and he might have gone into the civil service if the fellowship had not been available.[22]

A more obvious connection with the war was that he followed up his book on Twenty-First Army Group with two regimental histories – of the Inniskilling Fusiliers, and a more narrowly focused history of the Royal Warwickshire Regiment from 1919–55, referred to earlier. Both were published in the 1950s. These are good books of their type, although the Inniskillings' history suffers from the fact that an institutional history written over a period of centuries, with an ever-changing background, has of necessity to spend time establishing context without much chance of doing so very effectively. The Warwickshires' history works better, in my view. Both were far removed from Cunliffe's main academic interests by then, however, and one suspects that he wrote them more for the remuneration than because he saw himself as a military historian.[23]

So the war, and his own front-line experience, was only peripherally relevant to Cunliffe's professional career. Of course, its lessons about morality, about human nature, about courage and about loss must have been profound and it was perhaps those which made him feel in later life that the war was a formative experience.

It is therefore fitting that he should have the last word. This is a section towards the end of his chapter on the two Royal Warwickshire battalions in Normandy, the 2nd and the 1/7th. The two battalions, Cunliffe wrote,

> shared a whole mass of general impressions familiar to all front-line soldiers in the Normandy campaign. They would remember things as disparate as: the first unwary sip of some farmer's brew of Calvados; the black chimneys of the factory at Colombelles; the glitter of fireflies along the hedgerows; the heat of a weapon after firing, and the lingering reek of cordite; the letters and newspapers from home, amazingly recent in despatch, yet sometimes a world away in mood; the air armadas drumming in the sky; the angry Typhoons, diving (sometimes too close for comfort) to release their thudding rockets; the lavish guns, firing and firing through all hours at the wretched enemy; the muddy ersatz taste of powdered tea; the stillness of some place patrolled, one's creaking nerves, the sweat making one's hands clammy; the weight of the steel helmet, and the cool relief of removing it; the leaden irritability of hot days after nights without sleep; the maddening mosquitoes near the Orne; the sad, oppressive task of writing letters home to next of kin; the extraordinary pleasure of a bath and a change of clothes; the sight of German prisoners filing forward, hands in air, jackbooted, lank-haired, scared and grimy; the endless digging, in haste before the mortaring starts . . .[24]

It could only have been written by one who was there.

Abbreviations and Glossary

Artillery
British Army artillery pieces in 1944–5 were likely to be either 25-pounder field guns or 4.5in or 5.5in medium guns. Technically the 25-pounder and the 5.5in were 'gun-howitzers', i.e. they could fire at a high angle if necessary. Close-range barrages were fired by 25-pounders, which were very accurate.

AVRE (Armoured Vehicle Royal Engineers)
Manned by Royal Engineers, these were based on the Churchill tank and carried demolition charges and a large mortar which enabled pillboxes etc. to be blown up from a distance. Variants carried fascines to fill ditches and bridge-building equipment. See Chapter 2 for use of the first type, Chapter 5 for use of other types. The name was originally 'Assault Vehicle' but 'Armoured Vehicle' came into use at the end of the war and was applied retrospectively (Wikipedia, 'AVRE').

Barrage (artillery)
Fire of a number of guns aimed at a line parallel to, and on or near, the enemy's defensive line(s). The barrage line would vary in length, depending on the attack frontage and number of guns. In attack, when the enemy was echeloned in depth, it was likely to be a creeping barrage which would pause on a particular line for a period then 'lift' and advance a number of yards to the next line. See Chapter 2 for a description of a barrage behind which 144th RAC advanced. The idea was to neutralise the enemy in their dug-outs or trenches, while the infantry or tanks advanced close to the barrage line, ready, when it lifted, to suppress the enemy by fire or receive their surrender. (See also Concentration)

Brass up
Slang: to fire intensively at an area which might contain enemy; it was usually used of short-range fire from a tank's guns, whether heavier or machine guns, rather than longer range artillery fire. (See also 'Stonk')

Bren
Standard British light machine gun used by the infantry. The 'en' comes from the Royal Small Arms Factory, Enfield, as it did also for Polsten and Sten guns.

Bren-Gun Carrier – see Carrier

Brigade
Formation which, in the British Army, usually contained three main subsidiary units – battalions when infantry, regiments/battalions when armoured.

Brigade Major
Senior staff officer in a Brigade. An important position, even if the rank held was not very senior.

Buffalo
Amphibious vehicle described in Chapter 6.

Browning
Standard American machine gun fitted to Shermans; those used in British tanks were rechambered to take British .303 ammunition.

Carrier
Light tracked vehicle developed for the British Army before the war. Initially, mainly intended for armed reconnaissance and, as such, carrying a Bren Gun (hence Bren-Gun Carrier), they quickly became ubiquitous, used for supply, towing light guns etc.

Churchill (tank)
A relatively slow-moving tank with substantial armour protection, used for infantry support work. See Chapter 1.

Coaxial
A coaxial machine gun was one mounted in a tank turret which swung on the same axis as the main gun. Shermans carried one plus a machine gun in the hull, firing forwards.

Concentration (artillery)
Fire of a number of guns aimed at a defined area, e.g. a farm or wood. The official term for a Stonk. (See also Barrage)

Crocodile (tank)
Based on the Churchill, these projected fuel through a front nozzle, while retaining their main gun. The fuel, carried in an armoured trailer, could be projected as a liquid, or ignited. As the Churchill was slow, they were even

ABBREVIATIONS AND GLOSSARY

slower, but were a terrifying weapon to defenders. See Chapters 2 and 5.

Defilade
A position 'in defilade' is a defensive position which is concealed in some way from an approaching enemy, either artificially or by making use of the ground.

Division
Formation which controlled a number of subordinate formations – in British infantry divisions it would be three infantry brigades plus varying numbers of artillery units and, often, an independent tank/armoured brigade; a total of around 15,000 men. A British armoured division had an armoured brigade, an infantry brigade and various other units including artillery. The 79th Armoured Division, in which 144th RAC/4th RTR served at the end of the war, controlled the numerous specialised armoured vehicles – AVRES, Crocodiles, Flail tanks, Buffaloes etc. – which were then loaned out to more orthodox units for support roles.

Doctrine (military)
A flexible term, referring to the way in which a country's armed forces conducts operations. As such it might encompass all operations, or those in the different spheres of land, sea and air, or segments of them, e.g. the employment of tanks. Overarching British and Canadian land warfare doctrine in the later part of the war favoured well-prepared attacks which were closely controlled by higher commanders and supported by heavy artillery barrages and, possibly, preliminary bombing. Doctrine on the specific use of tanks, however, was rather less dogmatic and more flexible. See Chapters 1 and 2.

Echelon
It has two distinct meanings. A formation in echelon is one arranged diagonally or in a staggered pattern, frequent in defence and attack. Echelons were also groupings within a unit. Battalions, whether tanks or infantry, would have an A echelon which supplied the front-line troops/tanks and a 'B' echelon which comprised the rear transport carrying heavier stores etc. Strictly speaking the fighting units were the F echelon although the term was not so commonly used for them.

Firefly
Sherman tank equipped with a 17-pounder anti-tank gun. The usual complement was one Firefly in a troop of four tanks. See Chapter 1 and *passim*.

Flail tanks
Their official name was Sherman Crabs. They carried large rotating drums in the front whose iron chains detonated mines safely. There were variants based on other tanks.

GR (***Grenadier Regiment***)
German infantry regiment, equivalent to a British brigade.

Hull down
Of a tank: a position behind a hill crest or mound in which the hull is concealed and only the turret exposed, in order to minimise exposure to the enemy.

ID (***Infanterie Division***)
German infantry division.

LCT (Landing Craft Tanks)
Small vessels produced in large numbers for seaborne assaults, and supply subsequent to the assault. They had a relatively flat bottom and hinged bow so could beach themselves in order to unload tanks or other vehicles straight on to land. There were various types of LCTs; the largest in use on cross-Channel operations carried up to nine Shermans. However, Marcus Cunliffe remembered the ones 144th RAC crossed in as 'blunt-nosed little barges that held four tanks' (Reid and White, 'Pastmaster', p. 4).

LVT (Landing Vehicle Tracked)
The official designation for the Buffalo (q.v.).

Ofenrohre – see ***Panzerfaust*** and ***Panzerschreck***

'O' Group (Orders Group)
Self-explanatory – group of subordinate commanders brought together to receive orders; in 144th RAC these might involve discussion and a degree of 'give and take'.

Operational (military)
The stage of military conceptualisation between strategic (high level, to do with overall objectives) and tactical (to do with the actual fighting of battles). The planning of a campaign, such as that in North-Western Europe, would be at the operational level.

ABBREVIATIONS AND GLOSSARY

Panzerfaust and *Panzerschreck*
German handheld anti-tank devices. The former were simple 'guns', i.e. steel tubes (which were thrown away once used) which fired a projectile; the latter rather more sophisticated devices firing a mini-rocket. *Panzerschrecke* produced black smoke when fired which led to them being nicknamed *Ofenrohre* (stove pipes). The 144th RAC seems to have adopted this nomenclature, although it misspelt them *Offenrohre*; it does not appear to have distinguished between the different types. It also called them bazookas, after the American equivalent.

Polsten
An 'autocannon' – a small bore (20mm) rapid-fire weapon, firing explosive shells. Designed as an auxiliary weapon for armoured vehicles or for light anti-aircraft use. Polish engineers derived it from the Oerlikon but it was simpler and cheaper. It was fitted to Buffaloes. (See also Bren)

RAC (Royal Armoured Corps)
Founded in 1939 as an umbrella organisation uniting the Royal Tank Regiment (q.v.) and the various cavalry regiments which had mechanised in the 1930s. During the war numerous new regiments designated by number, such as the 144th, were added to the RAC's establishment. The 144th's conversion to 4th Battalion Royal Tank Regiment (RTR) meant that, while it remained in the RAC, its membership of the RTR made it more likely to have a permanent place in the army after the war – as indeed happened.

RHQ (Regimental Headquarters)

RTR (Royal Tank Regiment)
The earliest tanks, of 1916, were in the Machine Gun Corps but in 1917 were grouped in their own Tank Corps. After the First World War this became the Royal Tank Corps and in 1939, on the formation of the RAC (q.v.), it became the Royal Tank Regiment.

Sherman (tank)
By 1944, the standard Allied tank. British variants had a five-man crew: commander, driver, co-driver/hull machine-gunner, gunner, loader/radio operator (usually referred to as 'operator'). For other details and discussion, see Chapter 1.

SP gun
Self-propelled gun. As used in the context of 144th RAC, this would

usually mean an anti-tank gun mounted in a tank chassis (so the gun would not revolve as in a tank proper). The Germans had some very powerful SP guns. Standard artillery could also be self-propelled, although the Allies had far more of this than the Germans.

Spandau
British Army slang for German machine guns. It originated in the First World War when some of the guns were produced at the Spandau Arsenal in Berlin. The original type of machine guns to which the name was attached was replaced, but the name lived on.

Sten
A light British submachine gun, developed to be easily and cheaply manufactured, which seems to have been carried by all tank commanders, judging by the number of times it is mentioned. (See Bren)

Stonk
A 'stonk' was slang for concentrated artillery fire, whether the enemy's or one's own. It was a flexible word: e.g. one might refer to 'a good stonking', while 144th RAC applied it to 'Stonk Wood' where they experienced heavy enemy shellfire. It might also be used of mortar fire, if heavy. Derived from the artillery term 'STandard cONCentration' (Jary, 'Gunners', p. 56).

Tannoy
During the war the word became a colloquialism for public-address systems, being the name of the British firm which manufactured such systems.

Waffen SS
The Armed SS, i.e. SS fighting formations. These served alongside the regular German Army units. They often had better equipment and a disproportionate number were Panzer Divisions.

Zoot or Zuit suits
Term used by Lieutenant Phillips (see Chapters 5 and 6) for his overalls. Suits with distinctive baggy trousers cut narrow at the ankle and wide lapelled jackets, and popularised by jazz musicians in the 1940s (Wikipedia). Presumably the term became popularised as a nickname for the overalls, although they don't bear much resemblance to each other.

Notes

Chapter 1

1. L.F. Ellis, *Victory in the West, Vol. 1: The Battle of Normandy*, London, HMSO, 1962, Appendix IV.
2. See description in Sources and Bibliography.
3. Alan Jolly, *Blue Flash: The Story of an Armoured Regiment*, London, privately published, 1952.
4. Robert W. Thorne, 'World War 2 reminiscences' (henceforth Thorne, 'WW2').
5. George Washington University (henceforth GWU) Special Collections, MS0125.UA. Full details are in Sources and bibliography. There are diaries from 1942–3, which were not photographed.
6. For instance Cunliffe, 'Diary', 26 November 1944: 'Spent the remainder of the morning writing up a narrative of the fighting in August for the Colonel'; also 17 December.
7. Details of Cunliffe's life are taken from: Brian Holden Reid, 'Cunliffe, Marcus Falkner', *Oxford Dictionary of National Biography*, Oxford, OUP, n.d., and Brian Holden Reid and John White, 'Marcus Cunliffe: a Pastmaster' in Brian Holden Reid and John White (eds), *Americana: Essays in Memory of Marcus Cunliffe*, Hull, Hull University Press, 1998.
8. TNA WO 166/1433 (date of joining 144th RAC).
9. Cunliffe, 'Diary', 5 April 1944. In this Cunliffe was looking back to a year earlier, and describes himself then as a troop commander.
10. There are a number of references in Cunliffe's diary to his role as Intelligence Officer. His diary has only been used occasionally before May 1944, when it stopped. Its main use has been for the period from October 1944, when he restarted it, until the end of the war.
11. TNA WO 171/878, 17 and 18 September 1944; Lieutenant R.E. Bowyer started writing the war diary on the 17th, and the next day recorded that Cunliffe had taken over the Recce Troop. Stuart Hills, *By Tank into Normandy*, London, Cassell (Kindle edn), original edn 2002, notes a similar switch: after a long spell as a troop leader he became Intelligence Officer (Chapter 10) and then commander of the Recce Troop (Chapter 11), 'a position I had long coveted'.
12. Reid and White, 'Pastmaster', p. 5. Cunliffe was not writing his diary in August 1945 so there are no clues as to how he obtained such a desirable, for him, occupation. It may have arisen from the good offices of his friend Douglas Draycott, for whom see Chapter 8.
13. Marcus Cunliffe, *The Literature of the United States*, London, Penguin, 1954.

14. Reid, 'Cunliffe'.
15. For instance, on 4 January 1944 two pages of the diary discuss literature. Throughout the diary there are numerous notes, some of them lengthy, about books he has read. The short story, 'A Night Out', is in a folder cryptically entitled 'A Squadron' (GWU MS 0125.UA, Box 7, Folder 4).
16. Cunliffe, 'Diary', e.g. 7 September 1943.
17. *Ibid.*, 9 January 1944.
18. See discussion of 'The Other Side' in Sources and Bibliography.
19. Ken Tout, *Tank*, London, Robert Hale, 1985.
20. TNA WO 205/965 'The Night Attack'. This account of Totalize is not signed but it is obviously by Cunliffe. Apart from stylistic clues, it contains references to novels 'that always littered my turret', mentions of 'my brother' (Marcus and Keith were the only two officers who were brothers) and – typically Cunliffe – a reference to Gibbon!
21. Cunliffe, 'Diary', e.g. 11 and 20 March 1944, 16–17 July 1945.
22. Jolly, *Blue Flash*, pp. 1–3; TNA WO 166/1433, 144th RAC War Diary November/December 1941 – the actual inception of 144th was 22 November 1941.
23. Jolly, *Blue Flash*, p. 2.
24. John Buckley, *British Armour in the Normandy Campaign*, Abingdon, Routledge, 2004, pp. 113–14.
25. *Ibid.*, pp. 110–11.
26. *Ibid.*, pp. 111–12, 118–19, 127–9.
27. *Ibid.*, pp. 129–33, 145.
28. *Ibid.*, p. 80; Ellis, *The Battle of Normandy*, Appendix IV.
29. Buckley, *British Armour*, p. 78.
30. *Ibid.*, p. 81; Timothy Harrison-Place, *Military Training in the British Army, 1940–44: From Dunkirk to D-Day*, London, Frank Cass, 2000, p. 164.
31. Jolly, *Blue Flash*, pp. 2, 7, 73–80.
32. *Ibid.*, p. 67.
33. *Ibid.*, pp. 146–8.
34. *Ibid.*, p. 4.
35. *Ibid.*, p. 6.
36. Buckley, *British Armour*, p. 125.
37. Jolly, *Blue Flash*, p. 8; IWM Documents 18809, 'A Wartime Romance', letter 28 June.
38. First quote TNA WO 171/878, 10–12 June; other quotes from Jolly, *Blue Flash*, p. 8.
39. Jolly, *Blue Flash*, p. 9; Reid and White, 'Pastmaster', p. 4; Thorne, 'WW2'.
40. Hugh Darby and Marcus Cunliffe, *A Short Story of 21 Army Group*, Aldershot, Gale and Polden, 1949; Martin Lindsay, *So Few Got Through*, London, Collins, 1946.

NOTES

41. David Stahel, *Operation Barbarossa and Germany's Defeat in the East*, Cambridge, Cambridge University Press, 2009, pp. 98–102; Felix Romer, 'The Wehrmacht in the War of Ideologies: the Army and Hitler's Criminal Orders on the Eastern Front', in Alex Kay, Jeff Rutherford and David Stahel (eds), *Nazi Policy on the Eastern Front, 1941*, Rochester, New York, University of Rochester, 2012; for a general conspectus and much detail, Ben Shepherd, *Hitler's Soldiers: the German Army in the Third Reich*, London, Yale University Press, 2016, pp. xiv, 45, 110, 125, 128–9, 142, 148–9, 171–6, 214–17 and numerous further references.
42. For instance Max Hastings, *Overlord: D-Day and the Battle for Normandy 1944*, London, Michael Joseph, 1984.
43. These historians include Terry Copp, Stephen Hart and John Buckley.
44. The argument has been forcefully and well put by David Stahel in a number of books, for instance Stahel, *Operation Barbarossa*, pp. 83–5.
45. Evan Mawdsley, *Thunder in the East: the Nazi-Soviet War 1941–45*, London, Hodder Arnold, 2005, pp. 6–8, 41–2. David Stahel, 'The Wehrmacht and National Socialist Military Thinking', *War in History*, Vol. 24, No. 3, July 2017, pp. 336–61, esp. p. 339.
46. Subsequent paragraphs owe much to John Buckley, *Monty's Men: the British Army and the Liberation of Europe*, London, Yale University Press, 2013.

Chapter 2
1. Viscount Montgomery of Alamein, *Normandy to the Baltic,* London, Hutchinson, 1946, p. 16.
2. Chester Wilmot, *The Struggle for Europe*, London, Collins, 1952, pp. 214–15; Carlo D'Este, *Decision in Normandy*, London, Collins, 1983, pp. 476–8.
3. Jolly, *Blue Flash*, pp. 9–11.
4. Anthony Beevor, *D-Day: The Battle for Normandy*, London, Viking, 2009, pp. 267–9.
5. Jolly, *Blue Flash*, pp. 14–15 (quotes p. 15).
6. Buckley, *British Armour*, pp. 33–7; Wilmot, *Struggle*, map facing p. 337 and discussion pp. 356–7.
7. Buckley, *Monty's Men*, has two paragraphs on the operations which is more than most authors. There is also a useful Wikipedia article.
8. Buckley, *British Armour*, pp. 79, 100, 101 (quote).
9. TNA WO 171/878, '"The Battle of Noyers", 16–18 Jul 44: Action of 144 R.A.C.' (henceforth 'Regimental Account'), pp. 1–2 (quote p. 2). German units from TNA WO 171/571, 59th Division 'G' Branch, Intelligence Summaries, 16 and 17 July.
10. TNA CAB 106/1065, 'Pomegranate' Battlefield Tour, Appendix L.
11. TNA, WO 171/878 'Regimental Account', *passim* and p. 19; quote p. 5.
12. *Ibid.*, pp. 4–5.

13. *Ibid.*, p. 5.
14. *Ibid.*, p. 6 for Sergeant Critchley's action.
15. *Ibid.*, pp. 6–7.
16. *Ibid.*, p. 7.
17. *Ibid.*, pp. 7–8, 15–16.
18. *Ibid.*, p. 8.
19. Jolly, *Blue Flash*, p. 24.
20. *Ibid.*, p. 24.
21. *Ibid.*, p. 25.
22. Sydney Jary with 'Carbuncle', 'Gunners', *British Army Review*, No. 116, August 1997, pp. 56–64.
23. TNA WO 171/878, 'Regimental Account', p. 10.
24. *Ibid.*, p. 10.
25. *Ibid.*, p. 11.
26. *Ibid.*, p. 11.
27. *Ibid.*, pp. 14 and 16.
28. *Ibid.*, p. 15.
29. *Ibid.*, pp. 18 and 21.
30. Jolly, *Blue Flash*, p. 33; TNA WO 171/571, 59th Division, War Diary, 19 July.
31. Wilmot, *Struggle*, p. 357.
32. Beevor, *D-Day*, p. 309.
33. *Ibid.*, map facing p. 312.
34. 'Second Battle of the Odon', Wikipedia, accessed 07.09.2017.
35. TNA WO 171/337, XXX Corps G Branch, Intelligence Summary, 18 July, for Pomegranate; TNA WO 171/310, XII Corps G Branch, Intelligence Notes for Greenline; 'Second Battle of the Odon', Wikipedia.
36. Wilmost, *Struggle*, pp. 386 and 389.
37. TNA WO 171/878, 'Regimental Account', p. 10; TNA CAB 106/1065, 'Pomegranate' Battlefield Tour, gives 2/6th's casualties in Charnwood as 247 – almost a third of the battalion's total personnel – not all of whom had been replaced. The other two battalions in 177th Brigade had not suffered so badly.
38. TNA WO 171/878, 'Regimental Account', p. 21.
39. TNA CAB 106/1065, 'Pomegranate' Battlefield Tour.
40. Harrison-Place, *Military Training*, pp. 164–5.
41. TNA WO 171/878, 'Regimental Account', p. 23; Harrison-Place, *Military Training*, pp. 131–2.
42. TNA WO 171/878, 'Regimental Account', p. 24.
43. Harrison-Place, *Military Training*, pp. 164–5, describes different tactics pursued by regiments of 27th Armoured Brigade in their early days in Normandy. The conclusion Harrison-Place draws is that these were the result of doctrinal uncertainty. But one could equally draw the conclusion that they

NOTES

were the result of different conditions in different circumstances. Buckley, *British Armour*, p. 81.
44. TNA WO 171/878, 'Regimental Account', p. 23.
45. *Ibid.*, p. 23.
46. Buckley, *British Armour*, pp. 114–17; Stephen A. Hart, *Operation Totalize 1944*, Oxford, Osprey, 2016, p. 16. Cromwell regiments were allocated some Sherman Fireflys.
47. TNA WO 171/878, 'Regimental Account', p. 24.
48. *Ibid.*, p. 12.
49. *Ibid.*, p. 22.
50. Jolly, *Blue Flash*, pp. 20–33.
51. E.g. Hills, *By Tank Into Normandy*, Chapter 5; Bill Bellamy, *Troop Leader*, Stroud, Sutton (Kindle edn) original edn 2005, Chapter 4.
52. TNA CAB 106/1065, 'Pomegranate' Battlefield Tour, Appendix L.

Chapter 3
1. C.P. Stacey, *The Victory Campaign: the Operations in North-West Europe 1944–45 (Vol. III of the Official History of the Canadian Army in the Second World War)*, Ottawa, Cloutier, 1960, pp. 195–6.
2. Jolly, *Blue Flash*, p. 34.
3. *Ibid.*, p. 34.
4. Brian Horrocks, *A Full Life*, London, Collins, 1960, pp. 153–4.
5. BAOR Battlefield Tour, 'Operation Totalize', 1947, TNA CAB 106/1047, p. 32. According to Buckley, *Monty's Men*, p. 97, Kangaroos had already been thought of, and had been considered by O'Connor for Goodwood. This seems to rely on a recollection by O'Connor twenty years later, whereas Simonds' claim was made not long after the war.
6. Brian Reid, *No Holding Back: Operation Totalize, Normandy, August 1944*, Mechanicsburg, Stackpoole, 2004.
7. Hart, *Totalize*, p. 32.
8. Reid, *No Holding Back*, p. 73.
9. *Ibid.*, pp. 167–8.
10. Battlefield Tour, 'Operation Totalize', TNA CAB 106/1047, p. 32.
11. Thorne, 'WW2'; Jolly, *Blue Flash*, p. 41.
12. Jolly, *Blue Flash*, p. 39.
13. Battlefield Tour, 'Operation Totalize', TNA CAB 106/1047, p. 40.
14. Reid, *No Holding Back*, p. 165.
15. Battlefield Tour, 'Operation Totalize', TNA CAB 106/1047, p. 41.
16. TNA WO 205/965 'The Night Attack'. See Chapter 1, n. 20, for a brief discussion of this.
17. Reid, *No Holding Back*, p. 209.
18. Battlefield Tour, 'Operation Totalize', TNA CAB 106/1047, p. 46. Moore

Family Tree website, Trooper Sydney Moore; accessed 21.10.2017.
19. Reid, *No Holding Back*, p. 209.
20. Jolly, *Blue Flash*, p. 47.
21. Reid, *No Holding Back*, p. 209.
22. Battlefield Tour, 'Operation Totalize', TNA CAB 106/1047, p. 46.
23. Beevor, *D-Day*, p. 432; Buckley, *Monty's Men*, p. 177 comes to a more optimistic verdict.
24. Reid, *No Holding Back*, chs 12–18 for details; Stephen Hart, 'The Black Day Unrealised', in John Buckley (ed.), *The Normandy Campaign 1944*, Abingdon, Routledge, 2006, pp. 104–17, makes similar points to Reid, although putting a different weight on the various factors.
25. Beevor, *D-Day*, p. 432.
26. Reid, *No Holding Back*, pp. 237–8.
27. *Ibid.*, pp. 241–4.
28. *Ibid.*, pp. 243–6; Jolly, *Blue Flash*, p. 51. The action of the Northamptonshire Yeomanry is vividly described in Tout, *Tank*, chs 3 and 4.
29. Buckley, *British Armour*, pp. 25–6; Wikipedia, 'Michael Wittman', accessed 14.10.2017.
30. Reid, *No Holding Back*, Appendix E.

Chapter 4
1. Stacey, *Victory Campaign*, pp. 265–6 has a very brief outline. John Buckley, as often, is the exception and devotes three pages to I Corps' advance, and another three to the siege of Le Havre; Buckley, *Monty's Men*, pp. 189–95.
2. Beevor, *D-Day*, p. 465.
3. Jolly, *Blue Flash*, p. 52.
4. Reid, *No Holding Back*, p. 354.
5. Jolly, *Blue Flash*, p. 55.
6. *Ibid.*, pp. 55 (quote)–7.
7. *Ibid.*, pp. 57 (quote)–8.
8. Cunliffe, 'Diary', 6 May 1945.
9. *Ibid.*, p. 58; Thorne, 'WW2'.
10. Jolly, *Blue Flash*, pp. 59–60.
11. *Ibid.*, pp. 60–1 (quote p. 61).
12. *Ibid.*, pp. 61–3.
13. TNA WO 171/878, Narrative War Diary, 15 August 1944 (quote); Jolly, *Blue Flash*, p. 62. The Shermans were equipped with small mortars to discharge smoke bombs, and could also fire smoke shells.
14. Jolly, *Blue Flash*, p. 62. The Brigade's war diary contains the following: '144th RAC moved off again to continue their advance . . . Advance was very slow'; TNA WO 171/640, 15 August.
15. Jolly, *Blue Flash*, pp. 63 (first two quotes) and 63–4 (final quote).

NOTES

16. *Ibid.*, p. 64.
17. Wilmot, *Struggle*, p. 422.
18. Jolly, *Blue Flash*, p. 64.
19. Charles More, *The Road to Dunkirk*, Barnsley, Frontline, 2013, pp. 83–8.
20. See Chapter 1, n. 40.
21. Lindsay, *So Few Got Through*, p. 53; Jolly, *Blue Flash*, p. 66.
22. Jolly, *Blue Flash*, p. 67.
23. Buckley, *British Armour*, p. 23.
24. Lindsay, *So Few Got Through*, pp. 62 and 176 (quote).
25. *Ibid.*, pp 57–61; Jolly, *Blue Flash*, p. 69.
26. Lindsay, *So Few Got Through*, pp. 62–3 (quotes); Wikipedia accessed 13.10.2017.
27. Buckley, *British Armour*, pp. 96 and 99; Buckley, *Monty's Men*, p. 60; Jolly, *Blue Flash*, p. 70. Bill Close, *Tank Commander*, Barnsley, Pen and Sword, (Kindle edn) 2013, Chapter 12 records British troops tank riding in Tunisia in 1943; its use in the British Army deserves research.
28. Jolly, *Blue Flash*, p. 70.
29. Lindsay, *So Few Got Through*, pp. 12 (quote) and 134; Wikipedia accessed 13.10.2017.
30. Jolly, *Blue Flash*, pp. 70, 71 (quote), 72 (quote).
31. Lindsay, *So Few Got Through*, pp. 65–7, quote p. 66.
32. Jolly, *Blue Flash*, p. 73.
33. Lindsay, *So Few Got Through*, p. 77; Jolly, *Blue Flash*, *passim*.
34. The Forêt de Brotonne advance was on 29 August; Jolly inaccurately calls it the Forêt de Bretonne. Jolly, *Blue Flash*, pp. 77–9 ('prophylactic' p. 78); see also Buckley, *Monty's Men*, pp. 191–2.
35. Buckley, *Monty's Men*, pp. 195–200.
36. *Ibid.*, pp. 193–4; Jolly, *Blue Flash*, p. 86.
37. Jolly, *Blue Flash*, pp. 88–9; Lindsay, *So Few Got Through*, pp. 84–6 (first quote pp. 84–5, then pp. 85 and 86).
38. TNA 205/965, 144th RAC 'Account of Operations Caen-Le Havre, Part VI'; Jolly, *Blue Flash*, pp. 88–9.
39. *Ibid.*, p. 90; Lindsay, *So Few Got Through*, p. 84; Buckley, *Monty's Men*, p. 195.
40. Jolly, *Blue Flash*, pp. 90–1.
41. Buckley, *Monty's Men*, p. 191; Wilmot, *Struggle*, p. 434.

Chapter 5

1. Buckley, *Monty's Men*, p. 203; Jolly, *Blue Flash*, pp. 92–3.
2. There are dozens of accounts of Market Garden and opinions on its merits and demerits. Buckley, *Monty's Men*, Chapter 8 for an up-to-date, balanced account.
3. Jolly, *Blue Flash*, pp. 92 and 94 (quote).

4. *Ibid.*, p. 96.
5. Buckley, *Monty's Men*, pp. 243–4. 'Colin' was part of the larger Operation Pheasant, which encompassed a simultaneous Canadian offensive (Website Codenames of World War 2, http.codenames.info).
6. Jolly, *Blue Flash*, pp. 103 and 104 (quote).
7. *Ibid.*, pp. 104 (first quote), 105 (second quote).
8. *Ibid.*, p. 102; TNA WO 171/1266, 29 October.
9. Jolly, *Blue Flash*, pp. 98 and 100.
10. *Ibid.*, p. 100 (quotes). The account in *Blue Flash* is garbled. Jolly has 7th Armoured Division threatening to turn up, but not doing so, on 25 October and then turning up again on the 26th, when allegedly the double-banking incident took place. The war diary, however, has only one appearance of 7th Armoured, on the 25th, and this is when the double-banking occurred. This is confirmed by Cunliffe's personal diary, parts of which are reproduced in Chapter 7, 'Waiting'. He describes Jolly and the other colonel arguing with each other.
11. *Ibid.*, pp 100–2; XII Corps' Intelligence summaries, TNA WO 171/311, 22 October–5 November. for prisoner totals: on six days no separate totals were given, so presumably there were only a few prisoners; the total recorded for the other days was 3,320. The summaries also note on several occasions the successful retreat of Germans northwards.
12. Buckley, *Monty's Men*, pp. 236–8.
13. *Ibid.*, p. 239.
14. Jolly, *Blue Flash*, p. 106.
15. Cunliffe, 'Diary', 14 November 1944.
16. Jolly, *Blue Flash*, p. 108 (quote); Lindsay, *So Few Got Through*, p. 128.
17. Jolly, *Blue Flash*, pp. 109–10; Lindsay, *So Few Got Through*, pp. 131–2.
18. Cunliffe, 'Diary', 16 November 1944.
19. Jolly, *Blue Flash*, p. 112; Cunliffe, 'Diary', 17 December 1945; Buckley, *Monty's Men*, p. 260.
20. Cunliffe, 'Diary', 20 December (quote); Jolly, *Blue Flash*, p. 112.
21. Jolly, *Blue Flash*, pp. 114–15; Peter Caddick-Adams, *Snow and Steel: Battle of the Bulge 1944–45*, London, Preface, 2014, pp. 507–14.
22. Jolly, *Blue Flash*, p. 116 (quote) and pp. 118–24 (casualties).
23. *Ibid.*, p. 120 (quote); Anon., *History of the East Lancashire Regiment in the War, 1939–45*, Manchester, Rawson, 1953, p. 135.
24. Jolly, *Blue Flash*, p. 121; *History of the East Lancashire Regiment*, pp. 136 and 141.
25. Jolly, *Blue Flash*, p. 121; *History of the East Lancashire Regiment*, pp. 134–42 for some (not all) daily casualty figures which show that only a small minority were killed, and for a final figure which gives total casualties but not a breakdown between killed, wounded and missing.
26. Cunliffe, 'Diary', 24 November 1944. Phillips can be identified as the author

NOTES

as follows. The same National Archives file – TNA WO 205/965 – which contains the accounts of the Ardennes also contains two accounts of crossing the Rhine. One, whose author identifies himself as Lieutenant D. Wells of C Squadron, refers to the commander of C Squadron's 1 Troop as Phillips. The author of the other Rhine crossing account identifies himself as the commander of 1 Troop, and therefore must be Phillips. The author of the Ardennes' accounts also identifies himself as the commander of 1 Troop, and they are written in a style similar to that of the Rhine account. Finally, it is clear from *Blue Flash* (pp. 121–4) that the two Ardennes' incidents described in the accounts involved C Squadron. Phillips was the son of Hubert Phillips, a well-known journalist – see Chapter 8. His first name was John, but Cunliffe referred to him as Hilary, his second name. Presumably Phillips' two accounts started life as letters but ended up in The National Archives as part of Jolly's collection of material about the Regiment. There is another one, about the attack on 4–5 January, in Bovington Tank Museum Archives, but it was written later (BTMA RH88 MH.5 144 RAC E2008.566).

27. Jolly, *Blue Flash*, pp. 123–4.
28. *Ibid.*, p. 123, says anti-tank gun.
29. Jolly, *Blue Flash*, p. 122.
30. Charles B. MacDonald, *The European Theatre of Operations: the Last Offensive*, Washington DC, Office of the Chief of Military History, 1973, pp. 24–5; Caddick-Adams, *Snow and Steel*, p. 628.
31. Buckley, *Monty's Men*, pp. 260–4; Wilmot, *Struggle for Europe*, pp. 610–12 is useful on the press conference.

Chapter 6

1. Buckley, *Monty's Men*, pp. 270–9.
2. Wikipedia, accessed 12.12.2017; Jolly, *Blue Flash*, p. 126. According to a display board in Bovington Tank Museum, they had a crew of three. Jolly, however, names four in the vehicle he crossed in – commander, driver, gunner and operator; Phillips' account suggests that all Buffaloes had a radio suggesting that they all carried an operator.
3. Jolly, *Blue Flash*, pp. 127–8. See Chapter 8 for a description of this training.
4. *Ibid.*, pp. 93, 128–9; TNA WO 171/4709, 1 March.
5. Buckley, *Monty's Men*, p. 281.
6. *Ibid.*, p. 282; Wilmot, *Struggle*, p. 678.
7. Wilmot, *Struggle*, p. 682.
8. Buckley, *Monty's Men*, p. 282.
9. Jolly, *Blue Flash*, p. 137.
10. *Ibid.*, pp. 130 (first and second quotes), 136 (third quote).
11. *Ibid.*, p. 135.
12. Both in TNA, WO 205/965.

13. Jolly, *Blue Flash*, pp. 132 and map on p. 133; Buckley, *Monty's Men*, p. 282.
14. Lindsay, *So Few Got Through*, p. 231.
15. Jolly, *Blue Flash*, p. 134.
16. Tim Saunders, *Operation Plunder: Rhine Crossing*, Barnsley, Pen and Sword (Kindle edn), original edn 2006, Chapter 4, for the time of landing. The book is a useful survey of the entire operation. BTMA, RH87 4RTR/355.486.87./E2008.11/MH5.
17. *Ibid.*, pp. 136–7; Lindsay, *So Few Got Through*, p. 239.
18. Lindsay, *So Few Got Through*, pp. 238 (first quote) and 245 (second and third quotes).
19. Jolly, *Blue Flash*, pp. 137–8.
20. *Ibid.*, pp. 139 (first quote) and 140 (second quote).
21. *Ibid.*, p. 141.
22. Cited in Norman Scarfe, *Assault Division*, London, Collins, 1947, p. 259.
23. *Ibid.*, pp. 260–2, first and second quotes p. 261, third quote p. 262.
24. Jolly, *Blue Flash*, p. 142. *Blue Flash* has US 86th Airborne but this is an error; Darby and Cunliffe, *21 Army Group*, p. 137.
25. Jolly, *Blue Flash*, p. 142. According to the Wikipedia entry on 82nd Airborne, Omar Bradley, the commander of 12th Army Group, said in a 1975 interview that Montgomery was reluctant to cross the Elbe; the 82nd then crossed it, moved 36 miles in a day and captured large numbers of Germans. The statement is very misleading. Montgomery was typically cautious, and it is true that the Elbe could probably have been crossed sooner. But when the crossing did take place, in this area it was an operation of British Second Army; British VIII Corps was the first to cross on 29 April and, of course, 82nd Airborne was assisted by a British unit – 4th RTR. The haul of German prisoners was common to all the advancing units, British and American. Perhaps the main interest of Bradley's reminiscence is that, thirty years after the war, he was still irritated enough by Montgomery to drag up this half-remembered story. (Wikipedia, '82nd Airborne Division', accessed 05.01.2017; Buckley, *Monty's Men*, pp. 292–3.)

Chapter 7
1. This and following paragraphs: Cunliffe, 'Diary', 25 October 1944.
2. This and following paragraphs: Cunliffe, 'Diary', 14 November 1944.
3. Cunliffe, 'Diary', 18 March 1945.
4. IWM Documents 18809, 'A Wartime Romance', letter of 3 July.
5. Jolly, *Blue Flash*, p. 97.
6. This and the next paragraph: Cunliffe, 'Diary', 21 October 1944.
7. Cunliffe, 'Diary', 14 November 1944.
8. Jolly, *Blue Flash*, p. 111.
9. *Ibid.*, p. 127.
10. This and next paragraph: Cunliffe, 'Diary', 3 July 1945.

NOTES

11. Cunliffe, 'The Other Side'.
12. It seems likely that this was Escures-sur-Favières; it is actually about 15 miles south-east of Caen, but in other respects the description of the location in *Blue Flash*, and the number of prisoners, corresponds with Cunliffe's account. See Chapter 4.
13. Jolly, *Blue Flash*, p. 76.
14. TNA WO 171/337, XXX Corps 'G' Staff Intelligence Summary, D + 39 [16 July].
15. Cunliffe, 'Diary', 3 May 1945: Jolly, *Blue Flash*, p. 143.
16. Jolly, *Blue Flash*, p. 74.
17. Cunliffe, 'The Other Side'.
18. Jolly, *Blue Flash*, p. 75.
19. Cunliffe, 'Diary', 17 May 1945.
20. Lindsay, *So Few Got Through*, p. 107. See Chapter 9 for a further discussion.
21. Cunliffe, 'The Other Side'.
22. TNA WO 171/878, 27 August 1944; Jolly, *Blue Flash*, p. 70.
23. Jolly, *Blue Flash*, pp. 79–80, 93 (final quote).
24. *Ibid.*, p. 80.
25. Cunliffe, 'Diary', 11 May 1945.
26. This and following paragraphs: Cunliffe, 'Diary', 15 May 1945.

Chapter 8
1. Cunliffe, 'Diary', 19 November 1944 for MacGregor; Jolly, *Blue Flash*, *passim* for the 144th RAC officers.
2. Cunliffe, 'Diary', 19 November 1944; Draycott had been seconded to 79th Armoured Division, the home of the specialised armoured weapons such as AVRES, Crocodiles etc. – and the formation to which the Regiment was attached when it later converted to Buffaloes. He was still with 144th RAC on 11 November 1944 but listed as attached to 79th Armoured on the 25th; TNA WO 171/878.
3. Cunliffe, 'Diary', 24th November 1944.
4. *Ibid.*, 5 February 1945.
5. Jolly, *Blue Flash*, p. 93.
6. Cunliffe, *Diary*, 5 February 1945.
7. *Ibid.*, 29 November 1944.
8. *Ibid.*, 9 April 1945; there is nothing about the mooted book in 79th Armoured Division's war diary, but for the most part this is very thin. Draycott by that time had been promoted to captain and was GSO3 (Operations); TNA WO 171/4297, 79th Armoured Division War Diary, February 1945.
9. See Chapter 1, n. 6, also 'Sources and Bibliography'.
10. Jolly, *Blue Flash*, p. 5.
11. Cunliffe, 'Diary', 19 February 1945.

12. IWM Documents 18809, 'A Wartime Romance' contains transcripts of the four letters from Bob Thorne. The contents of Mrs Pearson's letters to him can be inferred from his replies.
13. Buckley, *British Arnour*, p. 178 summarises the arguments.
14. *Ibid.*, Chapter 8 and esp., pp. 200–1.
15. Scarfe, *Assault Division*, pp. 176–80.
16. Cunliffe, 'Diary', 22 November 1944.
17. Harrison-Place, *Military Training*, pp. 109–10 (quote p. 110).
18. TNA WO 166/11111 (1943) and TNA WO 171/878 (1944) for the material below, unless otherwise footnoted. Diary entries are from the month mentioned in the text.
19. Cunliffe, 'Diary', 5 April 1944. Oddly enough his theme was 'Happiness', and he was remembering the evening of the day described in the passage when, filled with tired contentment, he with two fellow officers and two naval officers were sitting and chatting in the cramped little wardroom of the LCT.
20. Up to and including March 1944 the war diary is typed and unsigned. From then on it is handwritten and signed by Cunliffe.
21. Jolly, *Blue Flash,* and quotes, pp. 4–5.
22. A number of diaries of infantry divisions and brigades with which 144th RAC trained were consulted: 49th and 61st Divisions; 70th, 146th, 147th and 182nd Brigades. They yielded no useful information about training in conjunction with the Regiment.
23. IWM Documents 18809, 'A Wartime Romance', letters April 1944 (no day) and 10 May 1944.
24. Jolly, *Blue Flash*, pp. 38–9.
25. TNA WO 171/4720, '144 RAC Training Directive No. 1', 29 January 1945, and war diaries for February and March; Jolly, *Blue Flash*, p. 128 (quote).
26. Cunliffe, 'Diary', 3 February, 5 February 1945.
27. Cunliffe, 'Diary', 3 March 1945.
28. Not every Buffalo crossing was perfect: the East Riding Yeomanry landed several units of 227 Highland Brigade of 15th Division seriously out of position; Saunders, *Operation Plunder*, Chapter 5.
29. A 21st Army Group memo of the 12 February 1945 (TNA WO 171/3871) orders the impending disbandment of 144th RAC and transfer of all parts to 4th RTR; it is clearly giving effect to what had already been decided. There is a reference in this to a War Office memorandum from the Adjutant General's office. Some digging, which has not been done, might turn up further information there.
30. Jolly's memo is one of the items in TNA WO 205/965.
31. *Ibid.*

NOTES

Chapter 9
1. Buckley, *British Armour*, pp. 188–9.
2. E.g. Buckley, *Monty's Men*, p. 126.
3. *Ibid.*
4. See Chapter 2.
5. Hills, *By Tank into Normandy*, Chapter 3.
6. See More, *Road to Dunkirk*, pp. 84–8, 91–2, and elsewhere.
7. Saunders, *Operation Plunder*, Chapter 5.
8. See Chapter 4.
9. Jolly, *Blue Flash*, p. 27.
10. See Chapters 4 and 5.
11. Jolly, *Blue Flash*, p. 146.
12. Buckley, *Monty's Men*, Chapter 5, has a thorough and balanced discussion of these and related topics.
13. More, *Road to Dunkirk*.
14. Jolly, *Blue Flash*, Appendix 1 and p. 33; Lindsay, *So Few Got Through*, p. 74; Marcus Cunliffe, *History of the Royal Warwickshire Regiment 1919–1955*, London, William Clowes, 1952, p. 120.
15. Hastings, *Overlord*, p. 211.
16. Close, *Tank Commander*, Chapter 14.
17. E.g. Cunliffe, 'Diary', 4 September 1943, 4 April 1944, 3 March 1945.
18. *Ibid.*, 27 November 1943 and 27 February 1944.
19. *Ibid.*, 7 August 1945.
20. *Ibid.*, 9 March and 4 April 1944, 22 July 1945.
21. *The Times*, 5 September 1990, p. 12.
22. Marcus Cunliffe, 'Backward Glances', *Journal of American Studies*, Vol. 14, 1980, pp. 85–6.
23. Marcus Cunliffe, *The Royal Inniskilling Fusiliers 1993–1950*, Oxford, Oxford University Press, 1952. Cunliffe wrote another important book with, in part, a military theme, *Soldiers and Civilians: the Martial Spirit in America 1775–1865*, London, Eyre and Spottiswoode, 1969. As its title implies, however, this is essentially about attitudes to the military and does not contain the standard fare of most military histories.
24. Cunliffe, *Royal Warwicks*, p. 120.

Sources and Bibliography

144th RAC/4th RTR Material
Most of the material generated by the regiment and used here is in The National Archives (TNA). Much of it is duplicated in Bovington Tank Museum Archives (BTMA), which also has a limited amount of material not in TNA. The BTMA material, for those who might wish to consult it, is in the 144th RAC and 4th RTR boxes for the relevant dates. Most references in this book are to TNA.

The narrative war diaries of 144th RAC have been quoted from time to time, mainly for the period before D-Day when they were used for research into training; once the Regiment was in Normandy the supplementary material discussed below is usually fuller and more interesting while *Blue Flash*, the Regimental history, which is closely based on the diaries and the 'Account of Operations' (see below), is more amusingly written. They have been quoted more frequently. *Blue Flash* is sometimes inaccurate in detail, however, probably when Jolly relied on memory, so the diaries have been used to check and correct it.

144th RAC War Diaries
TNA WO 166/1433 (Nov.–Dec. 1941).
TNA WO 166/11111 (Jan.–Dec. 1943).
TNA WO 171/878 (Jan.–Dec. 1944).
TNA WO 171/4720 (Jan.–Feb. 1945).

4th RTR War Diary
TNA WO 171/4709 (from March 1945).

WO 171/878 also contains a detailed account of the Battle of Noyers, as well as the 'Account of Operations', relating to Normandy, which is essentially an expansion of the diary. It seems clear that a fair proportion of the latter, perhaps all, was compiled by Marcus Cunliffe at Jolly's behest, although it was based on a draft written by Jolly (see Chapter 8, 'Becoming 4th RTR'). The account of Noyers has been extensively used. It might have been compiled or partially compiled by Cunliffe but I am inclined to think that some was written by Jolly himself, and it certainly represents his views.

SOURCES AND BIBLIOGRAPHY

In a separate file, TNA WO 205/965, there are a number of personal accounts and other background material, as well as another copy of the 'Account of Operations' which is in a somewhat disorganised state. The personal accounts include Cunliffe's account of Totalize and Lieutenant Phillips' various accounts, both extensively quoted. There are also various miscellaneous papers, including the memo by Alan Jolly discussed in Chapter 8.

Other TNA Material
This is a miscellany, used because of its relevance to particular episodes in 144th RAC's history or to particular queries.
21 Army Group: TNA WO 171/3871.
Corps War Diaries: TNA 171/310 and 311 (XII Corps); TNA 171/337 (XXX Corps).
Divisional War Diaries: TNA WO 171/571 (59th Division); TNA WO 171/4297 (79th Armoured Division).
Armoured Brigade War Diaries: TNA WO 171/640 (33rd Armoured Brigade).
Infantry Battalion War Diaries: TNA WO 171/1266 (5th Black Watch).
Battlefield Tours (there were numerous such tours after the war, for the benefit of younger officers): TNA CAB 106/1065, 'Pomegranate'; TNA CAB 106/1047 'Operation Totalize'.

Marcus Cunliffe's Papers
Cunliffe's papers are in the George Washington University Special Collections research centre, Gelman Library, Collections Number MS0125.UA. They were deposited during her lifetime by his third wife, Professor Phyllis Palmer. Cunliffe's diaries were extensive: he kept them from 1939 until not long before his death. Only the diaries from the later wartime years have been used. Cunliffe himself referred to them as 'ODTAA' ('One damned thing after another' – Diary, 13 September 1943). Those I have looked at were not kept every day but written up at intervals, sometimes of a few days and sometimes a couple of weeks. However, it is easiest to refer to them as diaries because that is effectively what they were. They are in exercise books, and carry on until one book is finished, so the books overlap calendar years.

They comprise:

Diary 08/1943–5/1944, Box 2, Folder 2.
Diary 10/1944–11/1945 Box 2, Folder 3.

Cunliffe did not keep one between June and September 1944. Keeping a diary was forbidden, although numerous officers such as Martin Lindsay (see Chapter 4) seem to have ignored this. Cunliffe himself, in spite of his occasional strictures on the British Army, was fairly obedient; he referred on 11 April 1944 to having to stop writing his diary. However, there are a few excerpts for July and August 1944 in Box 7, Folder 5.

He restarted it on 1 October 1944, implying that the prohibition had been lifted, although perhaps it was just obvious by then that plenty of people kept one. He then stopped again between August and November 1945, explaining (Diary, 2 November 1945) that he had thought that he would write about his experiences in letters, but was not doing so because his correspondents were not writing much back (and presumably, therefore, he had less incentive to write to them). The book in which this diary was kept finished on 13 November 1945, so I have not looked at much material after August.

'The Other Side', Box 7, Folder 2. Several stories in Chapter 7 originate here. They are all accounts of incidents during the Normandy campaign. Cunliffe had clearly worked on the collection in the summer/autumn of 1944, as he refers to it in his diary of 16 December 1944 as a 'neglected notebook of inglorious episodes . . . all true'; however, the diary entry of 8 February 1945 implies that the stories had still not been completed. So they are not absolutely contemporaneous, although the detail in them suggests that they are based on notes made soon afterwards. There are a number of other contemporary papers in Box 7 but only one set (Folder 5 – see above) has been used. The rest are either irrelevant, lack interest or are in some cases illegible, being written in very faint pencil.

In passing, it is worth noting the scope of the Cunliffe collection. After the war, apart from the diaries, there are numerous folders containing letters connected with his professional life, lecture and course notes etc: all the materials for an intellectual biography.

Other Primary Sources
Imperial War Museum (IWM) Documents 18809, Private Papers of G.A. Pearson. These mainly consist of letters home from George Pearson, a driver in A Echelon, transcribed and compiled into a booklet by his brother, Anthony Pearson, which is called 'A Wartime Romance'. (Pearson was engaged to be married, although the engagement was broken off before he died.) The booklet also contains background detail on Pearson and transcripts of other letters, notably from Captain R.W. Thorne to Pearson's mother.

SOURCES AND BIBLIOGRAPHY

Reminiscences of Captain R.W. Thorne in the possession of the author (Thorne, 'WW2').

Published Primary Sources
Bellamy, Bill, *Troop Leader*, Stroud, Sutton (Kindle edn), original edn 2005.
Close, Bill, *Tank Commander*, Barnsley, Pen and Sword (Kindle edn) 2013.
Hills, Stuart, *By Tank into Normandy*, London, Cassell (Kindle edn), original edn 2002.
Horrocks, Brian, *A Full Life*, London, Collins, 1960.
Lindsay, Martin, *So Few Got Through*, London, Collins, 1946.
Montgomery, Viscount, of Alamein, *Normandy to the Baltic*, London, Hutchinson, 1946.

Published Secondary Sources
General Texts
Anon., Obituary, 'Alan Jolly', *The Times*, 16 September 1977.
Beevor, Anthony, *D-Day: the Battle for Normandy*, London, Viking, 2009.
Buckley, John, *British Armour in the Normandy Campaign*, Abingdon, Routledge, 2004.
Buckley, John, *Monty's Men: the British Army and the Liberation of Europe*, London, Yale University Press, 2013.
Caddick-Adams, Peter, *Snow and Steel: Battle of the Bulge 1944–45*, London, Preface, 2014.
Cunliffe, Marcus, 'Backward Glances', *Journal of American Studies*, Vol. 14, 1980, pp. 83–102.
Cunliffe, Marcus, *History of the Royal Warwickshire Regiment 1919–1955*, London, William Clowes, 1952.
Cunliffe, Marcus, *The Literature of the United States*, London, Penguin, 1954.
Cunliffe, Marcus, *Soldiers and Civilians: the Martial Spirit in America 1775–1865*, London, Eyre and Spottiswoode, 1969
Cunliffe, Marcus, *The Royal Inniskilling Fusiliers 1993–1950*, Oxford, Oxford University Press, 1952.
D'Este, Carlos, *Decision in Normandy*, London, Collins, 1983.
Darby, Hugh and Cunliffe, Marcus, *A Short Story of 21 Army Group*, Aldershot, Gale and Polden, 1949.
Ellis, L.F. *Victory in the West, Vol. 1: The Battle of Normandy*, London, HMSO, 1962; *Vol. 2: The Defeat of Germany*, London, HMSO, 1968.
Hart, Stephen, *Operation Totalize, 1944*, Oxford, Osprey, 2016.

Hart, Stephen, 'The Black Day Unrealised', in John Buckley (ed.), *The Normandy Campaign 1944*, Abingdon, Routledge, 2006, pp. 104–17.

Harrison-Place, Timothy, *Military Training in the British Army 1940–44: From Dunkirk to D-Day*, London, Frank Cass, 2000.

Hastings, Max, *Overlord: D-Day and the Battle for Normandy 1944*, London, Michael Joseph, 1984.

Jary, Sydney with 'Carbuncle', 'Gunners', *British Army Review*, No. 116, August 1997, pp. 56–64.

Kay, Alex, Rutherford, Jeff and Stahel, David (eds), *Nazi Policy on the Eastern Front, 1941*, Rochester, New York, University of Rochester, 2012.

Macdonald, Charles B., *The European Theatre of Operations: the Last Offensive*, Washington DC, Office of the Chief of Military History, 1973.

Mawdsley, Evan, *Thunder in the East: the Nazi-Soviet War 1941–5*, London, Hodder Arnold, 2005.

More, Charles, *The Road to Dunkirk*, Barnsley, Frontline, 2013.

Reid, Brian, *No Holding Back: Operation Totalize, Normandy, August 1944*, Mechanicsburg, Stackpoole, 2004.

Reid, Brian Holden, 'Cunliffe, Marcus Falkner', *Oxford Dictionary of National Biography*, Oxford, OUP, n.d.

Reid, Brian Holden, and White, John (eds), *Americana: Essays in Memory of Marcus Cunliffe*, Hull, Hull University Press, 1998.

Romer, Felix, 'The Wehrmacht in the War of Ideologies: the Army and Hitler's Criminal Orders on the Eastern Front', in Alex Kay, Jeff Rutherford and David Stahel (eds), *Nazi Policy on the Eastern Front, 1941*, Rochester, New York, University of Rochester, 2012.

Saunders, Tim, *Operation Plunder: Rhine Crossing*, Barnsley, Pen and Sword (Kindle edn), original edn 2006.

Shepherd, Ben, *Hitler's Soldiers: the German Army in the Third Reich*, London, Yale University Press, 2016.

Stacey, C.P., *The Victory Campaign: the Operations in North-West Europe 1944–45 (Vol. III of the Official History of the Canadian Army in the Second World War)*, Ottawa, Cloutier, 1960.

Stahel, David, *Operation Barbarossa and Germany's Defeat in the East*, Cambridge, Cambridge University Press, 2009.

Stahel, David, 'The Wehrmacht and National Socialist Military Thinking', *War in History*, Vol. 24, No. 3, July 2017, pp. 336–61.

Tout, Ken, *Tank*, London, Robert Hale, 1985.

SOURCES AND BIBLIOGRAPHY

Whiting, Charles, *The Battle of the Bulge: Britain's Untold Story*, Stroud, Sutton, 1999.
Wilmot, Chester, *The Struggle for Europe*, London, Collins, 1952.

Regimental and Unit Histories
Anon., *A History of the East Lancashire Regiment in the War, 1939–45*, Manchester, Rawson, 1953.
Jolly, Alan, *Blue Flash: The Story of an Armoured Regiment*, London, privately published, 1952.
Scarfe, Norman, *Assault Division*, London, Collins, 1947.

Internet Sources
Codenames of World War 2: http://codenames.info
Moore Family Tree website: http://moore-familytree.s3-website-eu-west-1.amazonaws.com/Moore-Sidney.htm
Wikipedia – valuable for details of weaponry, unit histories etc.

Index

A Echelon 2, 14, 67, 160, 168
affiliation 13, 71–2
Aftwaterings Canal 84
Aldershot 13, 14
Ambler, Sam 73
American Army 19, 21, 35, 42, 65, 69, 77, 90–92, 107, 108, 183
  armies
    First 90
    Ninth 110
  corps
    XVIII Airborne 124
  divisions
    9th Armoured 110
    82nd Airborne 124
Amiens, Battle of 50, 60
Antwerp 78, 82, 86, 90
APC 45, 73, 177, *see also* Kangaroo
Appeville 76, 144
Ardennes 5, 15, 72, 90, 108, 110, 126, 131, 143, 147, 175, 183
Arnhem 15, 81–2
Arromanches 1, 14, 156, 180
Avranches 42, 45
AVRE 25, 32–4, 78, 80

Barbarossa 16, 17
Barnes, Michael 151
Bastogne 90
'Battle of the Bulge' 5, 90
Bayeux 14
Beevor, Anthony 59
Belgium 1, 81, 86, 109, 131, 168, 170
Belvert 85

Berry, Sergeant 122
Beveridge Plan 182
Blackford Assault School 166
Bleckede 124
Blitzkrieg 179
Bluecoat (Operation) 42, 47
Blue Flash 109n
Blue Flash (book) 1, 3, 9, 13, 48, 50, 58–9, 66, 68, 71, 76–9, 95n, 106, 129–30, 137–8, 141, 146, 154, 156, 175–7
Boorsheim 131
Borg, Lieutenant 27, 40
Bourneville 144
Bovington 112
Bowyer, Captain T.E. 156
Bremen 1, 123–4, 142, 146, 170, 176
Brettevillette 26, 28, 31
British Army 17, 19, 20, 35, 42, 44, 77, 107, 108, 149, 172–3, 177–9
  army group
    21st Army Group 4, 11, 150, 171, 183
  armies
    British Army of the Rhine 4
    Second Army 4, 124
  corps
    I 63, 69, 75
    XII 22, 82, 86, 110
    XXX 22, 77, 91, 108, 110, 120, 122, 136
  divisions
    Guards Armoured 78
    7th Armoured 21, 74–5, 84–6

INDEX

79th Armoured 124, 155–7
3rd 123, 161, 176
6th Airborne 44
15th 84, 110, 176
49th 12, 36, 138
50th 161
51st (Highland) 7, 13, 48, 49, 58, 63, 68–9, 71, 75, 78, 82, 84, 86, 100, 110, 122, 161–2, 169, 181
53rd (Welsh) 5, 36, 84, 92n, 100
59th (Staffordshire) 20, 23, 35, 67
61st 165
brigades
  31st Tank 76
  33rd Armoured 7, 11, 12, 20, 32, 37, 48, 60, 63, 68, 72, 75, 82, 86, 90, 161, 168–9
  34th Armoured 78
  9th 123
  44th 74
  49th 12, 76–8
  147th 76
  152nd 49, 72, 78
  153rd 13, 71–2, 74, 78, 82, 85, 101, 126–7, 161, 173
  154th 49, 65–6, 72
  158th 91
  177th 23–5, 29, 32, 36, 39
  182nd 166
  185th 123
regiments/battalions
  2nd Armoured Irish Guards 164
  1st RTR 112
  4th RTR 12, 109–10, 121–4, 170–1
  148th RAC 49, 67, 171
  1st East Riding Yeomanry 72, 176
  1st Northamptonshire Yeomanry 7, 32, 60–1, 65, 174
  7th Argyll and Sutherland Highlanders 49, 169
  5th Black Watch 71, 84, 101, 113, 120
  7th Black Watch 49
  2nd Derbyshire Yeomanry 68
  7th Duke of Wellington 76, 138
  1st East Lancashire 92–4
  8th East Lancashire 8
  1st Gordon Highlanders 14, 70–6, 78–9, 84, 122, 143, 162, 180
  5/7th Gordon Highlanders 71, 74, 113
  Inniskilling Fusiliers 183–4
  1st Norfolk 169
  6th North Staffordshire 32
  1st Oxfordshire and Buckinghamshire 70–1
  2nd Royal Ulster Rifles 123–4, 170
  Royal Warwickshire Regiment 183–4
  2nd Royal Warwickshire 123–4, 184
  1/7th Royal Warwickshire 184
  8th Royal Warwickshire 70–1
  South Staffordshire Regiment 24
  5th South Staffs 28
  1/6th South Staffs 26
  2/6th South Staffs 29, 35, 39, 177
Brotonne, Forêt de 77, 81–2
Browne, Corporal 51–2, 59

Bruneval 82
Brussels 78, 91
Buckley, John 11–12, 13, 21–3, 31, 37, 72, 80, 160, 173
Buffalo 4, 72, 108–9, 111, 113–14, 117, 121–4, 126, 131, 153, 156, 159, 163, 169–70, 176, 180–1
Bury St Edmunds 166

Caddick-Adams, Peter 107
Caen 7, 19, 20, 21, 34–5, 40, 42, 44, 47, 49, 63, 133, 138, 151, 178
Caillouet 45
Callwood, Corporal 66, 151, 158
Calonne, River 76, 138n, 141
Cambrai, Battle of 112
Campbell, Lieutenant 120
Canadian Army 17, 19, 35, 42, 44, 57–8, 65, 69, 77, 82, 122–3, 178
  armies
    First 4, 50, 63
  corps
    II 44
  divisions
    4th Armoured 48, 49, 59
    1st 123
    2nd 48
  brigades
    2nd Armoured 48
  regiments/battalions
    Sherbrooke Fusiliers 60–1, 174
Carr, Sergeant 104–5
Charnwood (Operation) 20, 35
Chartres 69
Churchill (tank) 8, 9, 10–11, 13, 22, 37, 165, 173–5
Close, Bill 180
Cobra (Operation) 21, 35
Colin, Operation 82, 84–5

Collins, Trooper 33
Cotentin 45
Cothem 131
Couvre-Chef 20
Crabs (tank) *see* Flail (tank)
Cracroft, Lieutenant Colonel R.C. 67
Cramesnil 49, 57–8, 60, 143
Crerar, Harry 50, 60
Critchley, Sergeant 26–7, 40, 66
Crocodile (tank) 25, 32–4, 37, 78, 80, 84, 86
Cromwell (tank) 10, 173–4
Cumming-Bruce, Henry 74
Cunliffe, Harold 3
Cunliffe, Kathleen 3
Cunliffe, Keith 3, 28, 31n, 66, 151, 182
Cunliffe, Marcus 2, 4, 5–8, 14, 31n, 49–52, 57–9, 63, 66–7, 76–7, 79, 86, 90, 93, 100, 113, 124, 125–30, 132–4, 137–8, 142–4, 147–8, 149–64, 170–1, 172–3, 175–7, 180–4
  Intelligence Officer 3, 4, 67, 69, 134, 144, 157–9
  literary tastes 152, 154, 183
  Reconnaissance Troop commander 3, 4, 85, 88, 126–7, 155–7, 159–60

Darby, Hugh 4
D-Day 44, 125, 164, 174
Dives, River 69–71, 138
Dommel, River 85
Draycott, Douglas 150, 152, 155, 157
Dunkirk 70

Eberbach, Heinrich 77